WITH
MONSTER
GIRLS

Volume 5

THIS IS MY CHANCE! THIS IS MY CHANCE...

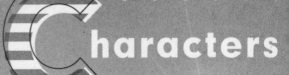

INTERVIEWS WITH MONSTER GIRLS

Characters

Vampire

Hikari Takanashi
Class 1-B

- Likes liver, tomato juice.
- Enjoys nibbling on arms.
- Receives blood from the government once a month.
- Opinions on romance: plenty; actual experience: none.

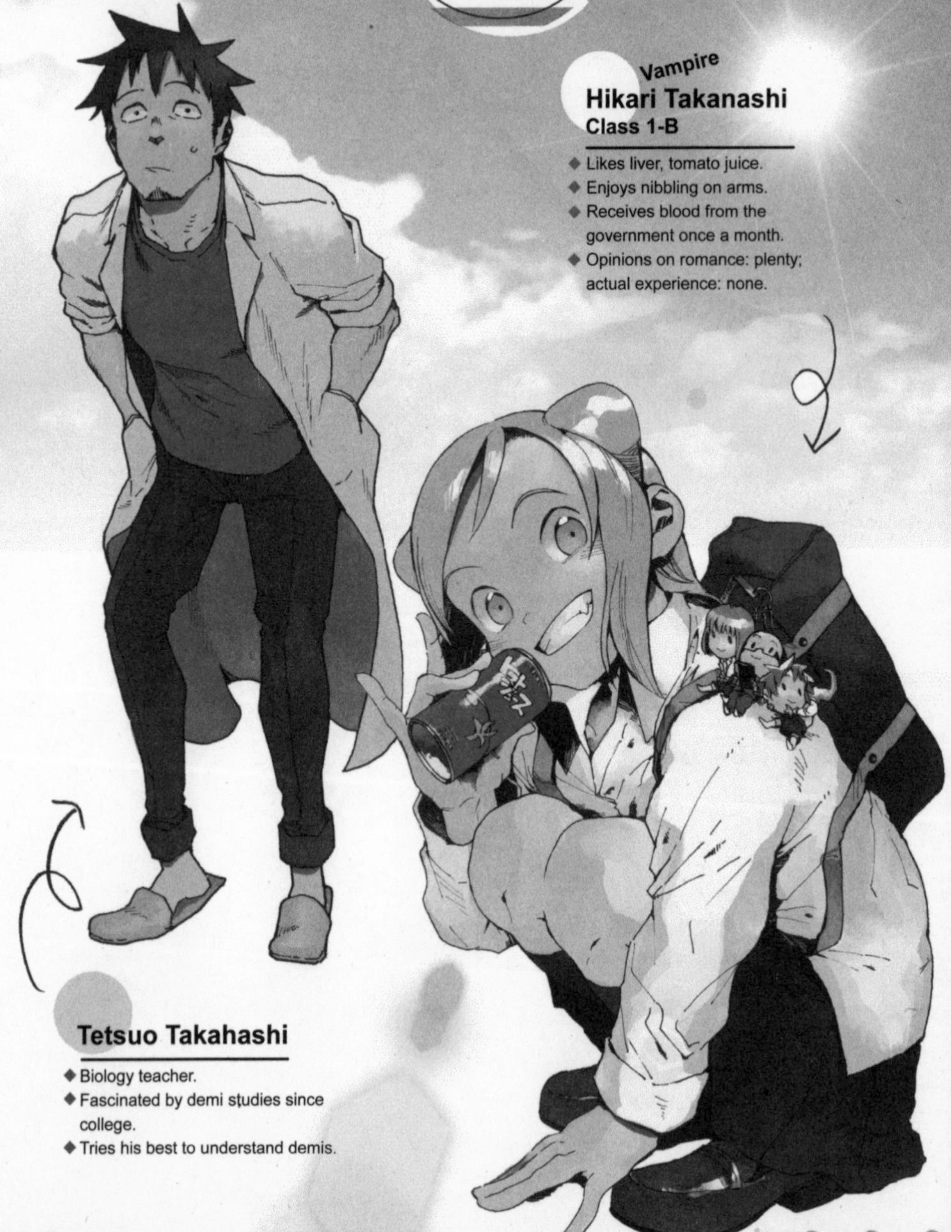

Tetsuo Takahashi

- Biology teacher.
- Fascinated by demi studies since college.
- Tries his best to understand demis.

Can: tomato juice

Dullahan
Kyoko Machi
Class 1-B

- A demi of Irish folklore whose head and body are separate.
- Likes her head to be held.
- In love with Takahashi-sensei.
- Top grades—has even been No. 1 in her class.

Succubus
Sakie Sato

- Math teacher.
- Lives in an isolated, dilapidated house so as not to unintentionally arouse anyone.
- Has a crush on Takahashi-sensei; has tried to arouse him.
- Romantic history: zilch.

Snow Woman
Yuki Kusakabe
Class 1-A

- Exudes cold air and weeps ice under stress.
- At first, avoided contact with others due to doubts about her own nature.
- Embarrassed to admit she likes gag manga; tries to hide it.

Himari Takanashi
Class 1-C

- Human
- Hikari's younger twin sister.
- Good grades, mature attitude—polar opposite of her sister.

Soma

- Assistant Professor at Musashino University of Science.
- Physicist.
- Takahashi-sensei's college classmate.

Koji Takanashi

- Father of Hikari and Himari; stay-at-home dad.
- On good terms with Kyoko's parents.
- Trying to learn not to shake too much while carrying Kyoko's head.

**"Demi-humans" are just a little different from us—
these days, they go by "Demis."
Their problems are as adorable as they are.**

*DEMIS: SHORT FOR "DEMI-HUMANS."

INTERVIEWS WITH MONSTER GIRLS

CONTENTS

Chapter 31: Summer's Just Around the Corner

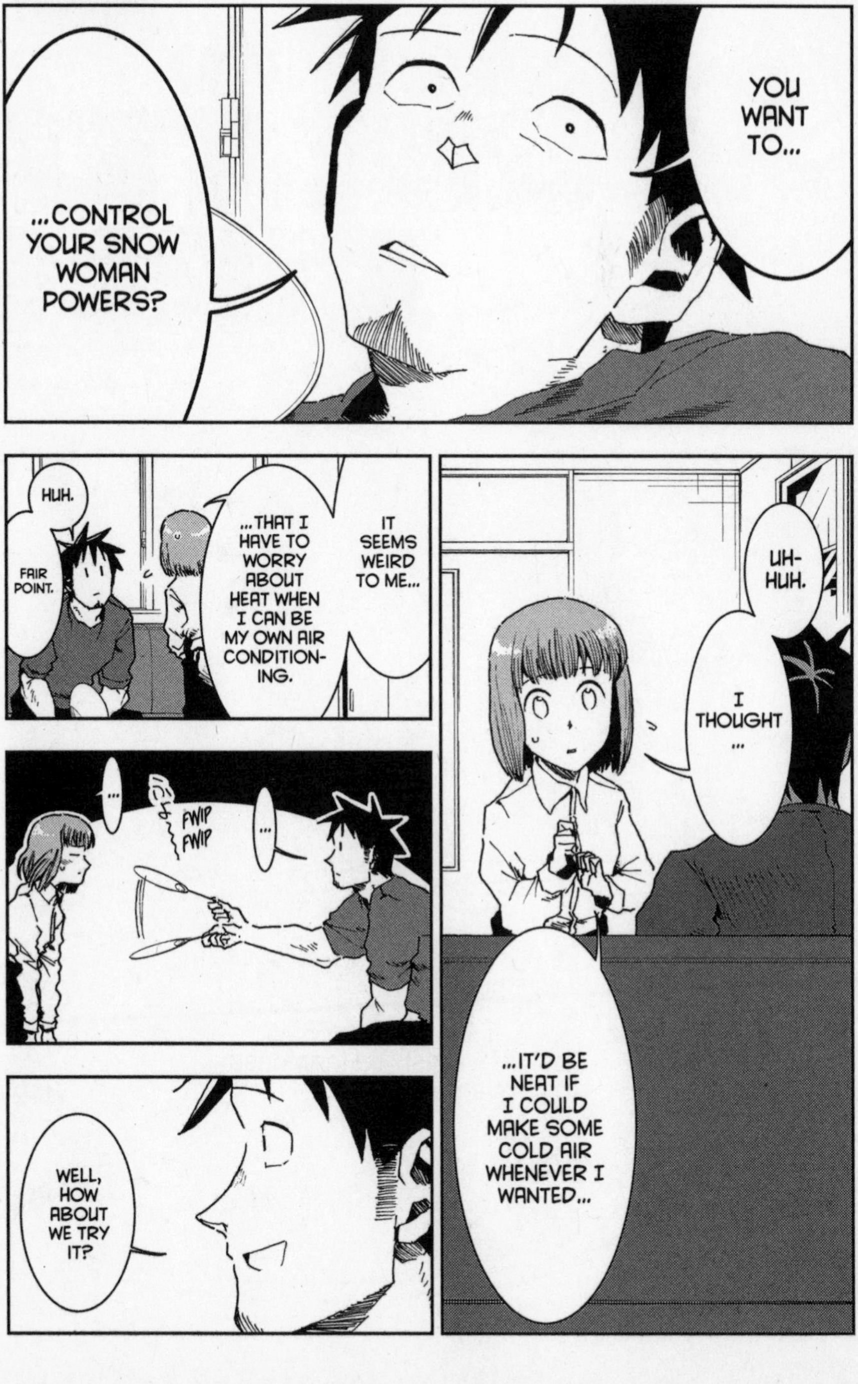
YOU WANT TO...
...CONTROL YOUR SNOW WOMAN POWERS?
UH-HUH.
I THOUGHT...
...IT'D BE NEAT IF I COULD MAKE SOME COLD AIR WHENEVER I WANTED...
IT SEEMS WEIRD TO ME...
...THAT I HAVE TO WORRY ABOUT HEAT WHEN I CAN BE MY OWN AIR CONDITIONING.
HUH.
FAIR POINT.
...
FWIP FWIP
...
WELL, HOW ABOUT WE TRY IT?

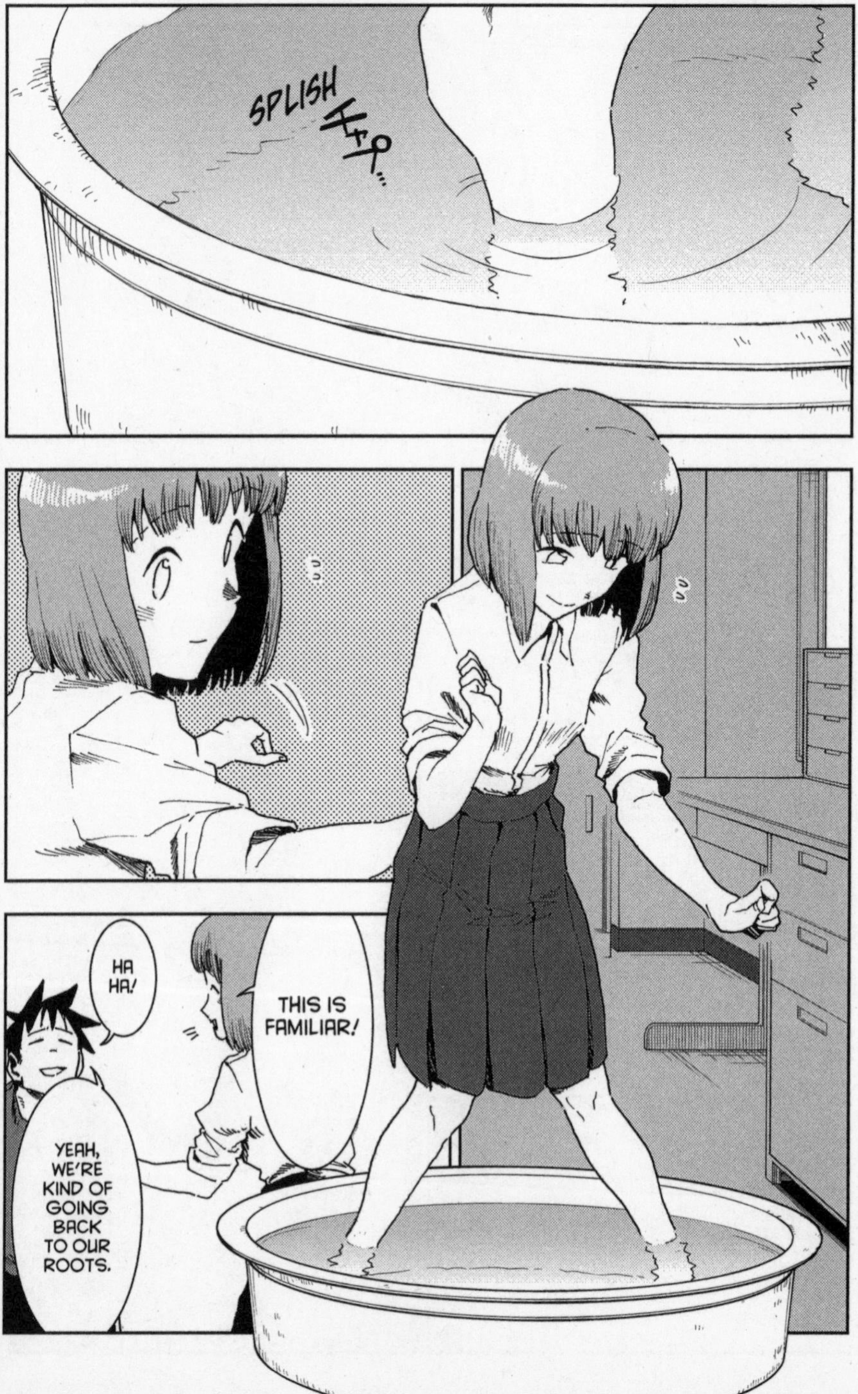
SPLISH
THIS IS FAMILIAR!
HA HA!
YEAH, WE'RE KIND OF GOING BACK TO OUR ROOTS.

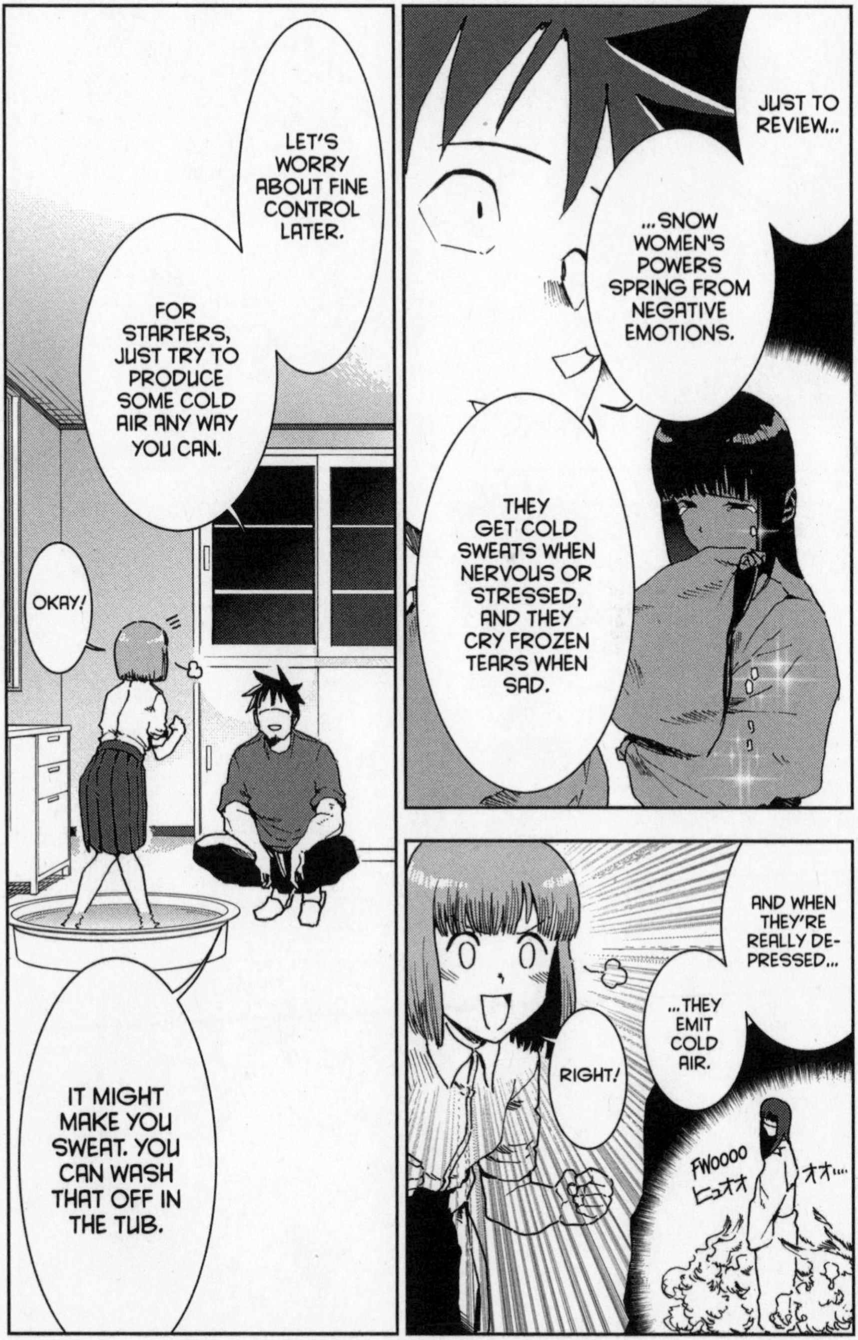
JUST TO REVIEW...
...SNOW WOMEN'S POWERS SPRING FROM NEGATIVE EMOTIONS.
THEY GET COLD SWEATS WHEN NERVOUS OR STRESSED, AND THEY CRY FROZEN TEARS WHEN SAD.
AND WHEN THEY'RE REALLY DE-PRESSED...
...THEY EMIT COLD AIR.
RIGHT!
FWOOOO
ヒュオオ
オオ...
LET'S WORRY ABOUT FINE CONTROL LATER.
FOR STARTERS, JUST TRY TO PRODUCE SOME COLD AIR ANY WAY YOU CAN.
OKAY!
IT MIGHT MAKE YOU SWEAT. YOU CAN WASH THAT OFF IN THE TUB.

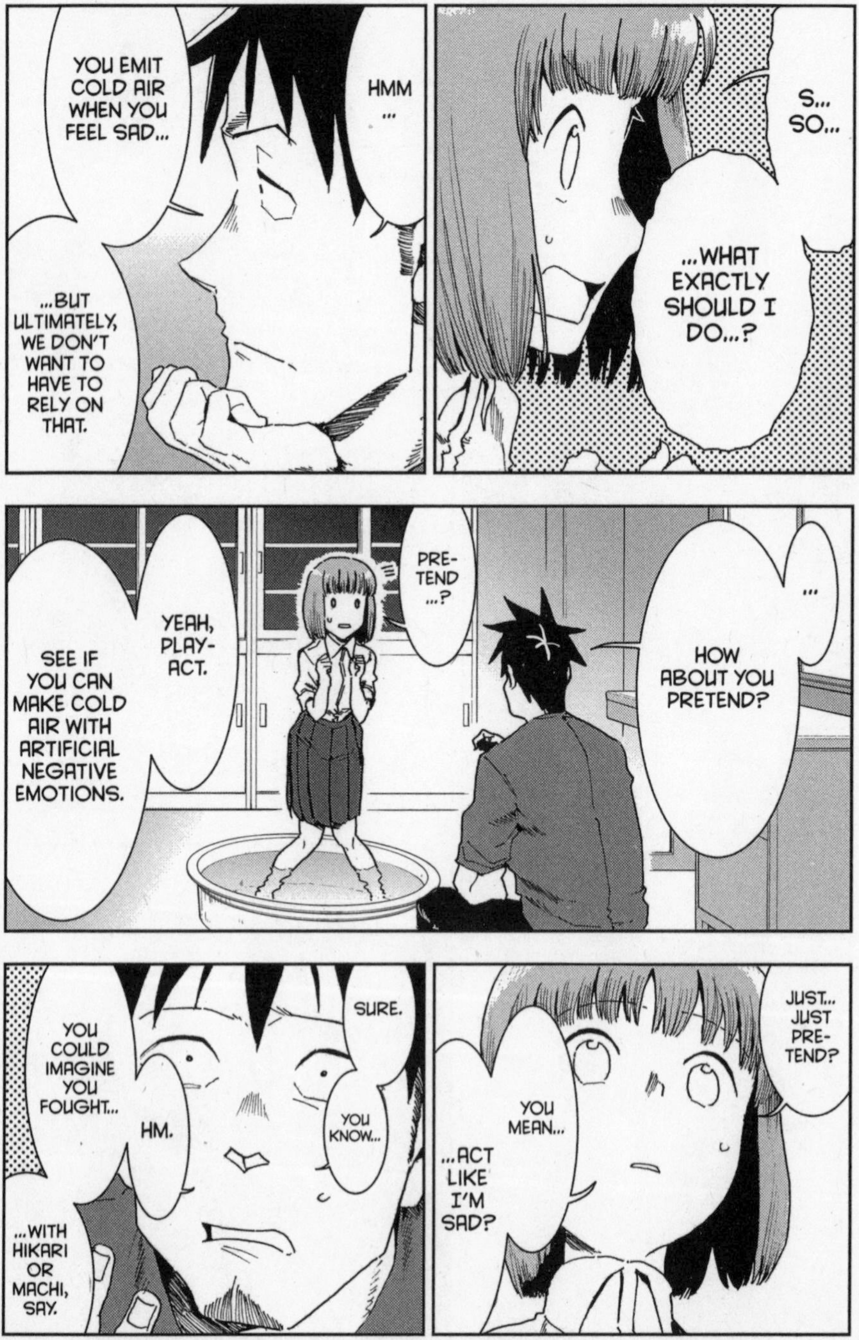
S... SO...
...WHAT EXACTLY SHOULD I DO...?
HMM ...
YOU EMIT COLD AIR WHEN YOU FEEL SAD...
...BUT ULTIMATELY, WE DON'T WANT TO HAVE TO RELY ON THAT.
...
HOW ABOUT YOU PRETEND?
PRE-TEND ...?
YEAH, PLAY-ACT.
SEE IF YOU CAN MAKE COLD AIR WITH ARTIFICIAL NEGATIVE EMOTIONS.
JUST... JUST PRE-TEND?
YOU MEAN...
...ACT LIKE I'M SAD?
SURE.
YOU KNOW...
HM.
YOU COULD IMAGINE YOU FOUGHT...
...WITH HIKARI OR MACHI, SAY.

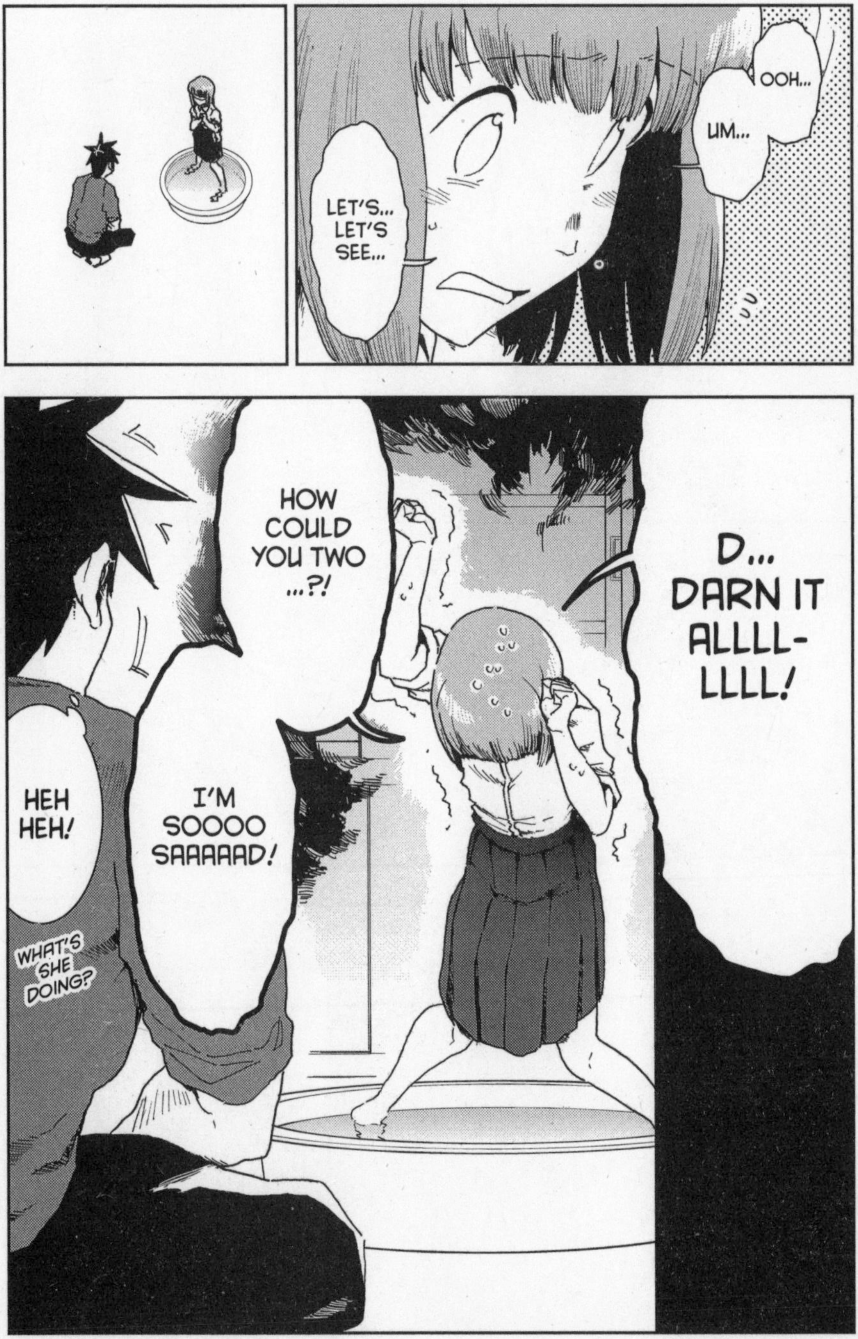
OOH...
UM...
LET'S... LET'S SEE...
D... DARN IT ALLLL-LLLL!
HOW COULD YOU TWO ...?!
I'M SOOOO SAAAAAD!
HEH HEH!
WHAT'S SHE DOING?

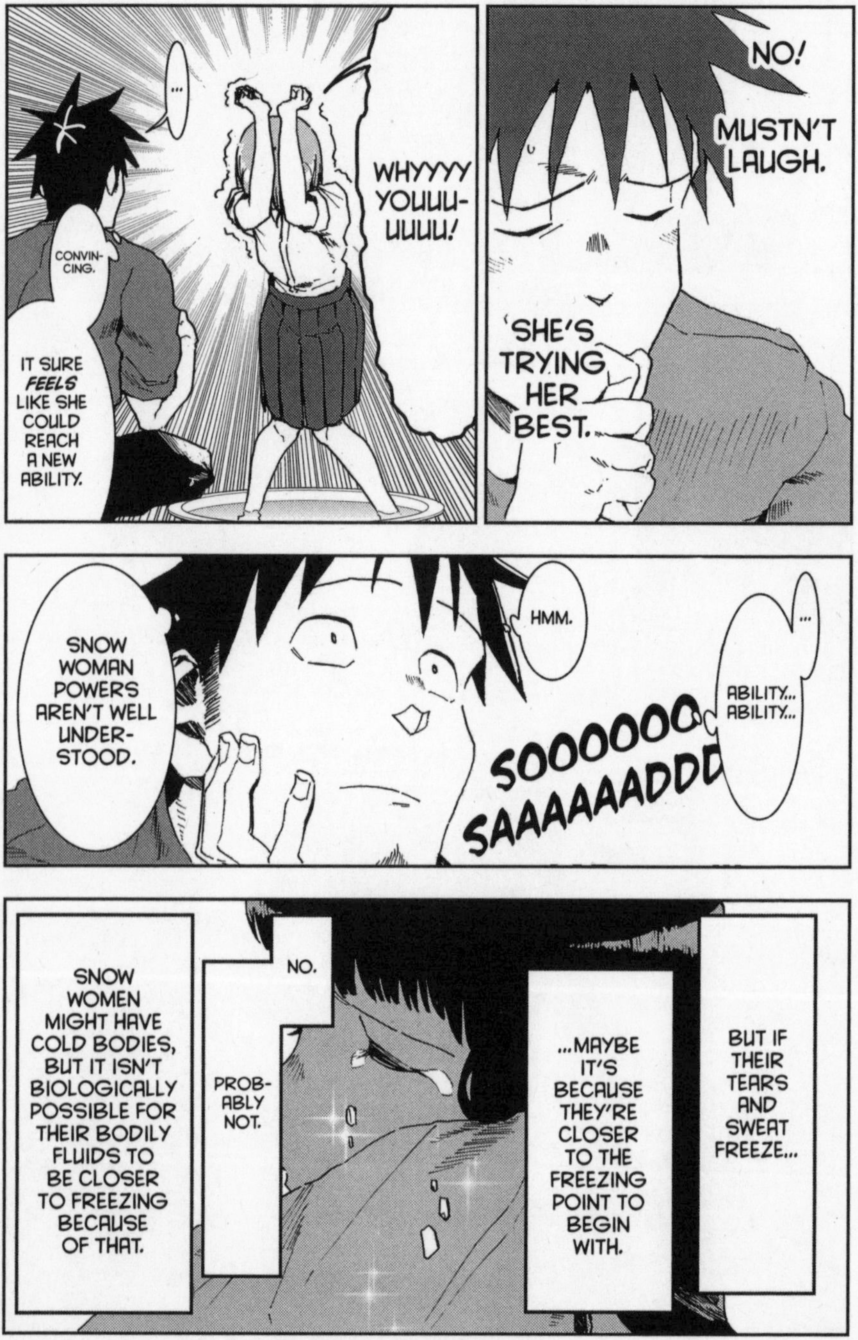
NO!
MUSTN'T LAUGH.
SHE'S TRYING HER BEST.
WHYYYY YOUUUU-UUUUU!
...
CONVIN-CING.
IT SURE *FEELS* LIKE SHE COULD REACH A NEW ABILITY.
...
ABILITY... ABILITY...
HMM.
SOOOOOO SAAAAAADDD
SNOW WOMAN POWERS AREN'T WELL UNDER-STOOD.
BUT IF THEIR TEARS AND SWEAT FREEZE...
...MAYBE IT'S BECAUSE THEY'RE CLOSER TO THE FREEZING POINT TO BEGIN WITH.
NO.
PROB-ABLY NOT.
SNOW WOMEN MIGHT HAVE COLD BODIES, BUT IT ISN'T BIOLOGICALLY POSSIBLE FOR THEIR BODILY FLUIDS TO BE CLOSER TO FREEZING BECAUSE OF THAT.

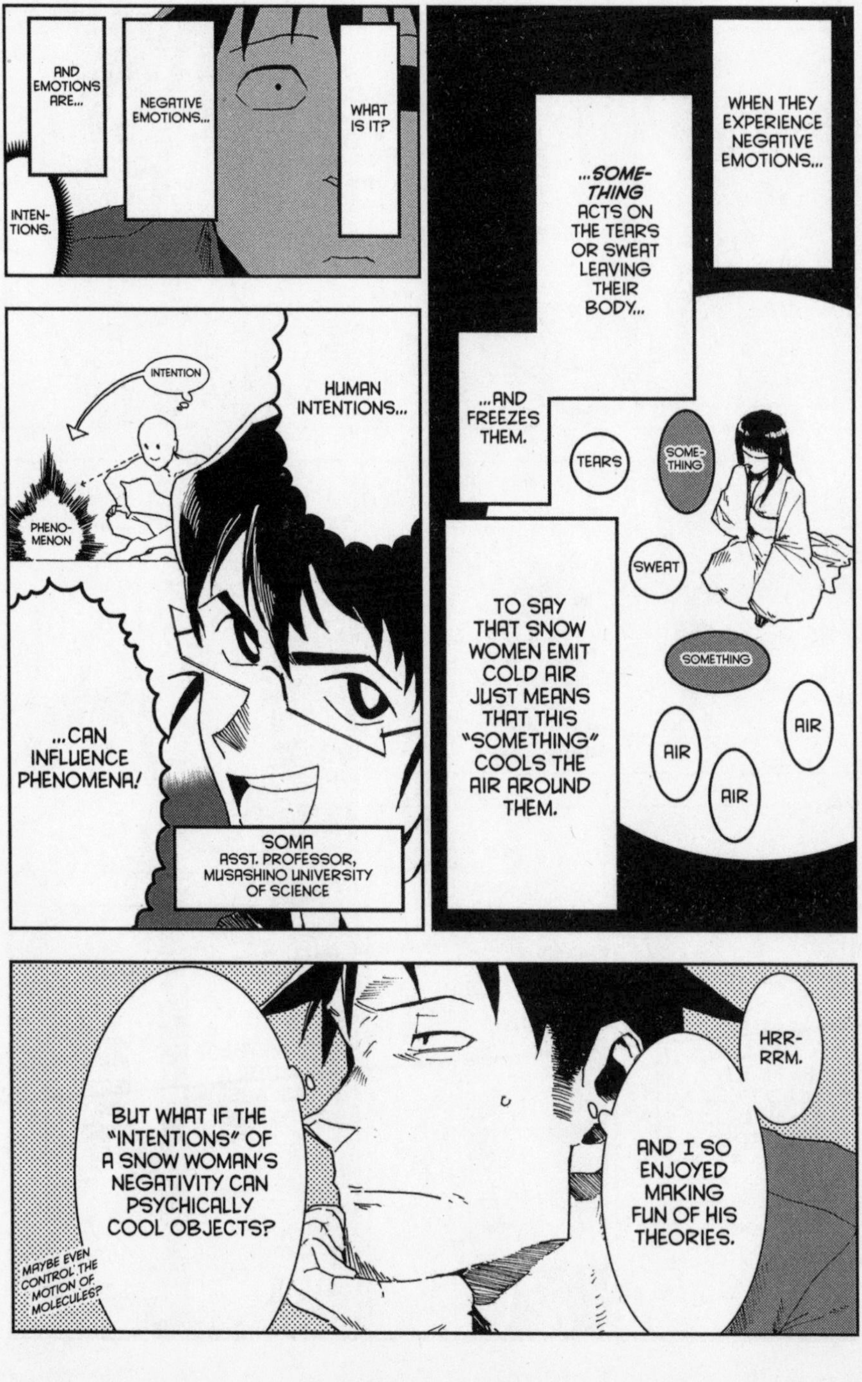
WHEN THEY EXPERIENCE NEGATIVE EMOTIONS...
...*SOMETHING* ACTS ON THE TEARS OR SWEAT LEAVING THEIR BODY...
...AND FREEZES THEM.
SOMETHING
TEARS
SWEAT
SOMETHING
AIR
AIR
AIR
TO SAY THAT SNOW WOMEN EMIT COLD AIR JUST MEANS THAT THIS "SOMETHING" COOLS THE AIR AROUND THEM.
WHAT IS IT?
NEGATIVE EMOTIONS...
AND EMOTIONS ARE...
INTENTIONS.
HUMAN INTENTIONS...
INTENTION
PHENOMENON
...CAN INFLUENCE PHENOMENA!
SOMA
ASST. PROFESSOR, MUSASHINO UNIVERSITY OF SCIENCE
HRR-RRM.
AND I SO ENJOYED MAKING FUN OF HIS THEORIES.
BUT WHAT IF THE "INTENTIONS" OF A SNOW WOMAN'S NEGATIVITY CAN PSYCHICALLY COOL OBJECTS?
MAYBE EVEN CONTROL THE MOTION OF MOLECULES?

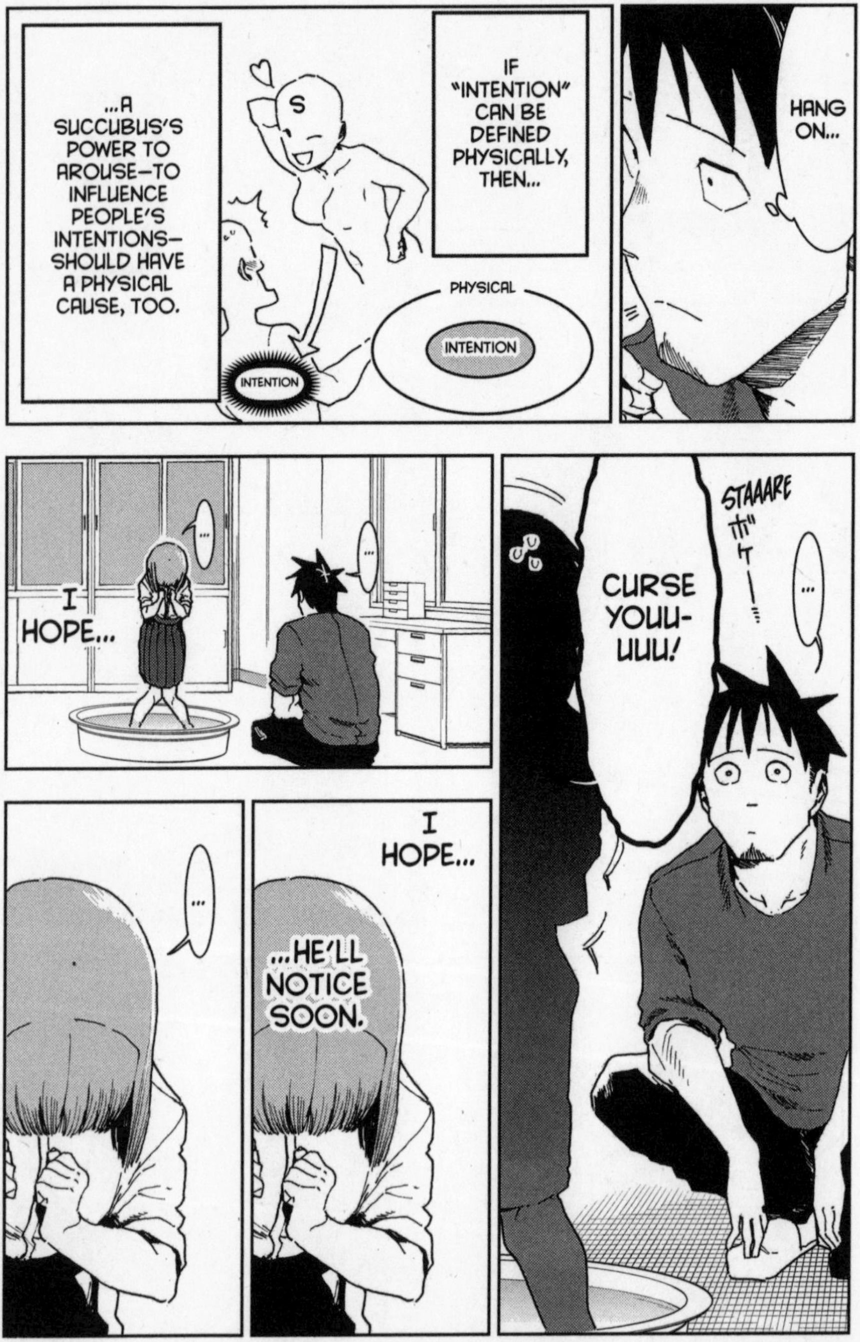
HANG ON...
IF "INTENTION" CAN BE DEFINED PHYSICALLY, THEN...
PHYSICAL
INTENTION
S
...A SUCCUBUS'S POWER TO AROUSE—TO INFLUENCE PEOPLE'S INTENTIONS—SHOULD HAVE A PHYSICAL CAUSE, TOO.
INTENTION
...
STAAARE
ボケー
CURSE YOUUU-UUU!
...
...
I HOPE...
I HOPE...
...HE'LL NOTICE SOON.
...

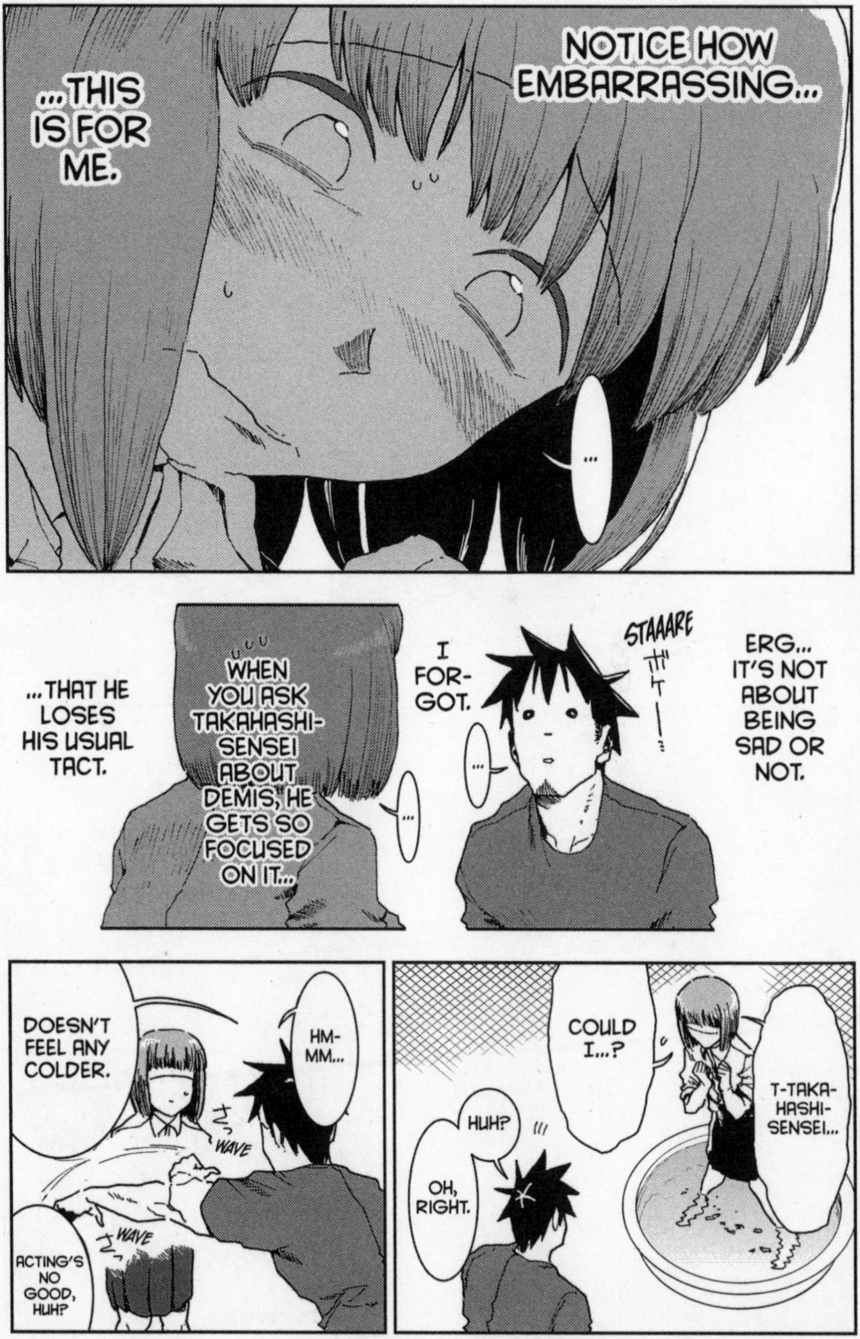
NOTICE HOW EMBARRASSING...
...THIS IS FOR ME.
...
ERG... IT'S NOT ABOUT BEING SAD OR NOT.
STAAARE
ボケー
I FOR-GOT.
...
WHEN YOU ASK TAKAHASHI-SENSEI ABOUT DEMIS, HE GETS SO FOCUSED ON IT...
...
...THAT HE LOSES HIS USUAL TACT.
T-TAKA-HASHI-SENSEI...
COULD I...?
HUH?
OH, RIGHT.
HM-MM...
DOESN'T FEEL ANY COLDER.
WAVE
WAVE
ACTING'S NO GOOD, HUH?

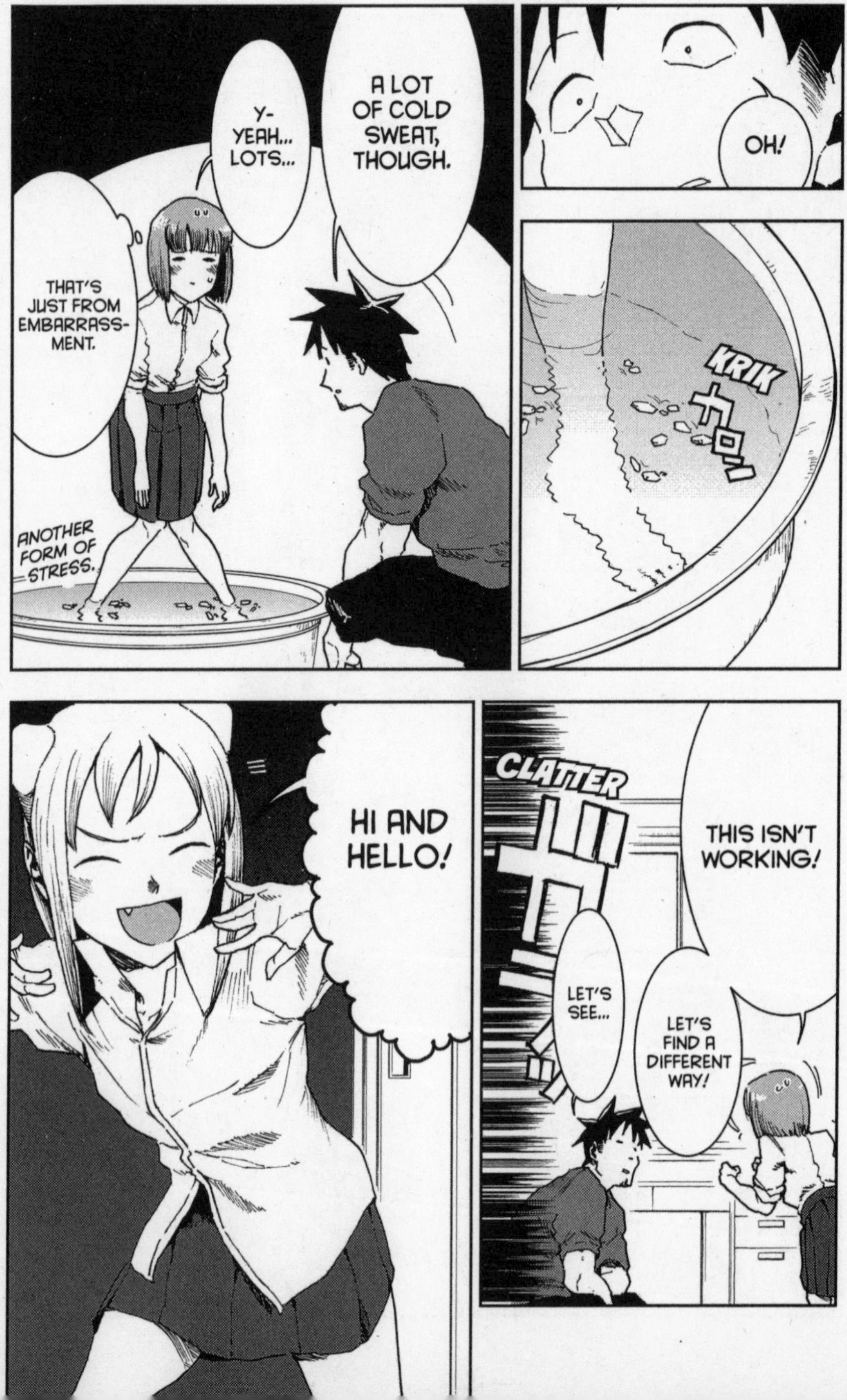
OH!
KRIK
A LOT OF COLD SWEAT, THOUGH.
Y-YEAH... LOTS...
THAT'S JUST FROM EMBARRASSMENT.
ANOTHER FORM OF STRESS.
CLATTER
THIS ISN'T WORKING!
LET'S FIND A DIFFERENT WAY!
LET'S SEE...
HI AND HELLO!

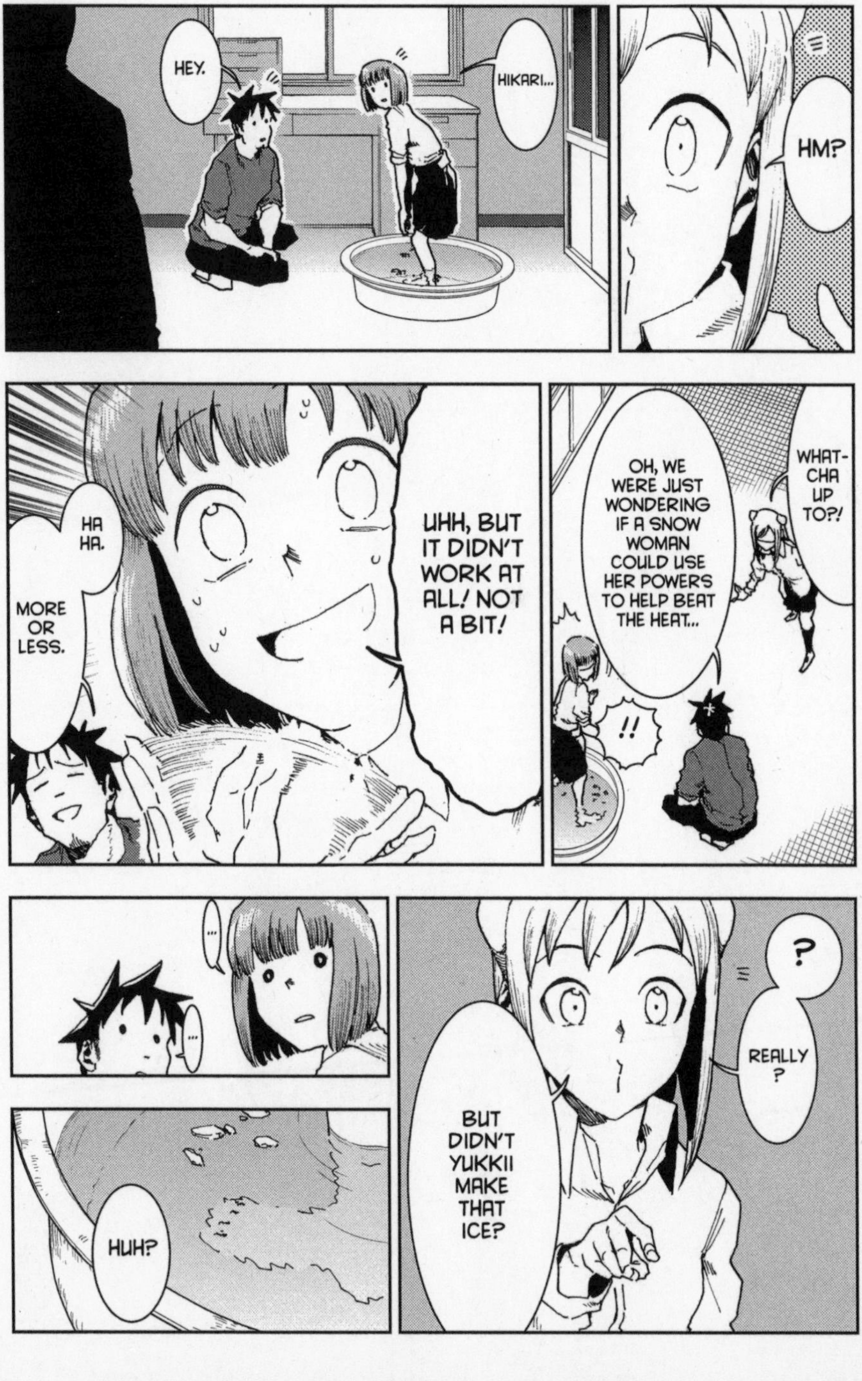
HM?
HIKARI...
HEY.
WHAT-CHA UP TO?!
OH, WE WERE JUST WONDERING IF A SNOW WOMAN COULD USE HER POWERS TO HELP BEAT THE HEAT...
!!
UHH, BUT IT DIDN'T WORK AT ALL! NOT A BIT!
HA HA.
MORE OR LESS.
?
REALLY?
BUT DIDN'T YUKKII MAKE THAT ICE?
...
...
HUH?

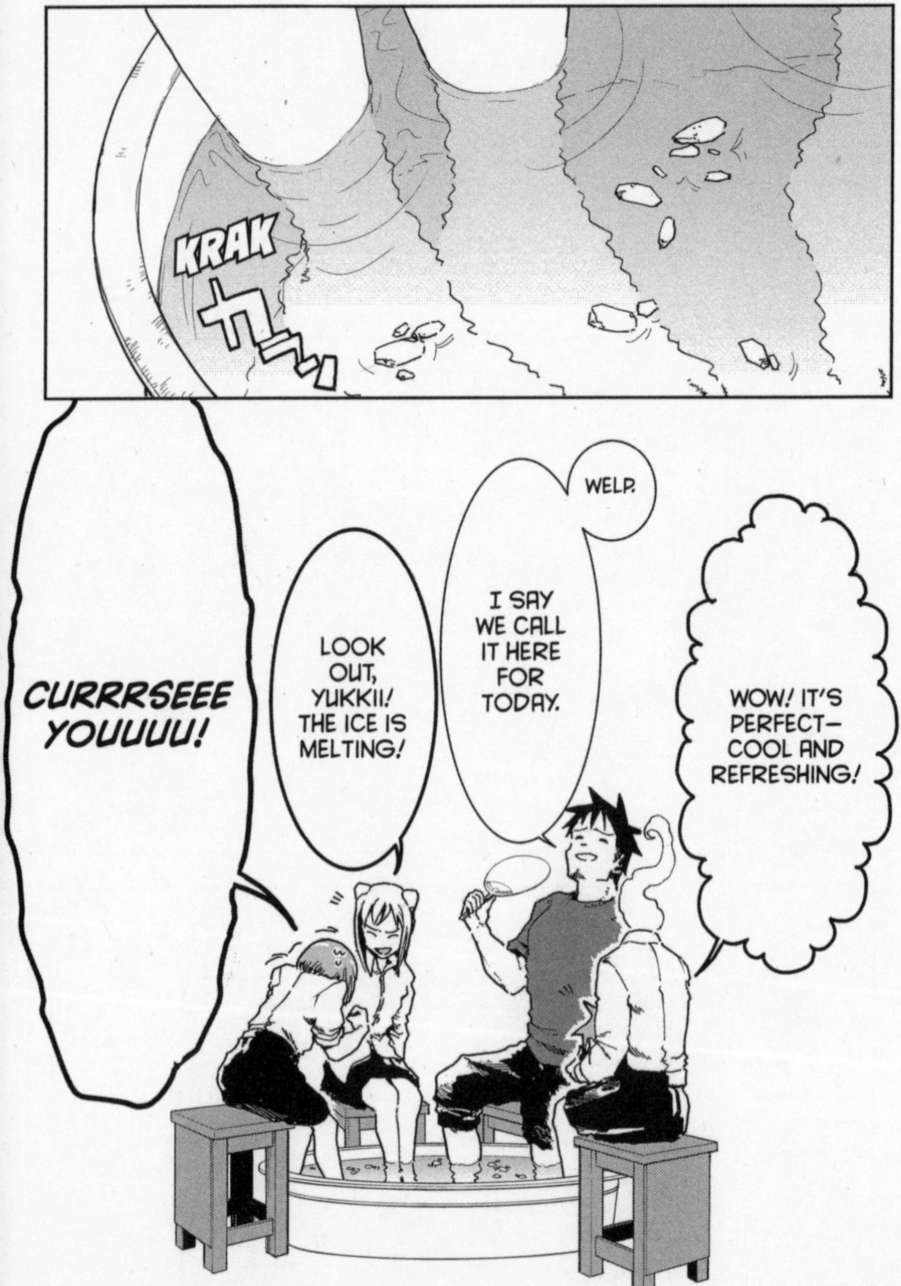
KRAK
WOW! IT'S PERFECT—COOL AND REFRESHING!
WELP.
I SAY WE CALL IT HERE FOR TODAY.
LOOK OUT, YUKKII! THE ICE IS MELTING!
CURRRSEEE YOUUUU!

DULLAHANS ARE NORMAL EXCEPT THEY HAVE WORMHOLES FOR NECKS.
SNOW WOMEN AND SUCCUBI ARE BASICALLY NORMAL, EXCEPT FOR POWERS THAT VERGE ON ESP.
...
SO ONLY VAMPIRES HAVE MARKED BIOLOGICAL DIFFERENCES FROM HUMANS.
...
BLOOD-SUCKING GETS THE MOST ATTENTION, BUT VAMPIRES' SENSES ARE MUCH SHARPER THAN HUMANS'. THEY MIGHT DRINK BLOOD IN ORDER TO FUEL THEIR "HIGH-SPEC" BODIES.
...
THAT'S JUST THE SORT OF STRANGE PATH EVOLUTION WOULD TAKE.
VWOOOP
HIS NECK IS SO FLEXIBLE.
LOST IN THOUGHT...

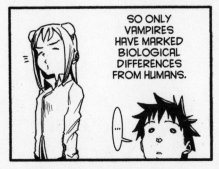

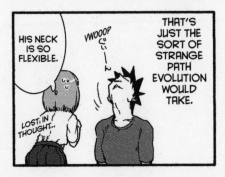

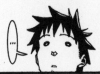

INTERVIEWS WITH MONSTER GIRLS

Chapter 32: Demis Want to Be Cool

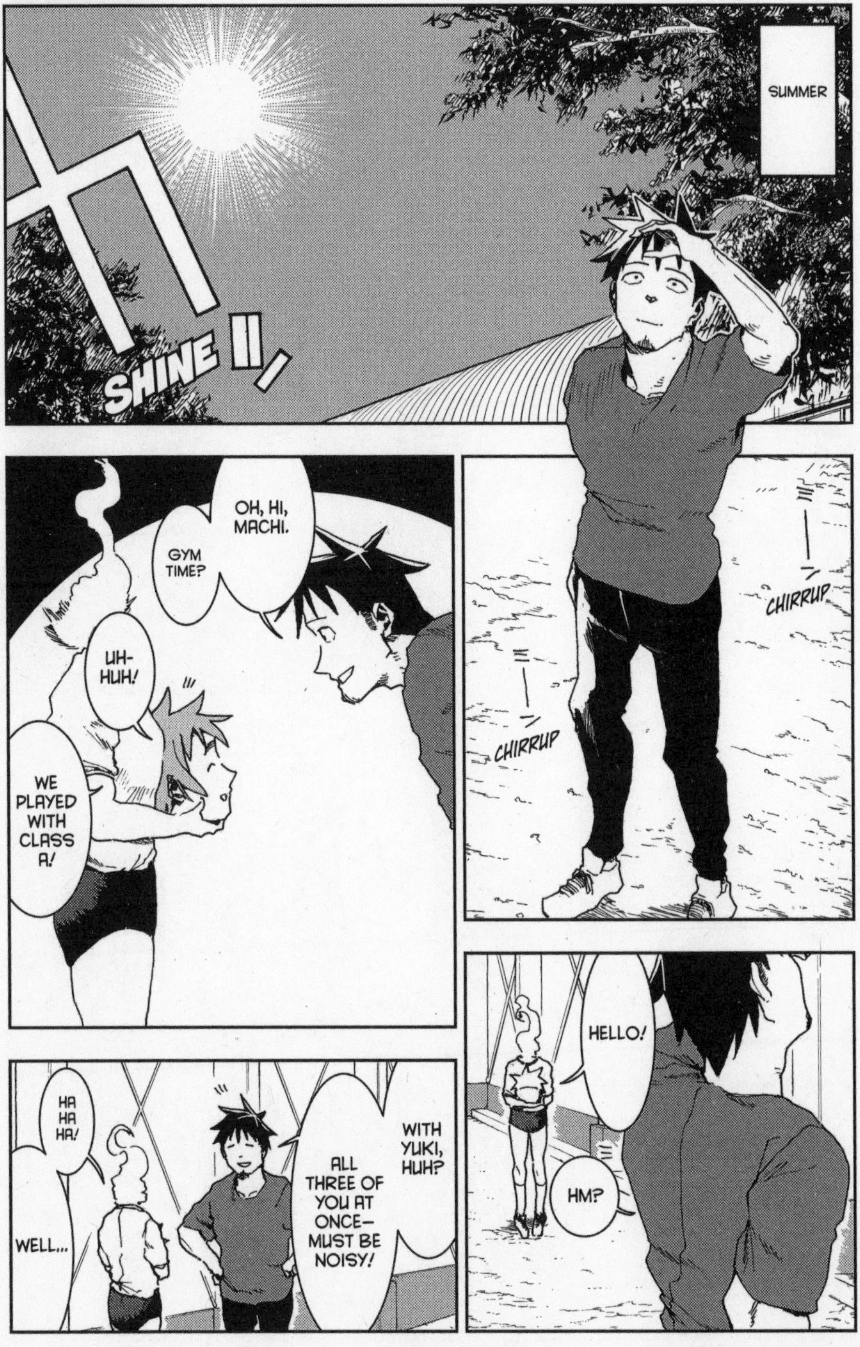
SUMMER
SHINE
CHIRRUP
CHIRRUP
OH, HI, MACHI.
GYM TIME?
UH-HUH!
WE PLAYED WITH CLASS A!
HELLO!
HM?
WITH YUKI, HUH?
ALL THREE OF YOU AT ONCE—MUST BE NOISY!
HA HA HA!
WELL...

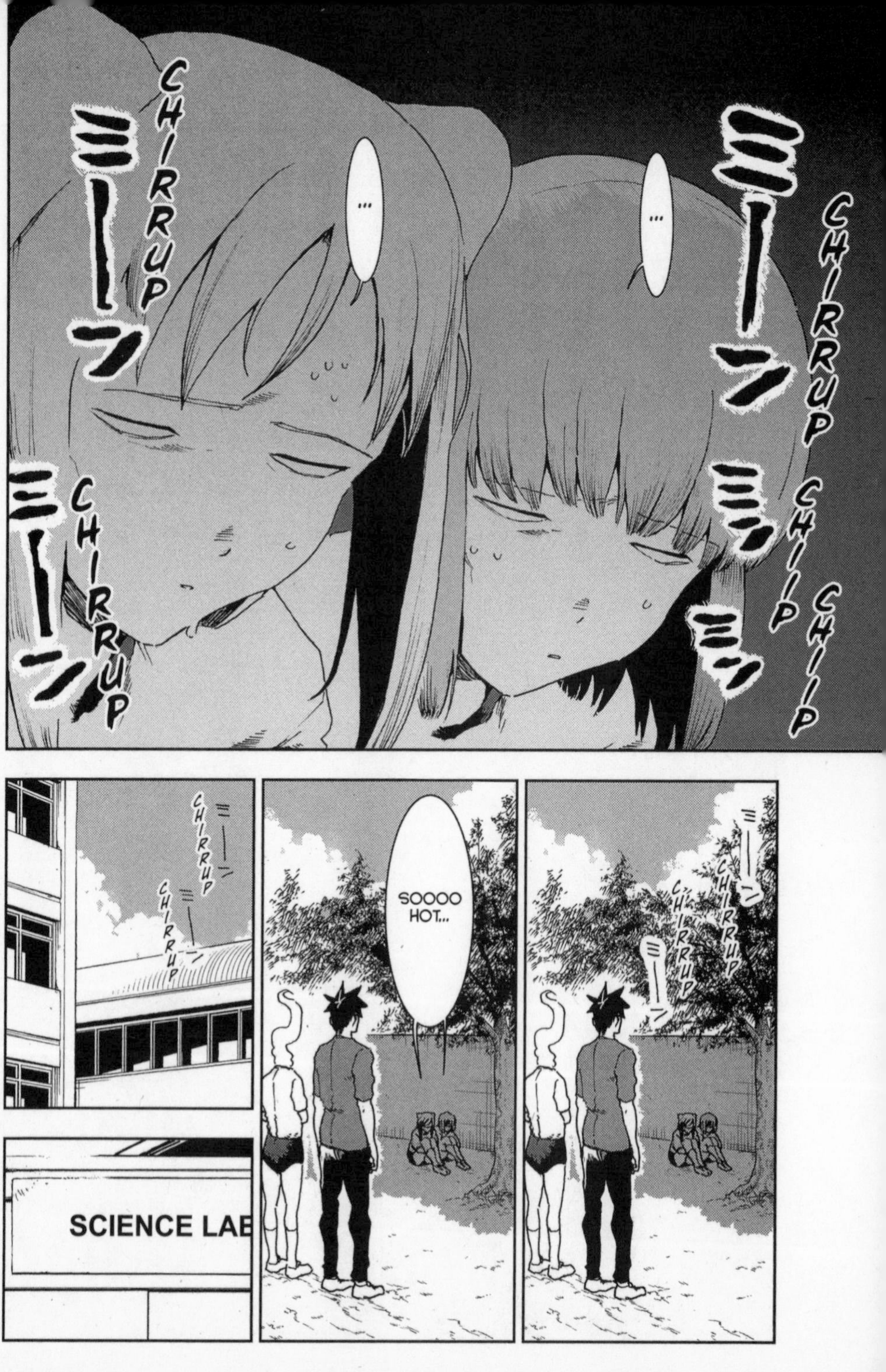
CHIRRRUP
CHIRP
CHIRP
...
...
CHIRRUP
CHIRRUP
CHIRRUP
CHIRRUP
SOOOO HOT...
CHIRRUP
CHIRRUP
SCIENCE LAB

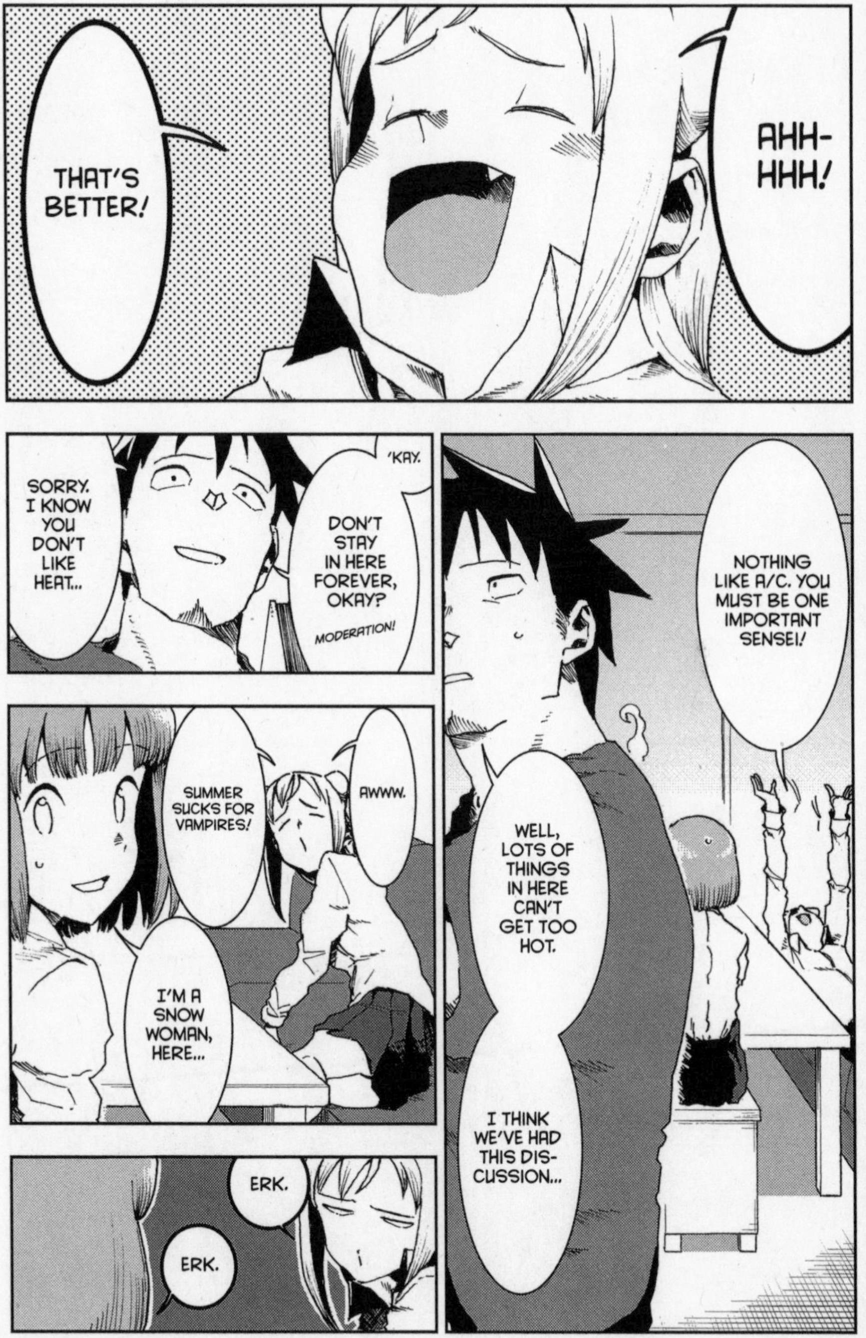
AHH-HHH!
THAT'S BETTER!
NOTHING LIKE A/C. YOU MUST BE ONE IMPORTANT SENSEI!
WELL, LOTS OF THINGS IN HERE CAN'T GET TOO HOT.
I THINK WE'VE HAD THIS DIS-CUSSION...
'KAY.
DON'T STAY IN HERE FOREVER, OKAY? MODERATION!
SORRY. I KNOW YOU DON'T LIKE HEAT...
AWWW.
SUMMER SUCKS FOR VAMPIRES!
I'M A SNOW WOMAN, HERE...
ERK.
ERK.

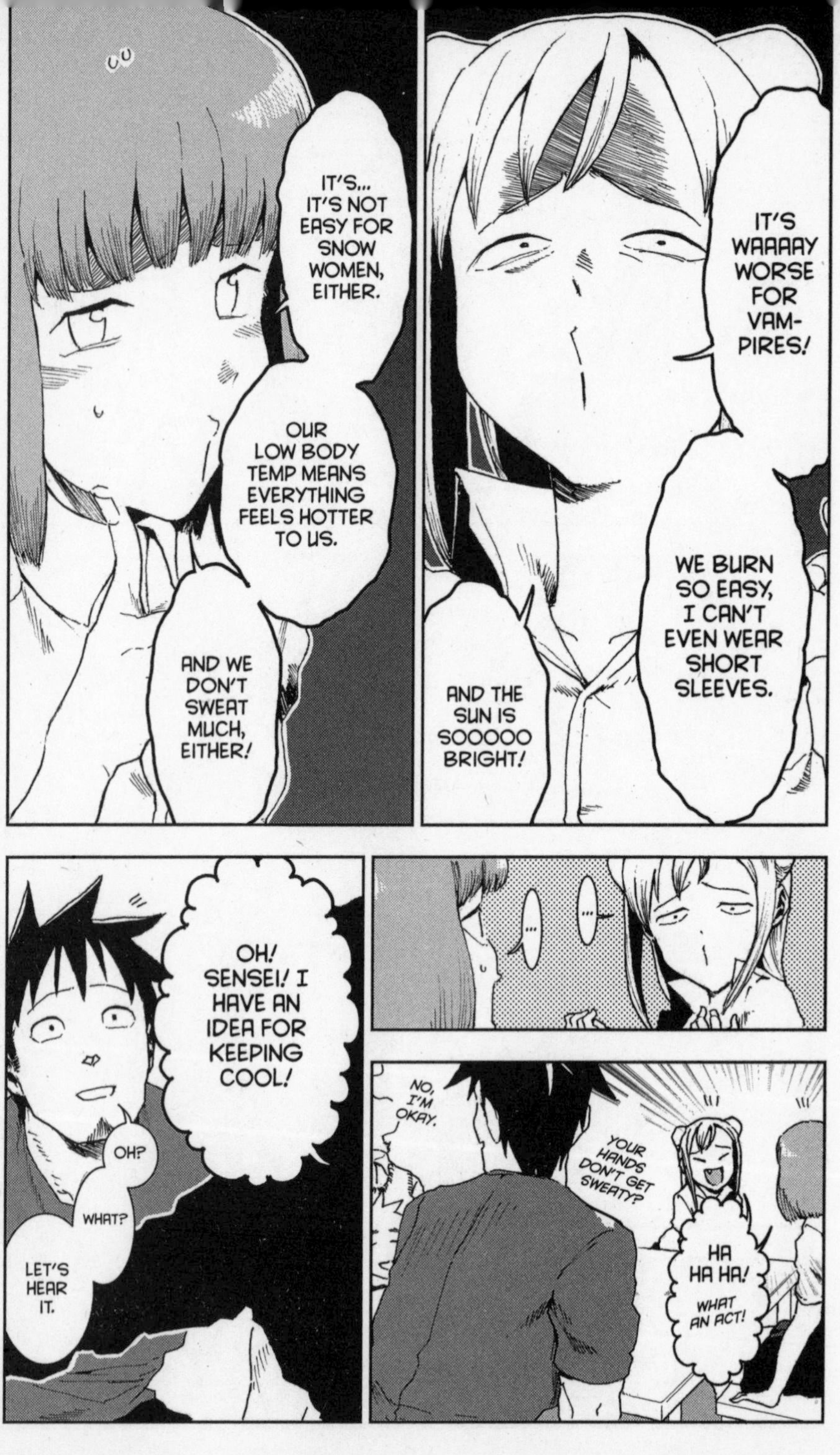
IT'S WAAAAY WORSE FOR VAM-PIRES!
WE BURN SO EASY, I CAN'T EVEN WEAR SHORT SLEEVES.
AND THE SUN IS SOOOOO BRIGHT!
IT'S... IT'S NOT EASY FOR SNOW WOMEN, EITHER.
OUR LOW BODY TEMP MEANS EVERYTHING FEELS HOTTER TO US.
AND WE DON'T SWEAT MUCH, EITHER!
...
...
YOUR HANDS DON'T GET SWEATY?
NO, I'M OKAY.
HA HA HA!
WHAT AN ACT!
OH! SENSEI! I HAVE AN IDEA FOR KEEPING COOL!
OH?
WHAT?
LET'S HEAR IT.

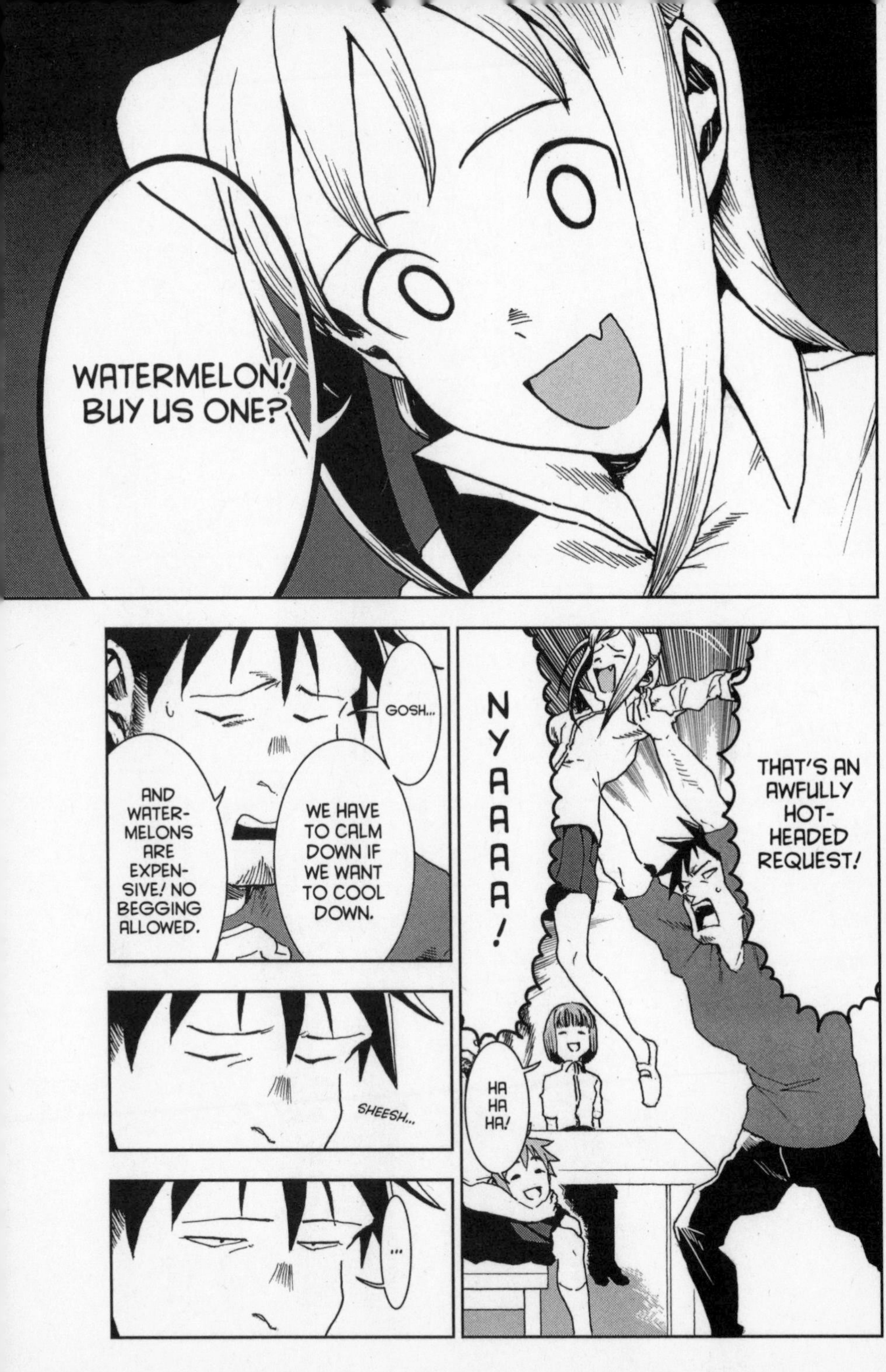
WATERMELON! BUY US ONE?
THAT'S AN AWFULLY HOT-HEADED REQUEST!
NYAAAA!
HA HA HA!
GOSH...
WE HAVE TO CALM DOWN IF WE WANT TO COOL DOWN.
AND WATER-MELONS ARE EXPEN-SIVE! NO BEGGING ALLOWED.
SHEESH...
...

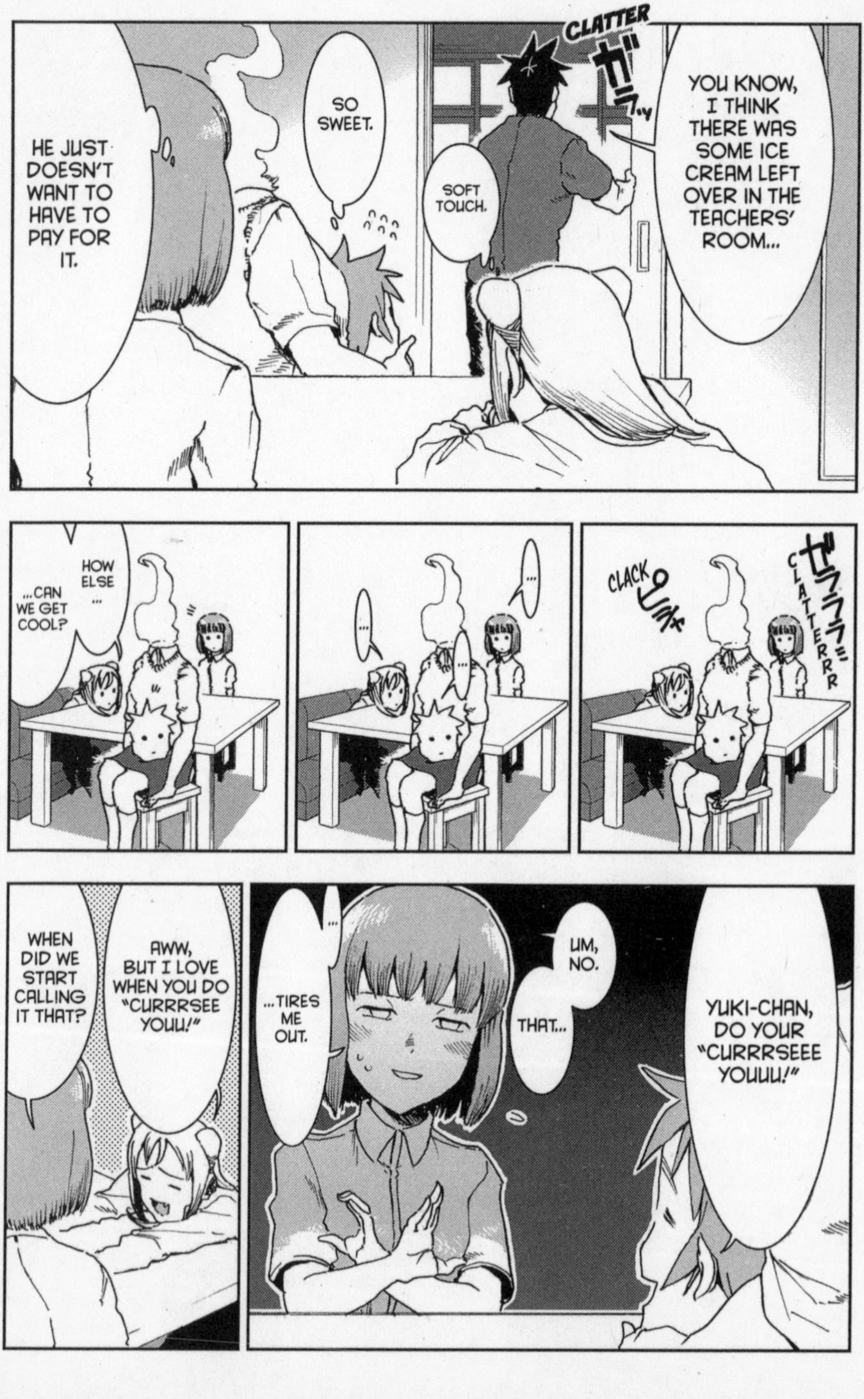
CLATTER
YOU KNOW, I THINK THERE WAS SOME ICE CREAM LEFT OVER IN THE TEACHERS' ROOM...
SO SWEET.
SOFT TOUCH.
HE JUST DOESN'T WANT TO HAVE TO PAY FOR IT.
CLATTERRR
CLACK
...
...
...
HOW ELSE...
...CAN WE GET COOL?
YUKI-CHAN, DO YOUR "CURRRSEEE YOUUU!"
UM, NO.
THAT...
...
...TIRES ME OUT.
AWW, BUT I LOVE WHEN YOU DO "CURRRSEE YOUU!"
WHEN DID WE START CALLING IT THAT?

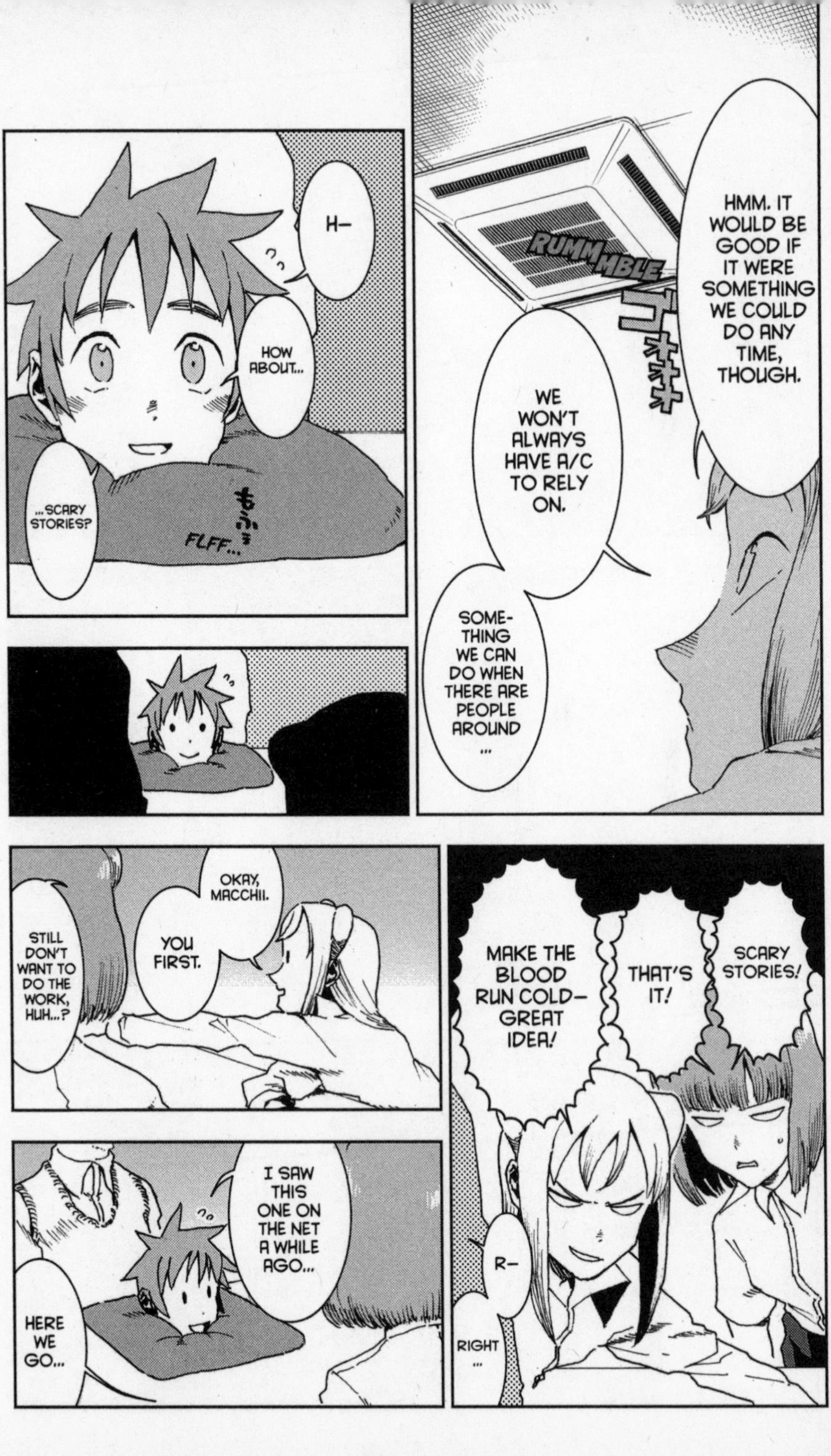
HMM. IT WOULD BE GOOD IF IT WERE SOMETHING WE COULD DO ANY TIME, THOUGH.
RUMMMBLE
WE WON'T ALWAYS HAVE A/C TO RELY ON.
SOMETHING WE CAN DO WHEN THERE ARE PEOPLE AROUND...
H—
HOW ABOUT...
...SCARY STORIES?
FLFF...
SCARY STORIES!
THAT'S IT!
MAKE THE BLOOD RUN COLD—GREAT IDEA!
R—
RIGHT...
OKAY, MACCHII.
YOU FIRST.
STILL DON'T WANT TO DO THE WORK, HUH...?
I SAW THIS ONE ON THE NET A WHILE AGO...
HERE WE GO...

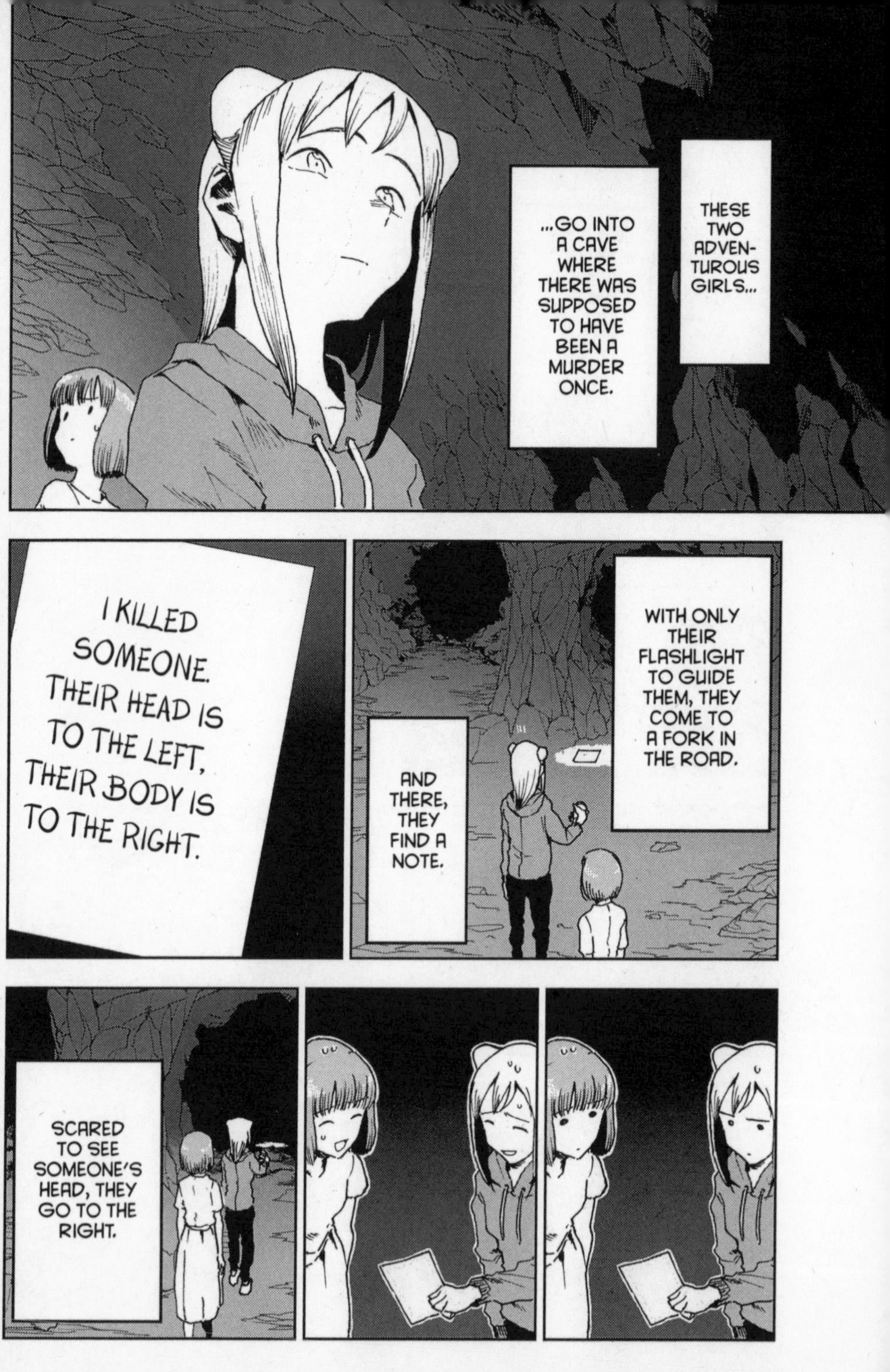
THESE TWO ADVEN-TUROUS GIRLS...
...GO INTO A CAVE WHERE THERE WAS SUPPOSED TO HAVE BEEN A MURDER ONCE.
WITH ONLY THEIR FLASHLIGHT TO GUIDE THEM, THEY COME TO A FORK IN THE ROAD.
AND THERE, THEY FIND A NOTE.
I KILLED SOMEONE. THEIR HEAD IS TO THE LEFT, THEIR BODY IS TO THE RIGHT.
SCARED TO SEE SOMEONE'S HEAD, THEY GO TO THE RIGHT.

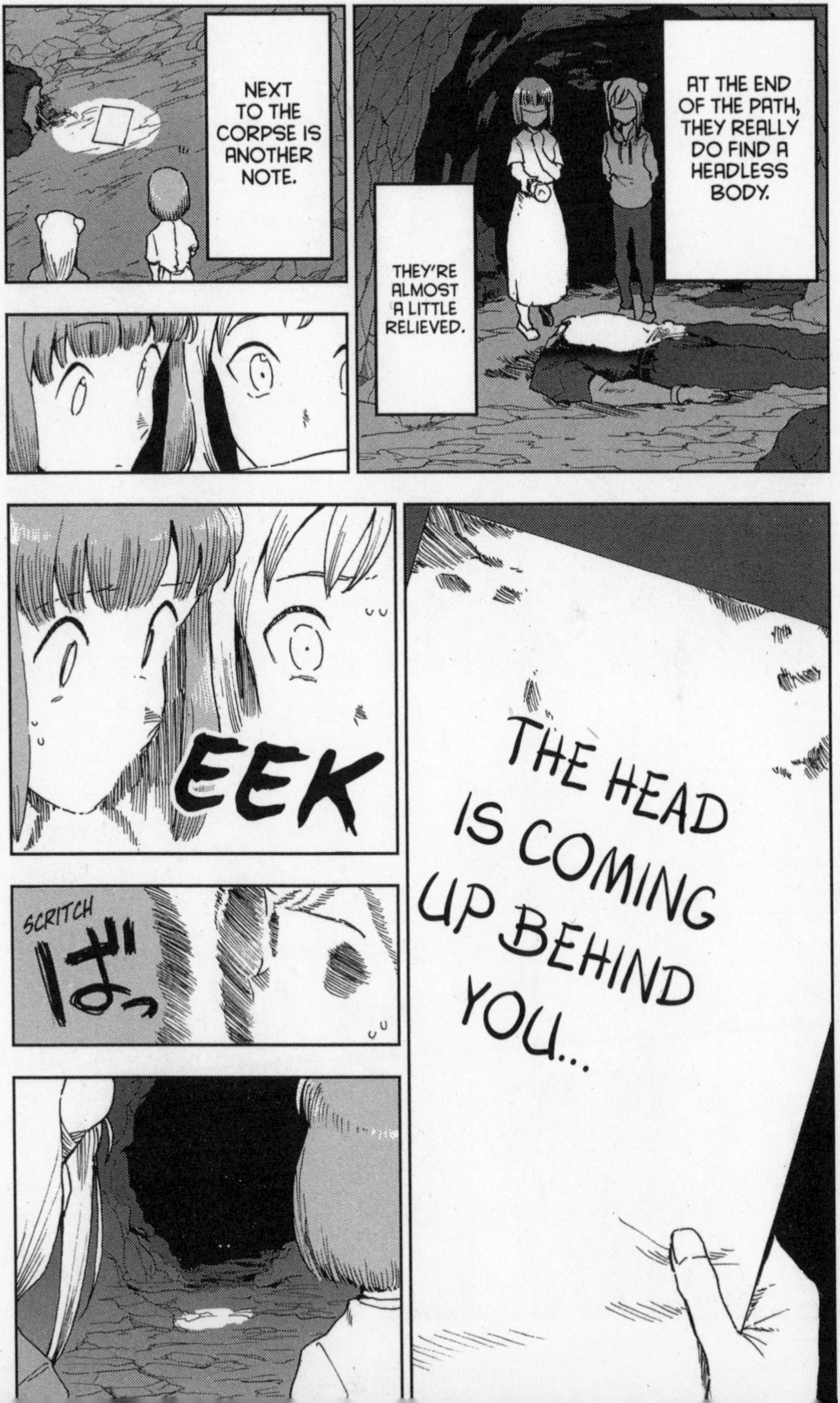
AT THE END OF THE PATH, THEY REALLY DO FIND A HEADLESS BODY.
THEY'RE ALMOST A LITTLE RELIEVED.
NEXT TO THE CORPSE IS ANOTHER NOTE.
THE HEAD IS COMING UP BEHIND YOU...
EEK
SCRITCH
ぱっ

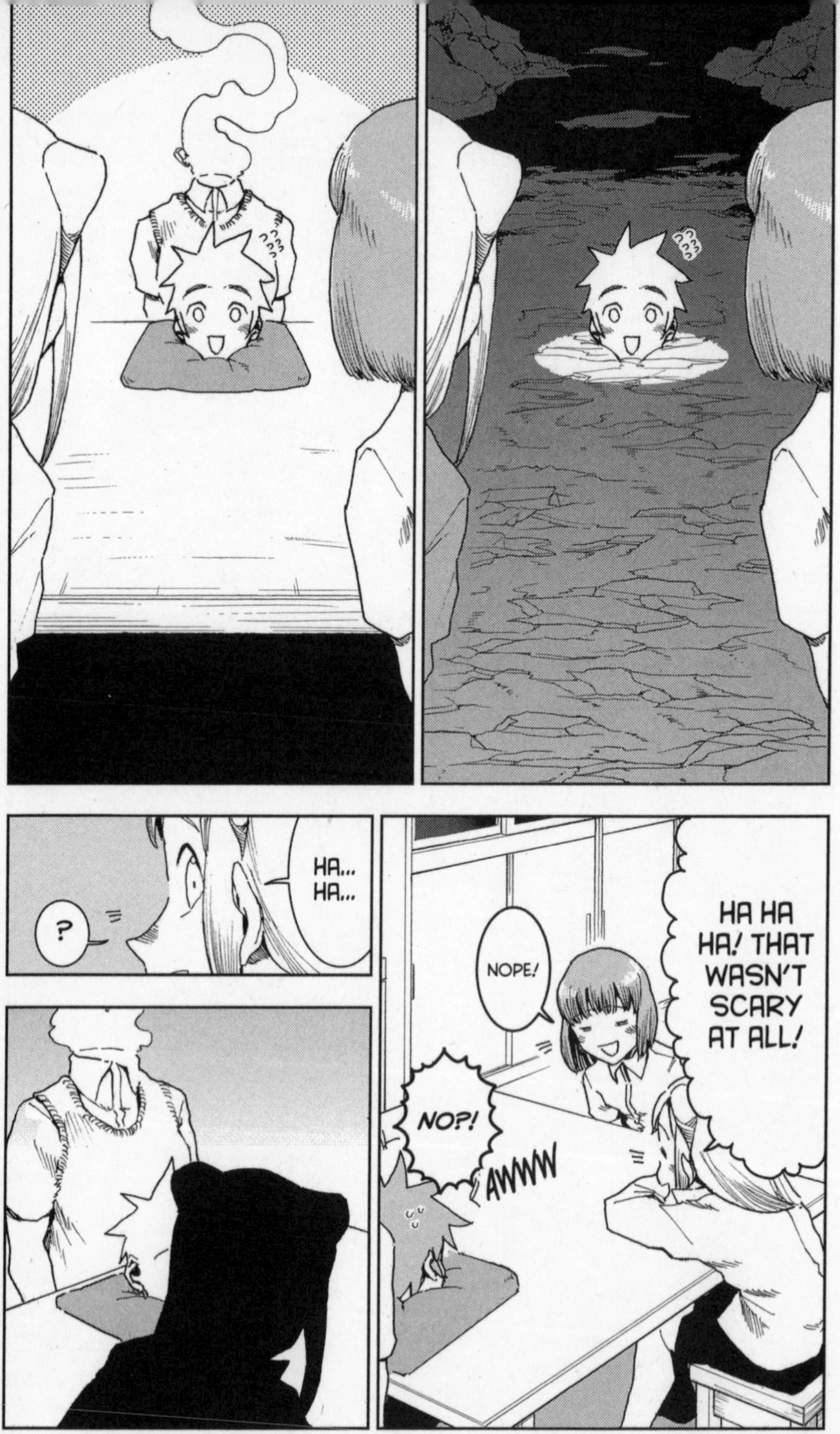
HA HA HA! THAT WASN'T SCARY AT ALL!
NOPE!
NO?!
AWWW
HA... HA...
?

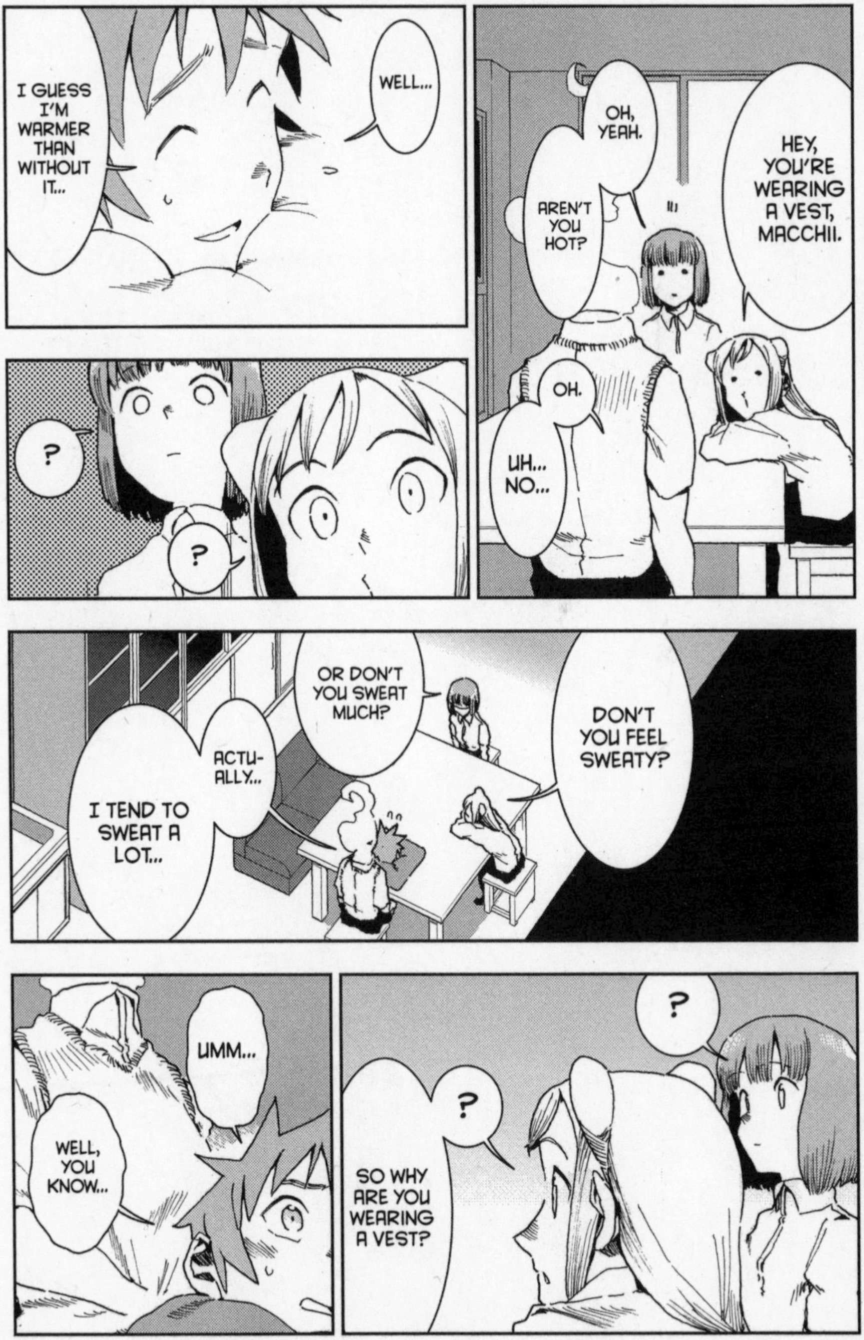
HEY, YOU'RE WEARING A VEST, MACCHII.
OH, YEAH.
AREN'T YOU HOT?
OH.
UH... NO...
WELL...
I GUESS I'M WARMER THAN WITHOUT IT...
?
?
DON'T YOU FEEL SWEATY?
OR DON'T YOU SWEAT MUCH?
ACTU-ALLY...
I TEND TO SWEAT A LOT...
?
?
SO WHY ARE YOU WEARING A VEST?
UMM...
WELL, YOU KNOW...

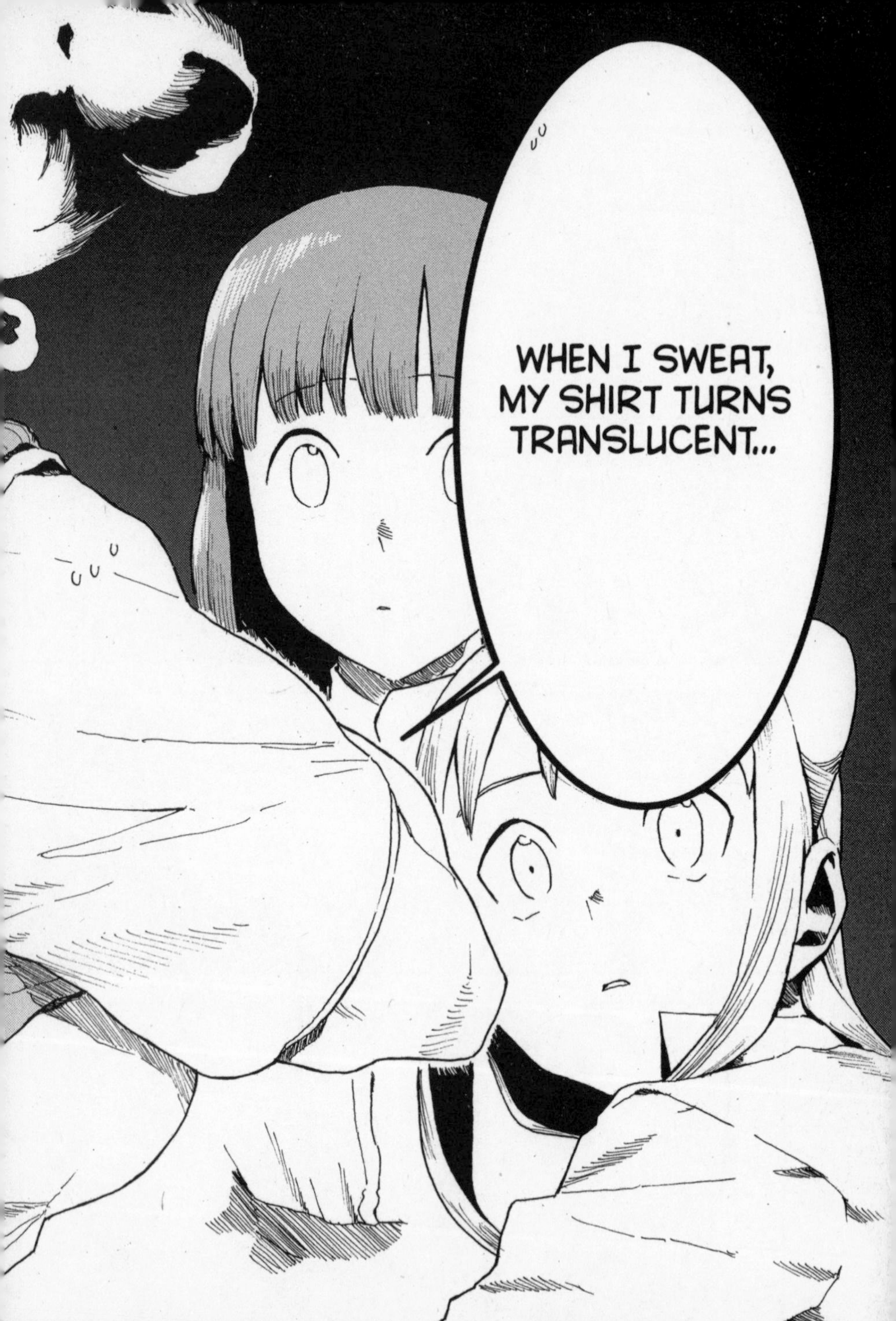
WHEN I SWEAT, MY SHIRT TURNS TRANSLUCENT...

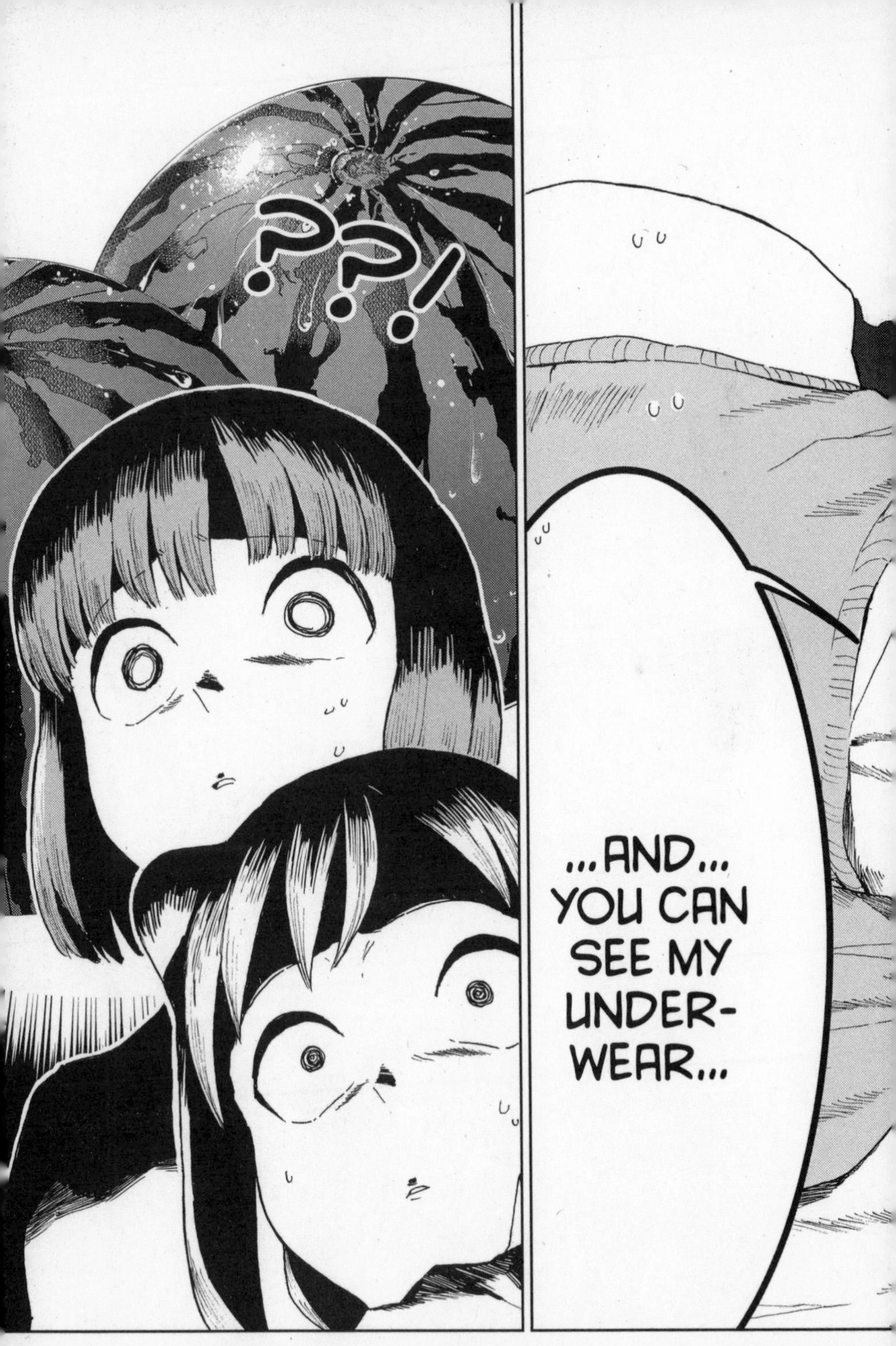
...AND... YOU CAN SEE MY UNDER-WEAR...
??!

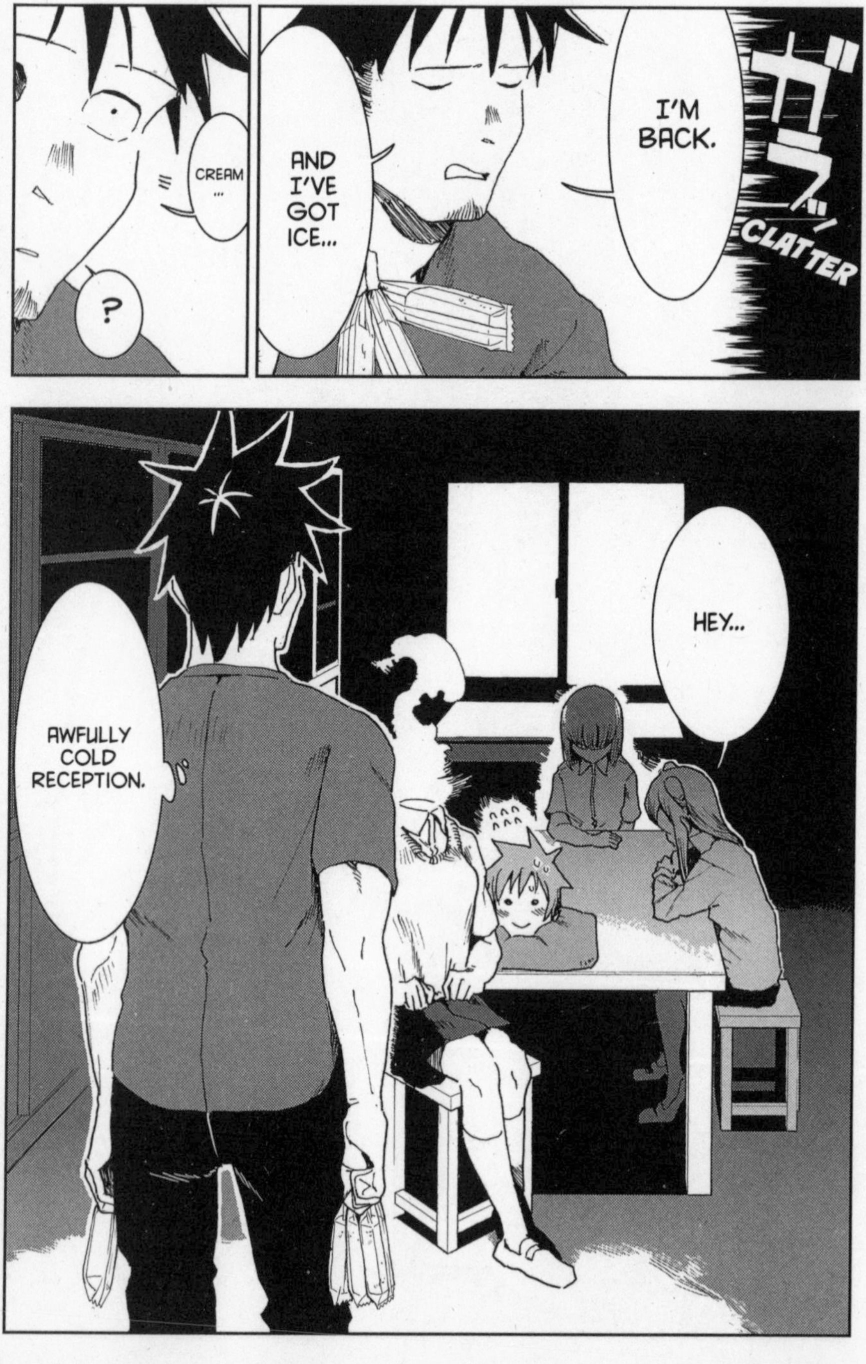
CLATTER
I'M BACK.
AND I'VE GOT ICE...
CREAM ...
?
HEY...
AWFULLY COLD RECEPTION.

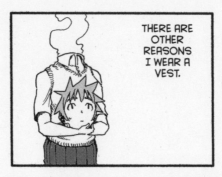

THERE ARE OTHER REASONS I WEAR A VEST.
WIPE WIPE
ふき ふき
LIKE, I CAN WIPE THE SWEAT OFF MY FACE.
KINDA GROSS, HUH?

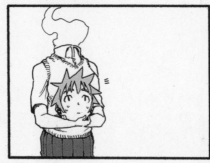

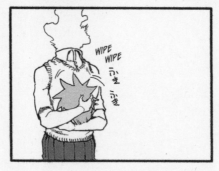

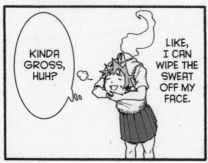

INTERVIEWS WITH MONSTER GIRLS

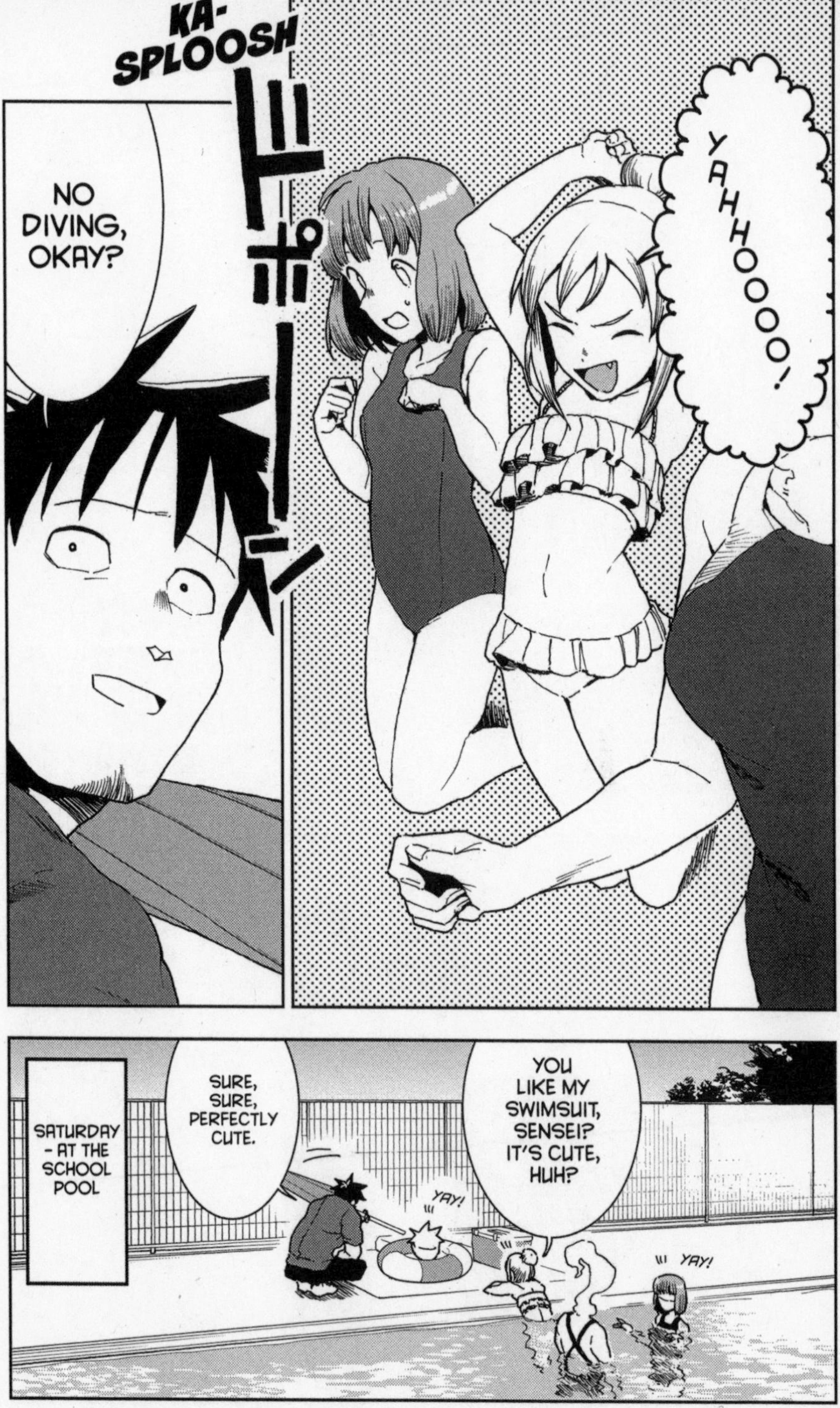
YAHHOOOO!
KA-SPLOOSH
ドポーン
NO DIVING, OKAY?
YOU LIKE MY SWIMSUIT, SENSEI? IT'S CUTE, HUH?
SURE, SURE, PERFECTLY CUTE.
SATURDAY - AT THE SCHOOL POOL
YAY!
YAY!

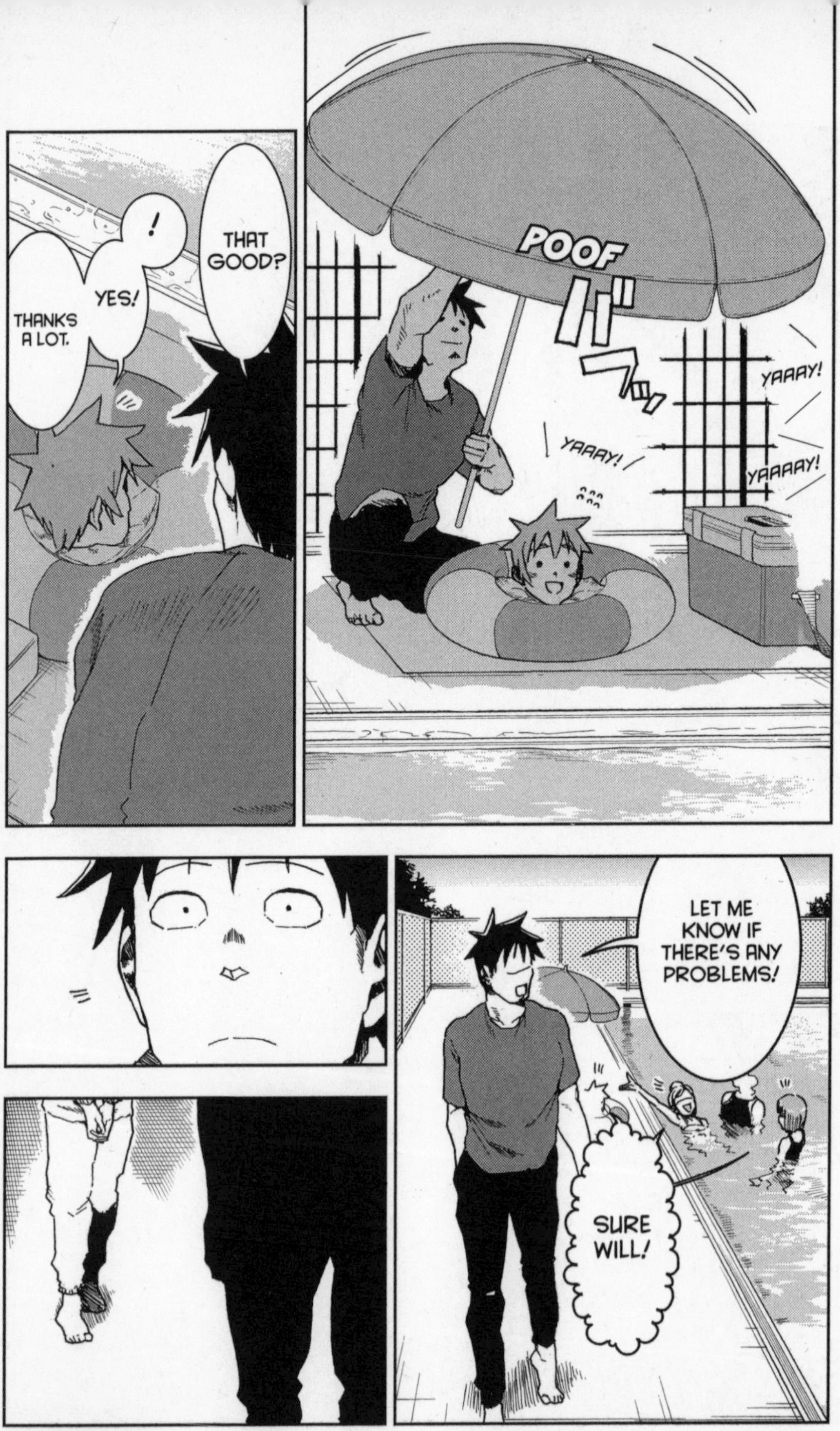
POOF
YAAAY!
YAAAAY!
YAAAY!
THAT GOOD?
!
YES!
THANKS A LOT.
LET ME KNOW IF THERE'S ANY PROBLEMS!
SURE WILL!

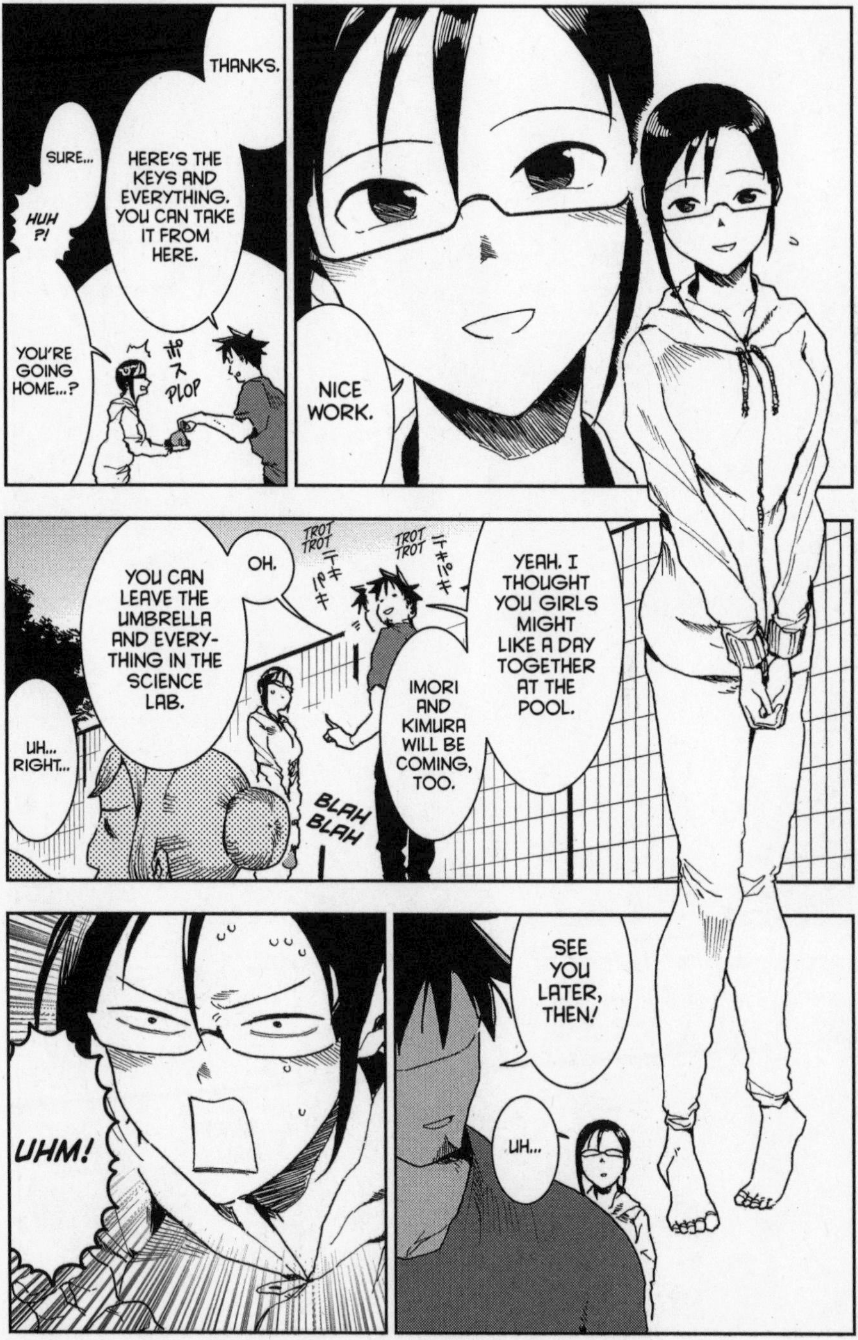
NICE WORK.
THANKS.
HERE'S THE KEYS AND EVERYTHING. YOU CAN TAKE IT FROM HERE.
SURE...
HUH ?!
ポス
PLOP
YOU'RE GOING HOME...?
YEAH. I THOUGHT YOU GIRLS MIGHT LIKE A DAY TOGETHER AT THE POOL.
テキパキ
TROT TROT
IMORI AND KIMURA WILL BE COMING, TOO.
OH.
テキパキ
TROT TROT
YOU CAN LEAVE THE UMBRELLA AND EVERY-THING IN THE SCIENCE LAB.
BLAH BLAH
UH... RIGHT...
SEE YOU LATER, THEN!
UH...
UHM!

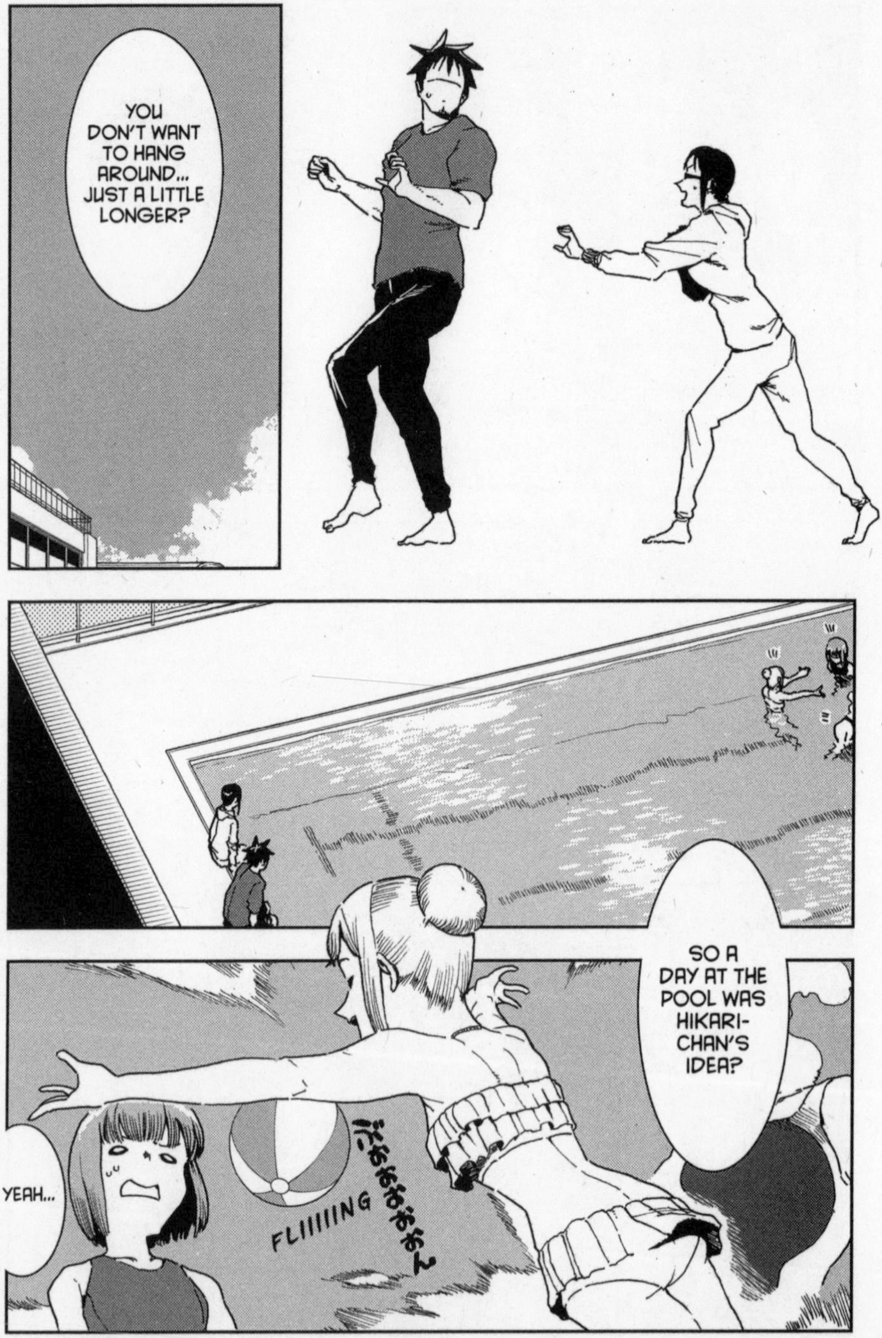
YOU DON'T WANT TO HANG AROUND... JUST A LITTLE LONGER?
SO A DAY AT THE POOL WAS HIKARI-CHAN'S IDEA?
ぶぉおおおぉん
FLIIIIING
YEAH...

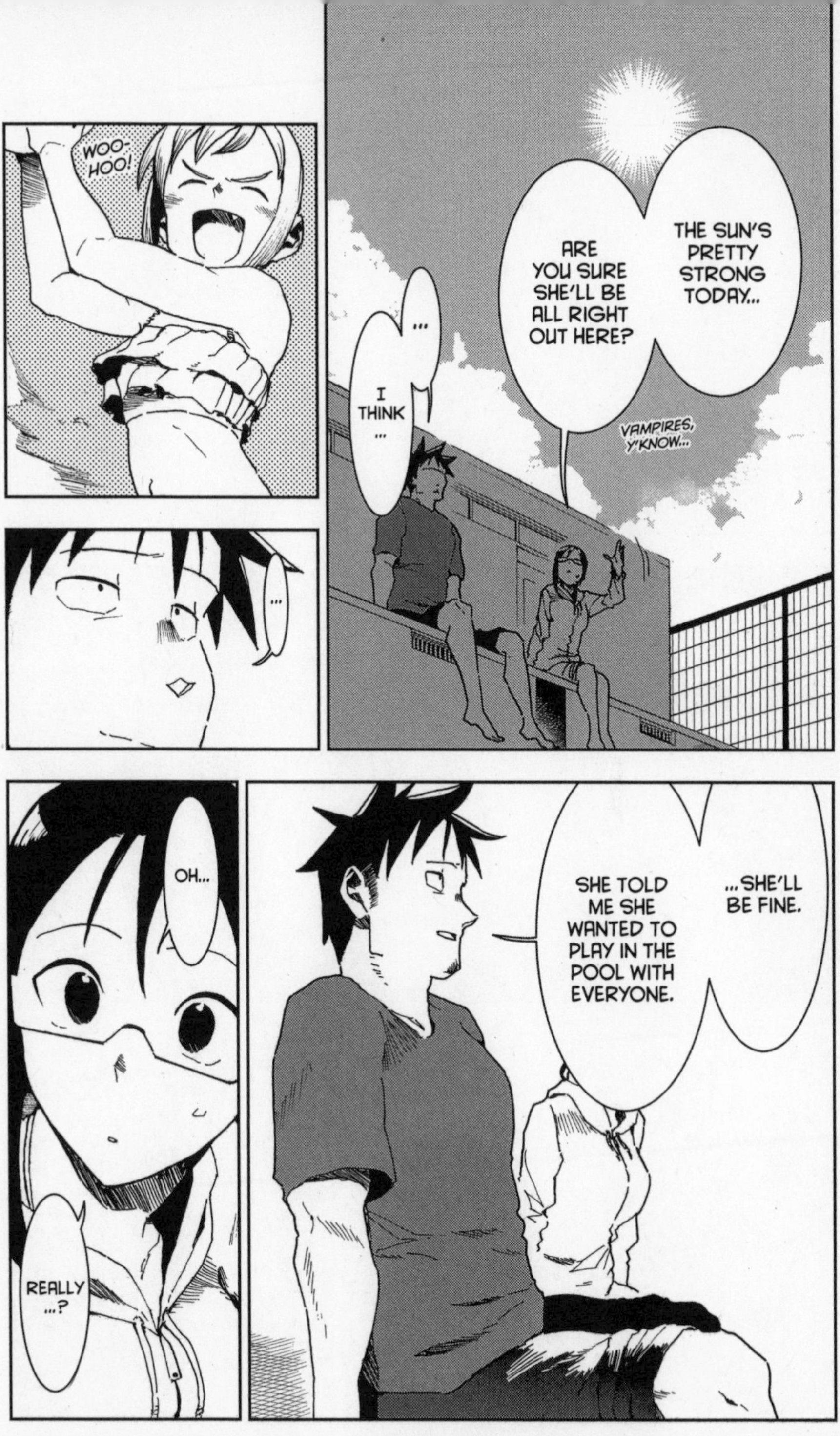
THE SUN'S PRETTY STRONG TODAY...
ARE YOU SURE SHE'LL BE ALL RIGHT OUT HERE?
VAMPIRES, Y'KNOW...
...
I THINK ...
WOO-HOO!
...
...SHE'LL BE FINE.
SHE TOLD ME SHE WANTED TO PLAY IN THE POOL WITH EVERYONE.
OH...
REALLY ...?

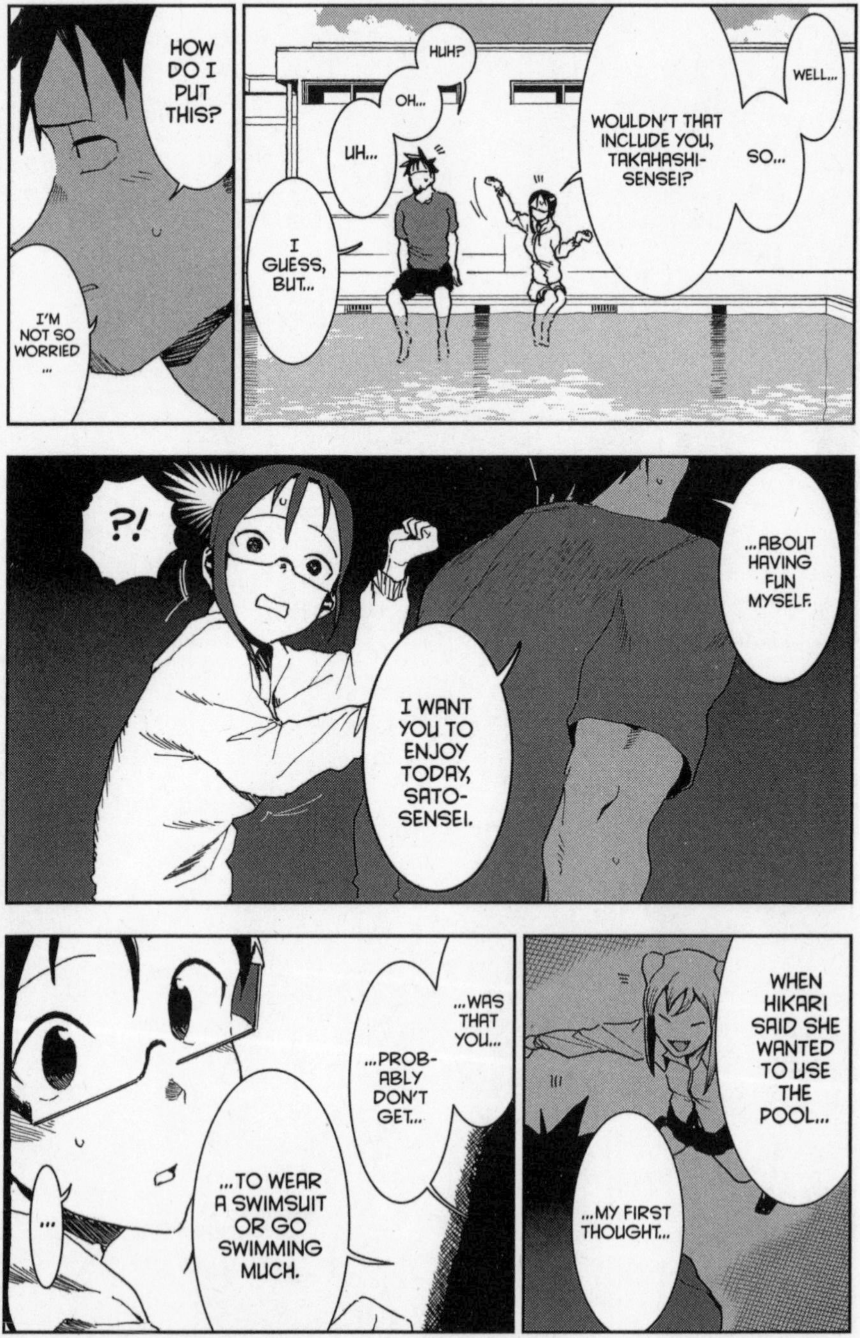
WELL...
SO...
WOULDN'T THAT INCLUDE YOU, TAKAHASHI-SENSEI?
HUH?
OH...
UH...
I GUESS, BUT...
HOW DO I PUT THIS?
I'M NOT SO WORRIED ...
...ABOUT HAVING FUN MYSELF.
I WANT YOU TO ENJOY TODAY, SATO-SENSEI.
?!
WHEN HIKARI SAID SHE WANTED TO USE THE POOL...
...MY FIRST THOUGHT...
...WAS THAT YOU...
...PROBABLY DON'T GET...
...TO WEAR A SWIMSUIT OR GO SWIMMING MUCH.
...

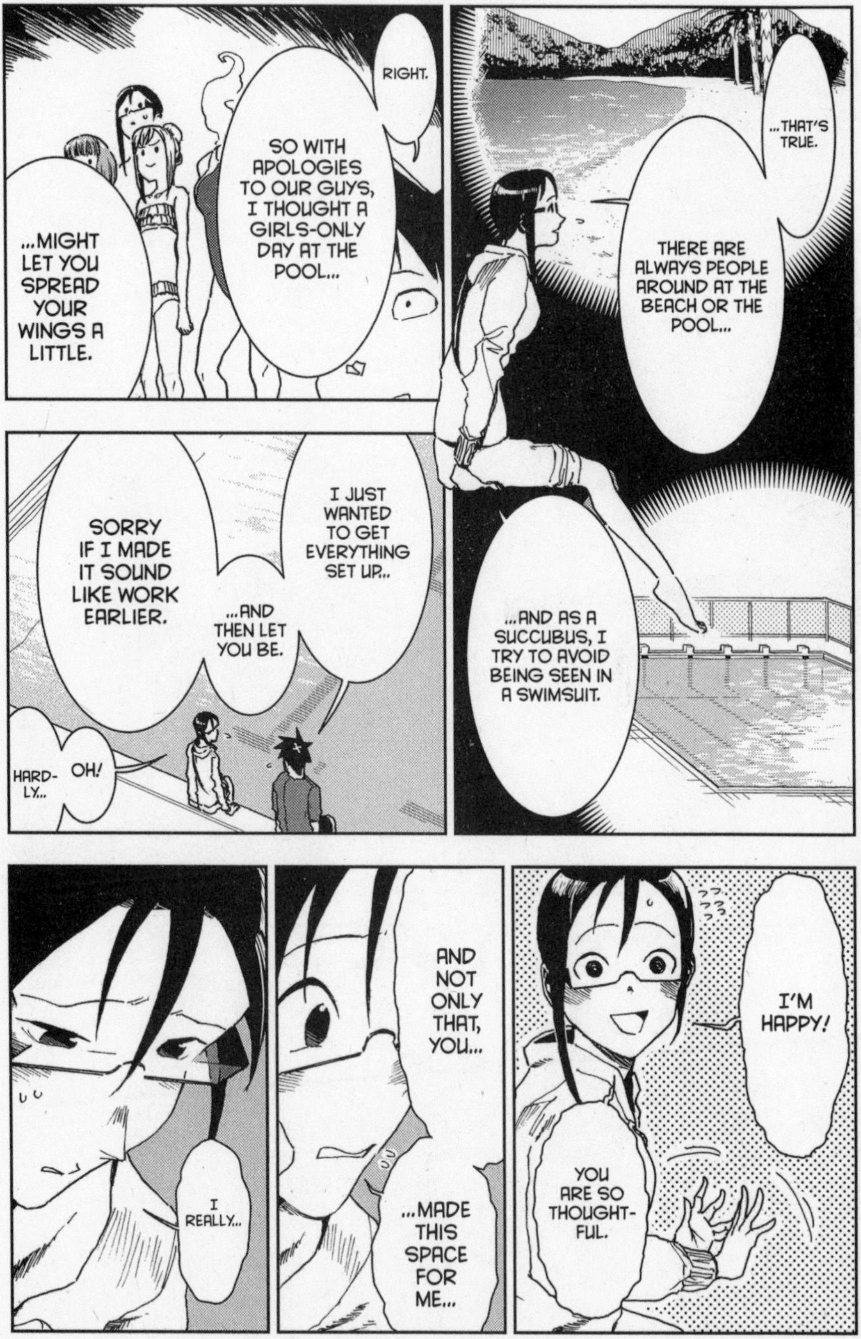
...THAT'S TRUE.
THERE ARE ALWAYS PEOPLE AROUND AT THE BEACH OR THE POOL...
...AND AS A SUCCUBUS, I TRY TO AVOID BEING SEEN IN A SWIMSUIT.
RIGHT.
SO WITH APOLOGIES TO OUR GUYS, I THOUGHT A GIRLS-ONLY DAY AT THE POOL...
...MIGHT LET YOU SPREAD YOUR WINGS A LITTLE.
I JUST WANTED TO GET EVERYTHING SET UP...
...AND THEN LET YOU BE.
SORRY IF I MADE IT SOUND LIKE WORK EARLIER.
OH!
HARD-LY...
I'M HAPPY!
YOU ARE SO THOUGHT-FUL.
AND NOT ONLY THAT, YOU...
...MADE THIS SPACE FOR ME...
I REALLY...

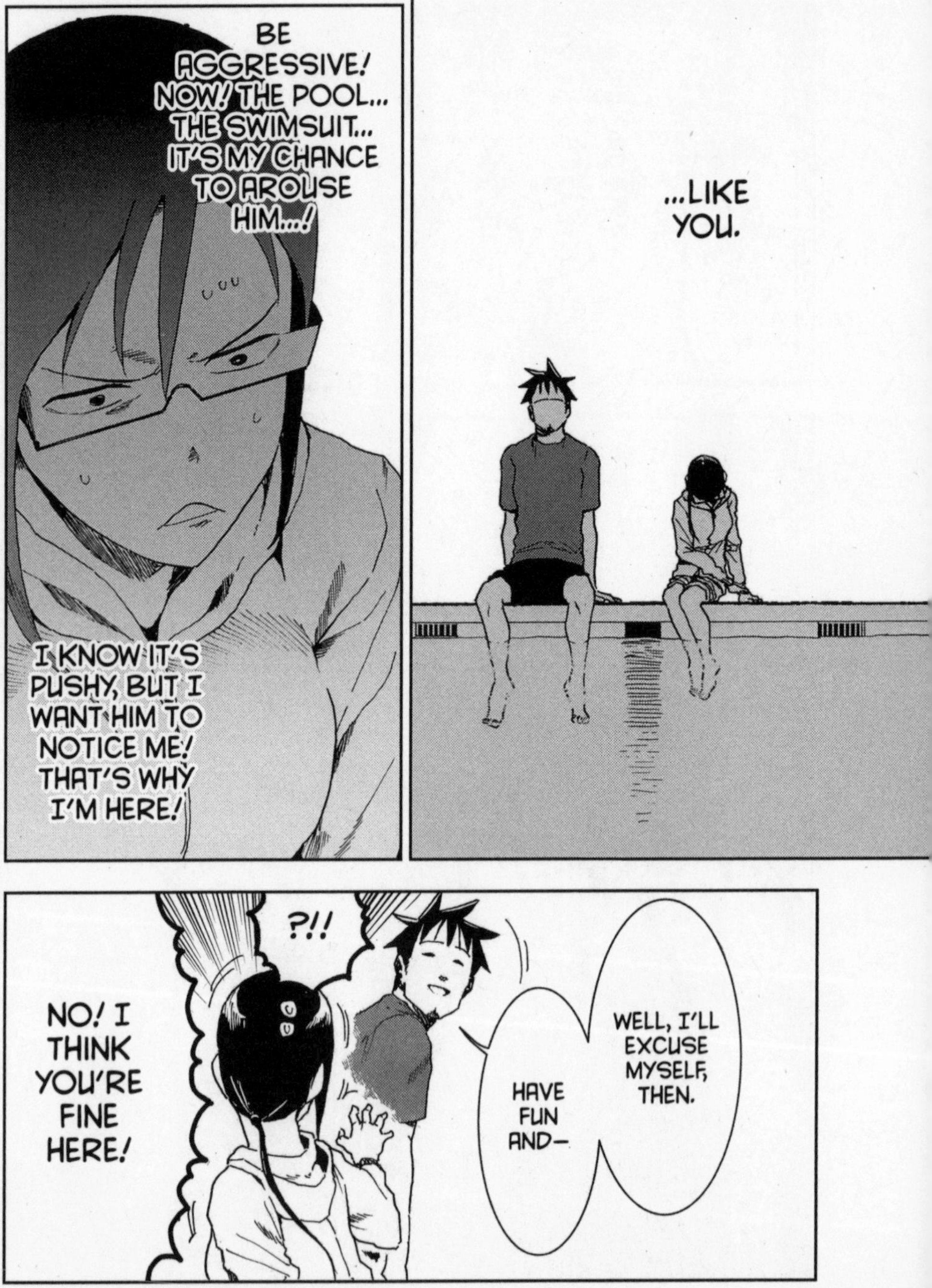
...LIKE YOU.
BE AGGRESSIVE! NOW! THE POOL... THE SWIMSUIT... IT'S MY CHANCE TO AROUSE HIM...!
I KNOW IT'S PUSHY, BUT I WANT HIM TO NOTICE ME! THAT'S WHY I'M HERE!
WELL, I'LL EXCUSE MYSELF, THEN.
HAVE FUN AND—
?!!
NO! I THINK YOU'RE FINE HERE!

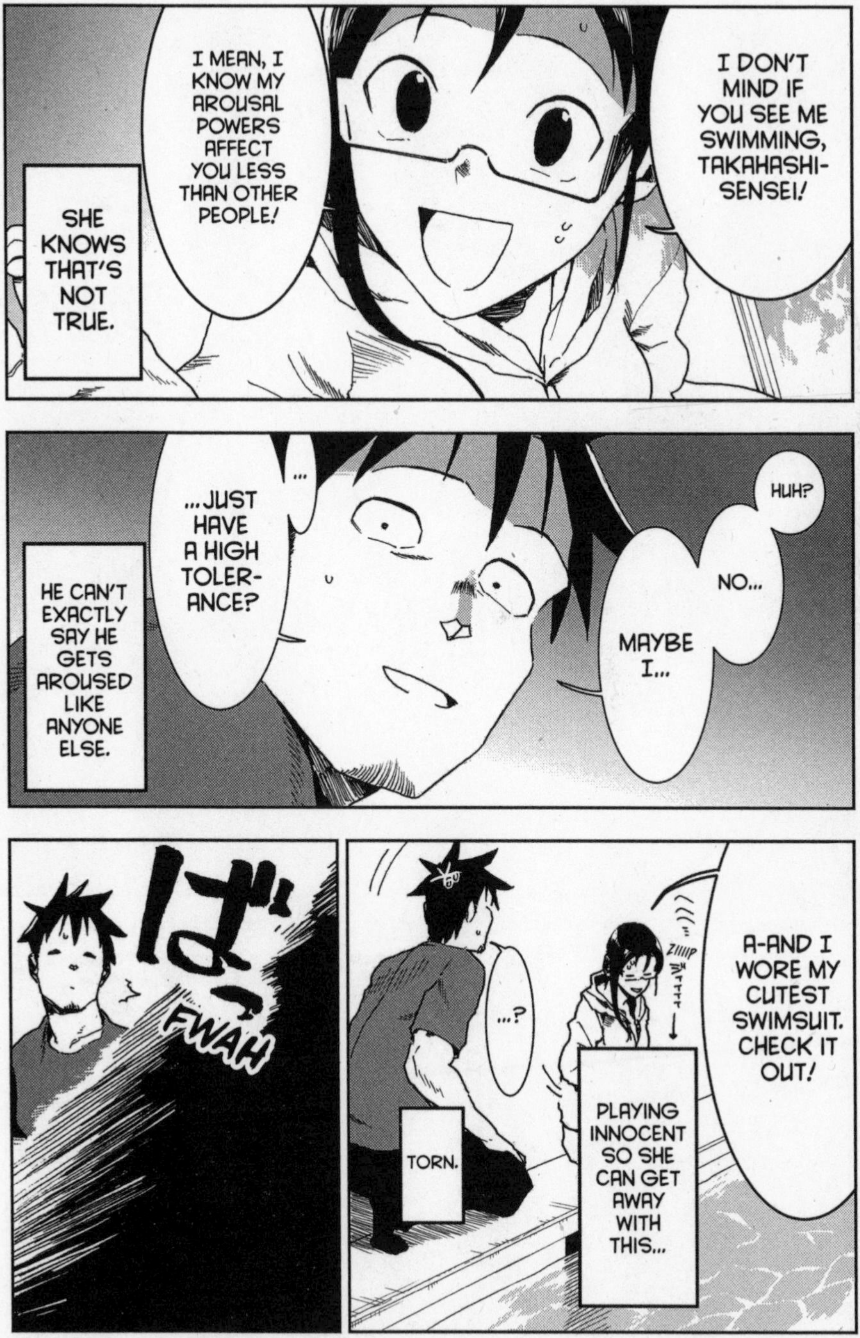
I DON'T MIND IF YOU SEE ME SWIMMING, TAKAHASHI-SENSEI!
I MEAN, I KNOW MY AROUSAL POWERS AFFECT YOU LESS THAN OTHER PEOPLE!
SHE KNOWS THAT'S NOT TRUE.
HUH?
NO...
MAYBE I...
...
...JUST HAVE A HIGH TOLERANCE?
HE CAN'T EXACTLY SAY HE GETS AROUSED LIKE ANYONE ELSE.
A-AND I WORE MY CUTEST SWIMSUIT. CHECK IT OUT!
ZIIIP
PLAYING INNOCENT SO SHE CAN GET AWAY WITH THIS...
...?
TORN.
ばっ
FWAH

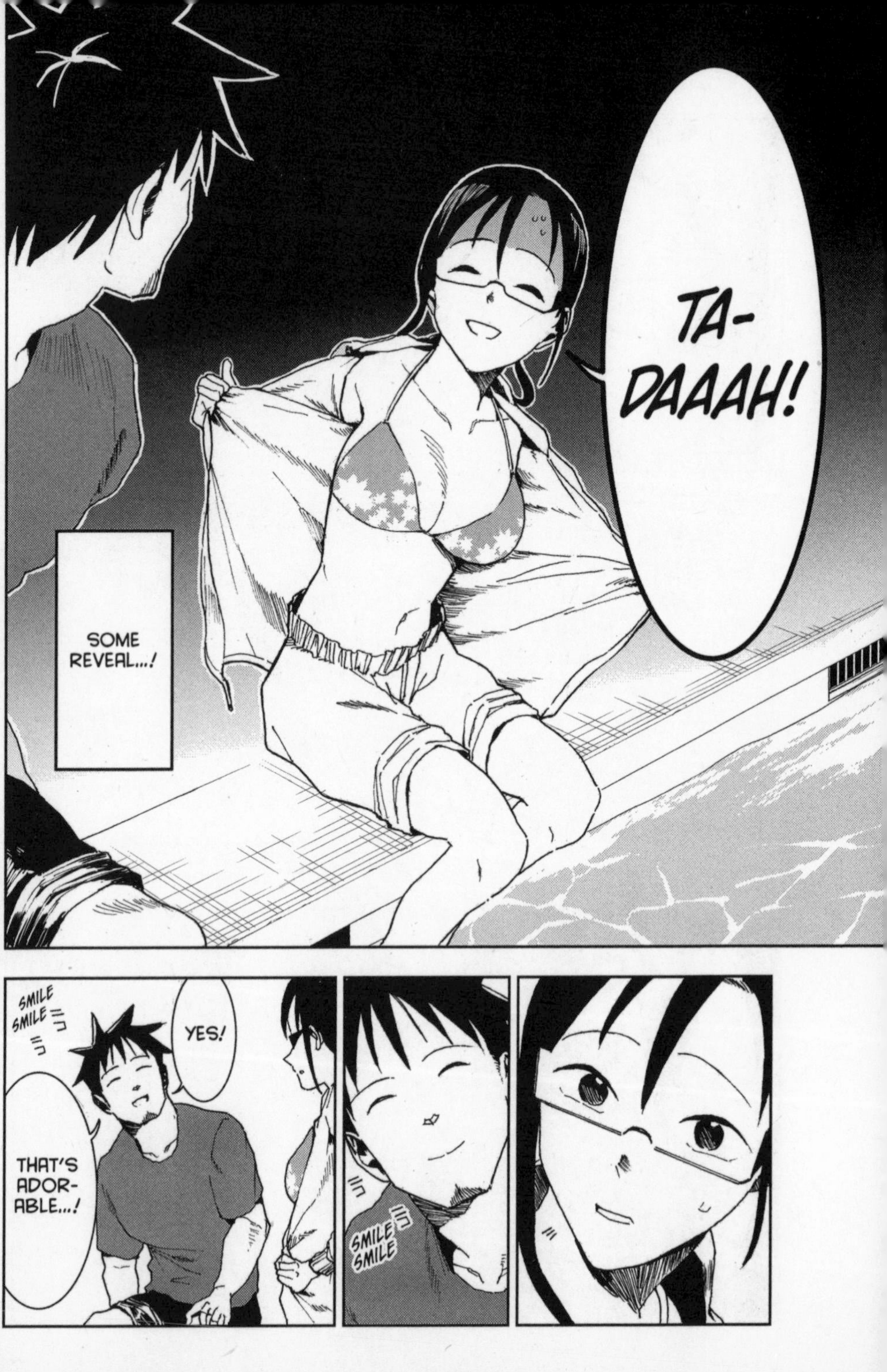
TA-DAAAH!
SOME REVEAL...!
SMILE SMILE
YES!
SMILE SMILE
THAT'S ADORABLE...!

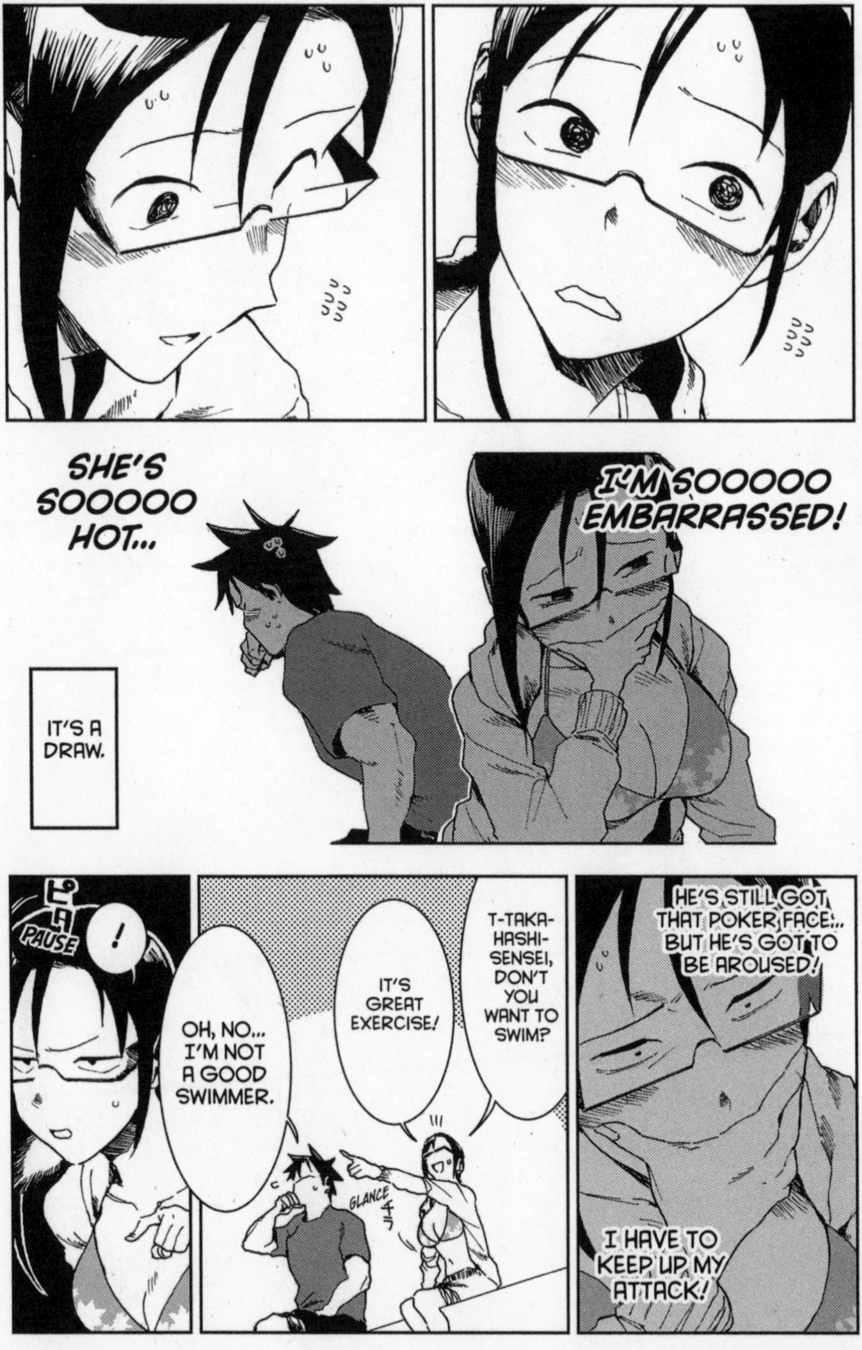
I'M SOOOOO EMBARRASSED!
SHE'S SOOOOO HOT...
IT'S A DRAW.
HE'S STILL GOT THAT POKER FACE... BUT HE'S GOT TO BE AROUSED!
I HAVE TO KEEP UP MY ATTACK!
T-TAKA-HASHI-SENSEI, DON'T YOU WANT TO SWIM?
IT'S GREAT EXERCISE!
GLANCE
OH, NO... I'M NOT A GOOD SWIMMER.
PAUSE
!

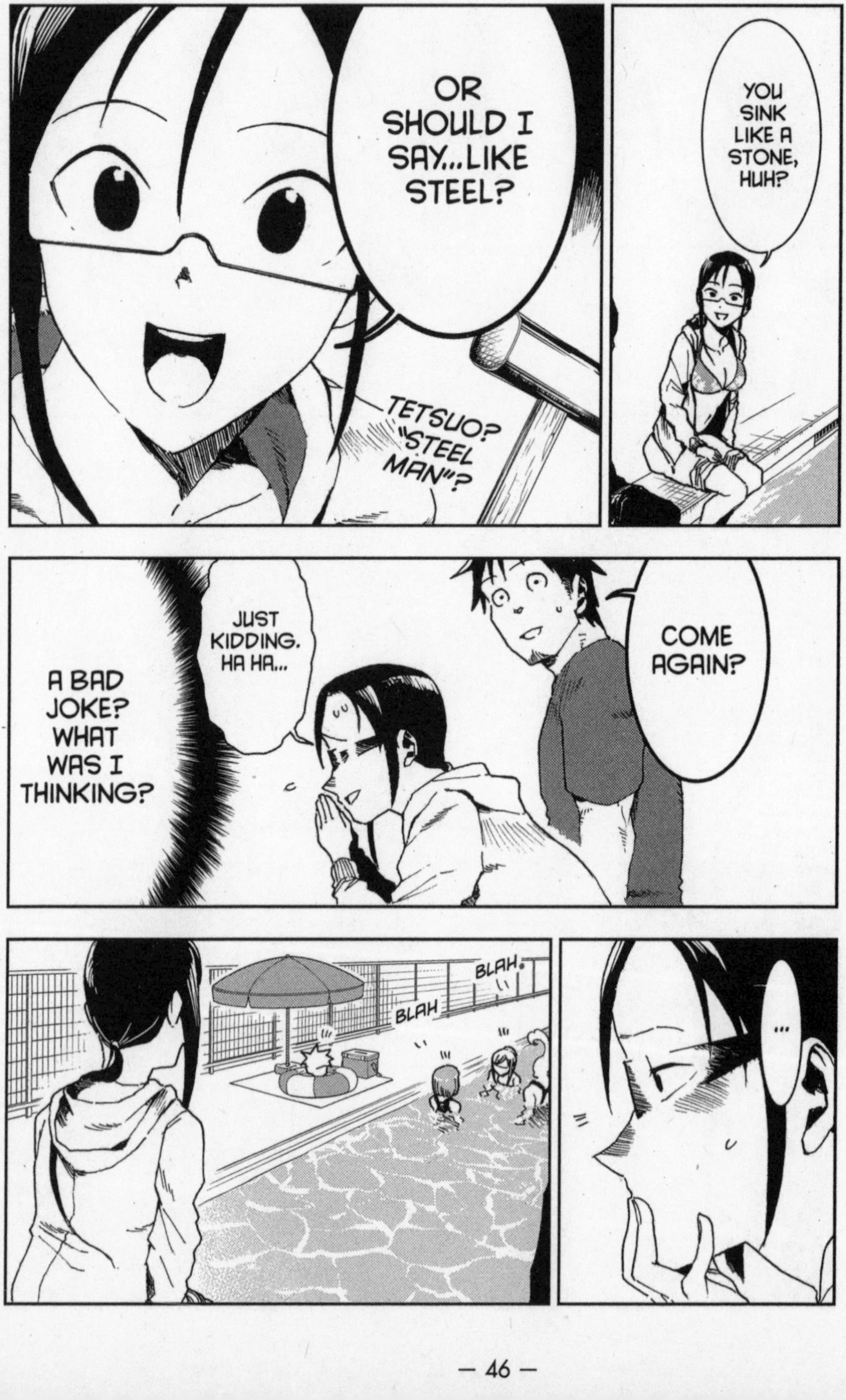
YOU SINK LIKE A STONE, HUH?
OR SHOULD I SAY...LIKE STEEL?
TETSUO? "STEEL MAN"?
COME AGAIN?
JUST KIDDING. HA HA...
A BAD JOKE? WHAT WAS I THINKING?
...
BLAH
BLAH

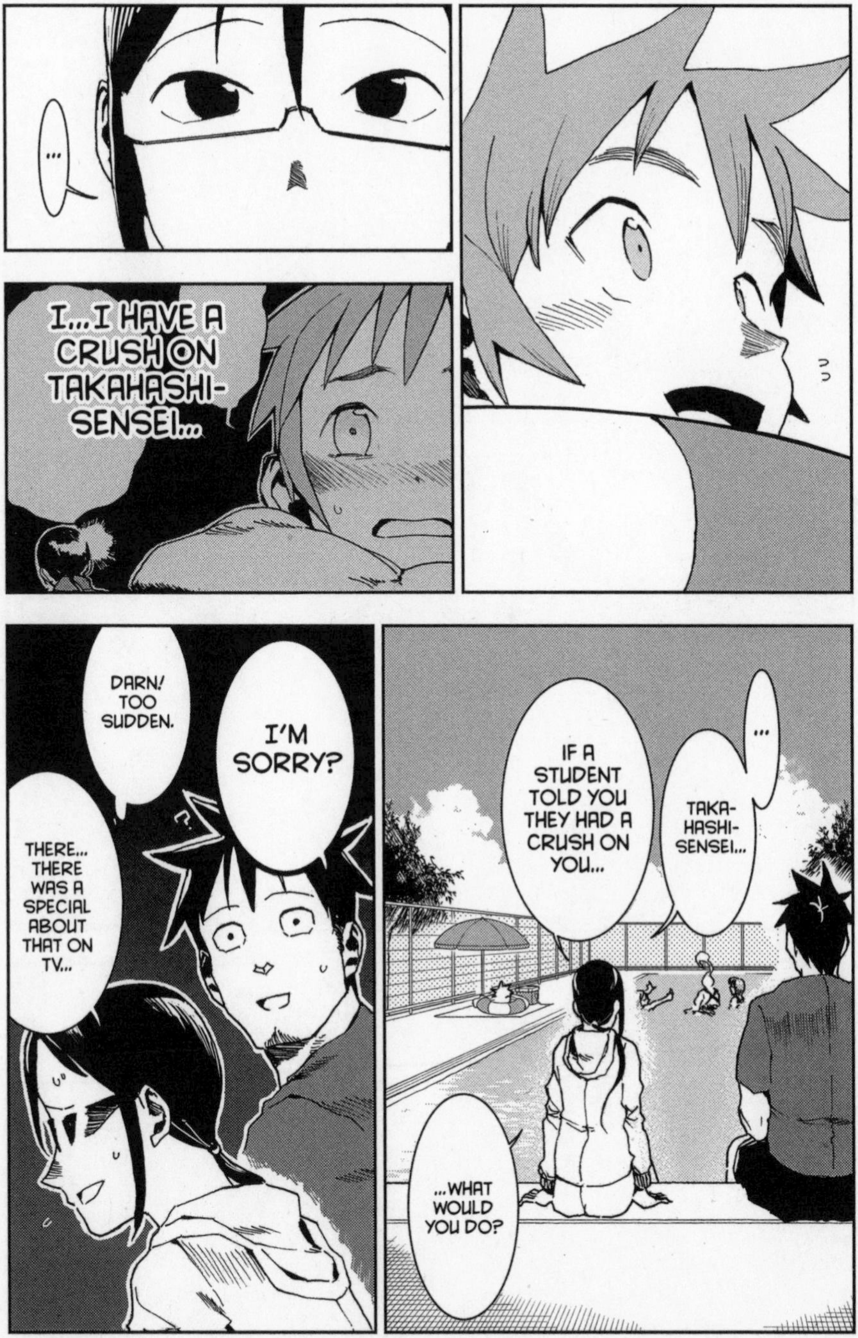
...
I... I HAVE A CRUSH ON TAKAHASHI-SENSEI...
...
TAKA-HASHI-SENSEI...
IF A STUDENT TOLD YOU THEY HAD A CRUSH ON YOU...
...WHAT WOULD YOU DO?
I'M SORRY?
DARN! TOO SUDDEN.
THERE... THERE WAS A SPECIAL ABOUT THAT ON TV...

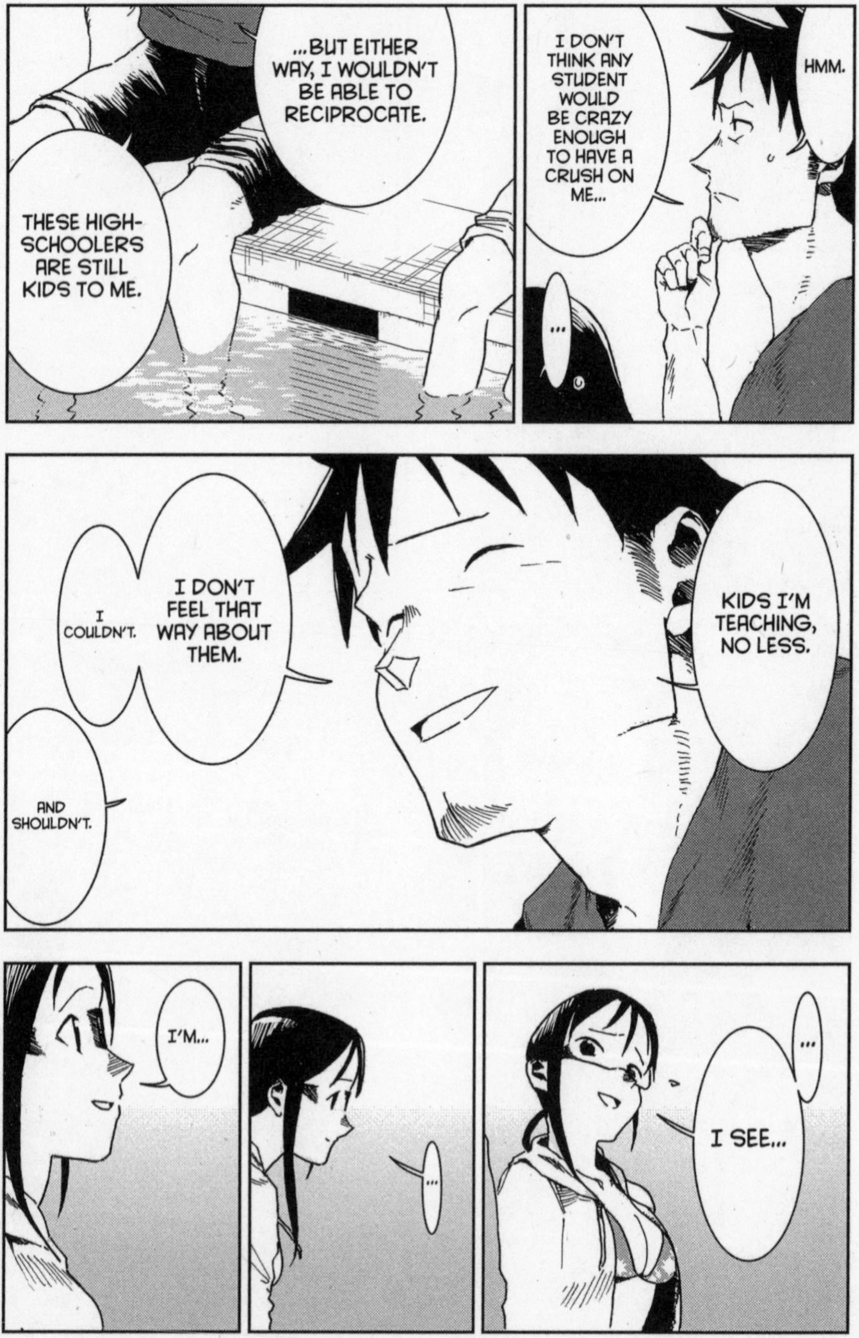
HMM.
I DON'T THINK ANY STUDENT WOULD BE CRAZY ENOUGH TO HAVE A CRUSH ON ME...
...
...BUT EITHER WAY, I WOULDN'T BE ABLE TO RECIPROCATE.
THESE HIGH-SCHOOLERS ARE STILL KIDS TO ME.
KIDS I'M TEACHING, NO LESS.
I DON'T FEEL THAT WAY ABOUT THEM.
I COULDN'T.
AND SHOULDN'T.
...
I SEE...
...
I'M...

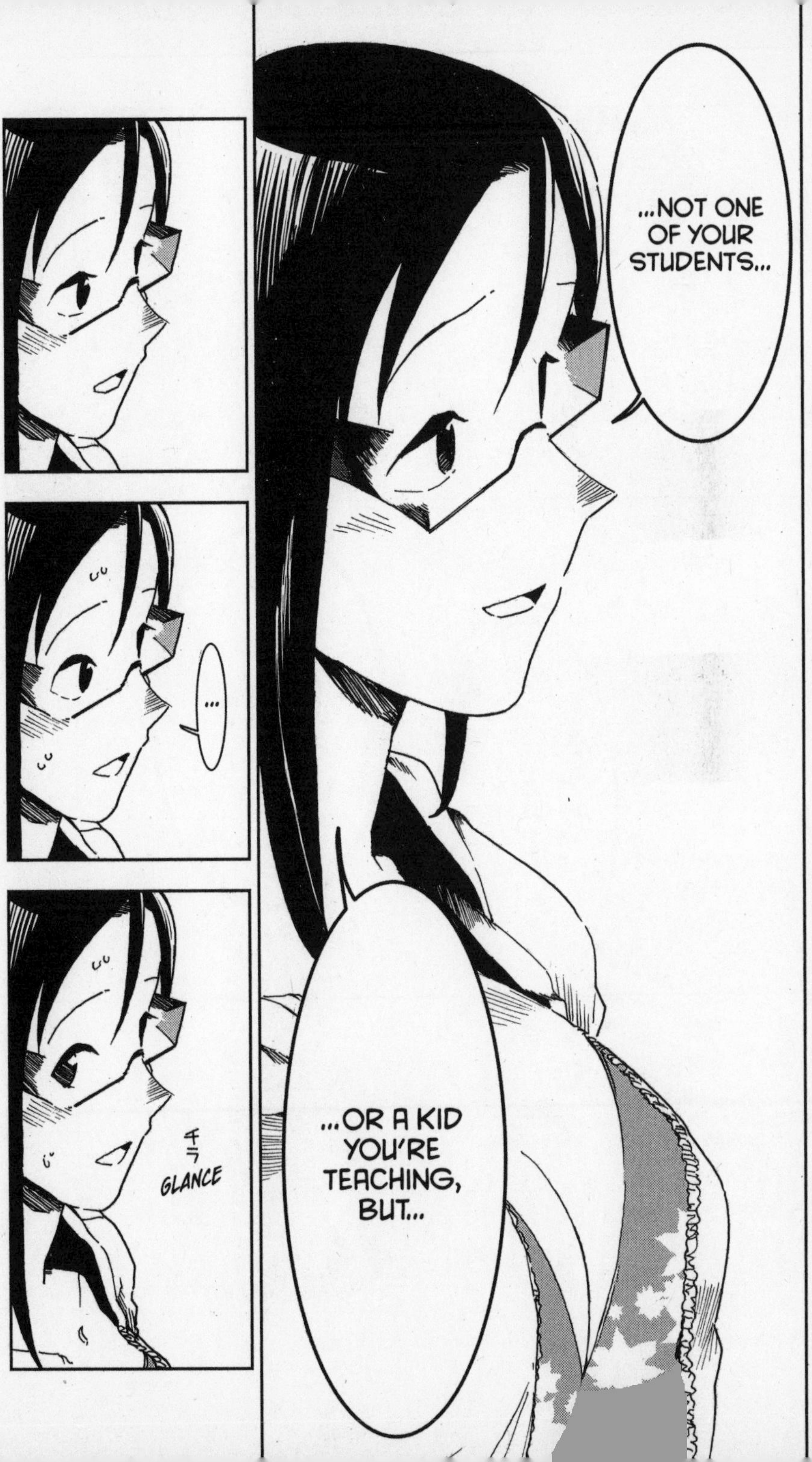
...NOT ONE OF YOUR STUDENTS...
...OR A KID YOU'RE TEACHING, BUT...
...
チラ
GLANCE

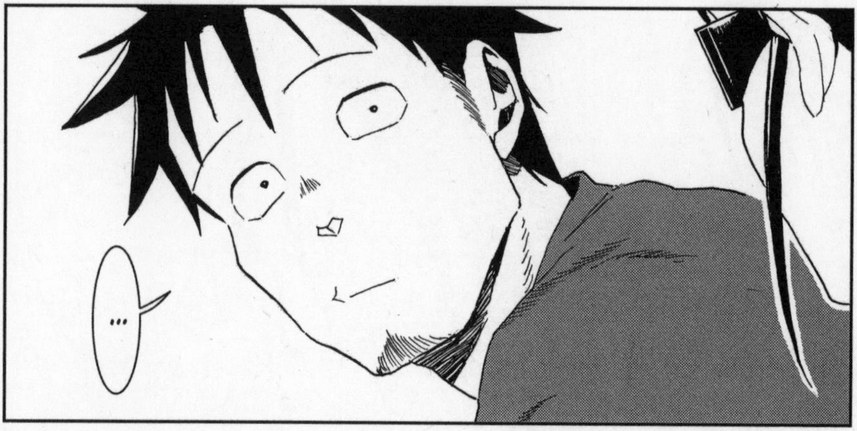
...

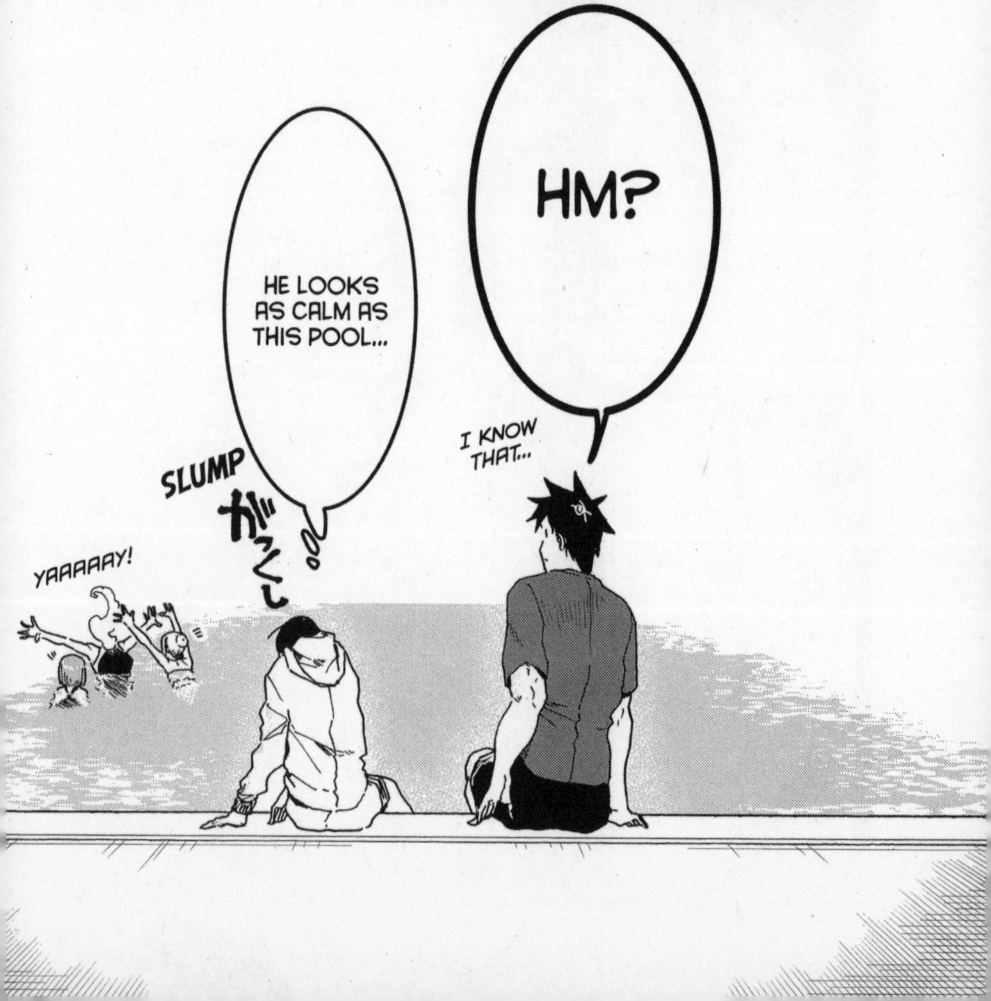
HM?
I KNOW THAT...
HE LOOKS AS CALM AS THIS POOL...
SLUMP
がっくし
YAAAAAY!

THE GIRLS ARE LEARNING TO RELY ON OTHER PEOPLE.
MAYBE IT'S TIME FOR ME TO BOW OUT.
YAY!
YAY!
...
I'LL JUST BE IN THE WAY.
WELL, I GUESS THEY DON'T COME TO ME AS MUCH AS THEY USED TO...
...
MEH!
A LITTLE LONGER...
WON'T HURT...
!

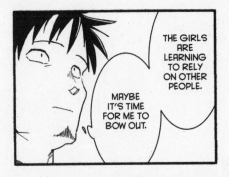

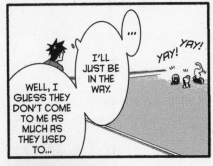

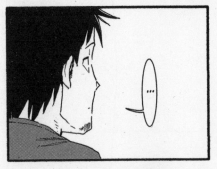

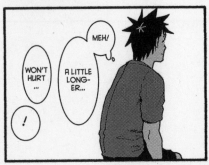

INTERVIEWS WITH MONSTER GIRLS

CHAPTER 34: TRY EVERYTHING ONCE

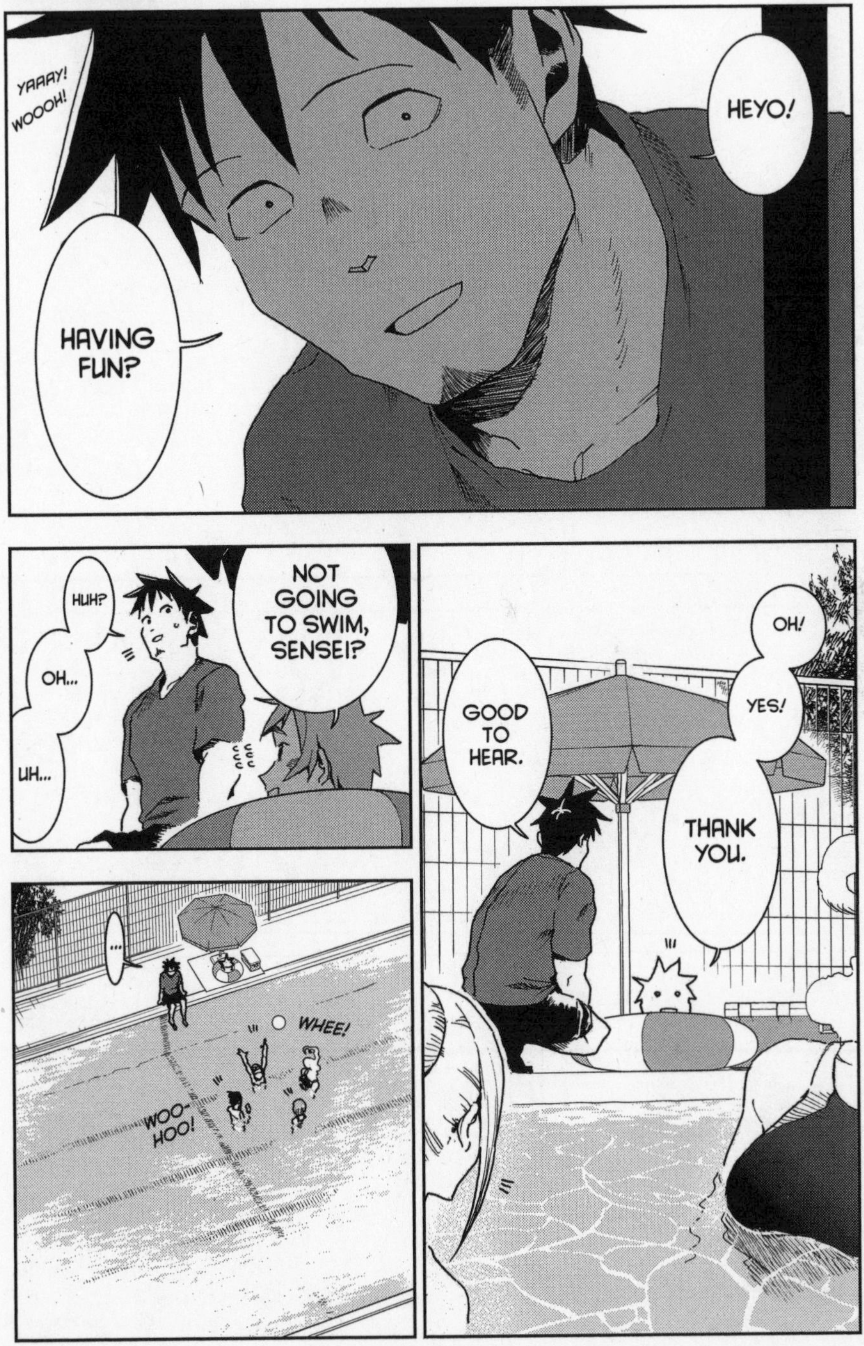
HEYO!
YAAAY! WOOOH!
HAVING FUN?
OH!
YES!
THANK YOU.
GOOD TO HEAR.
NOT GOING TO SWIM, SENSEI?
HUH?
OH...
UH...
...
WHEE!
WOO-HOO!

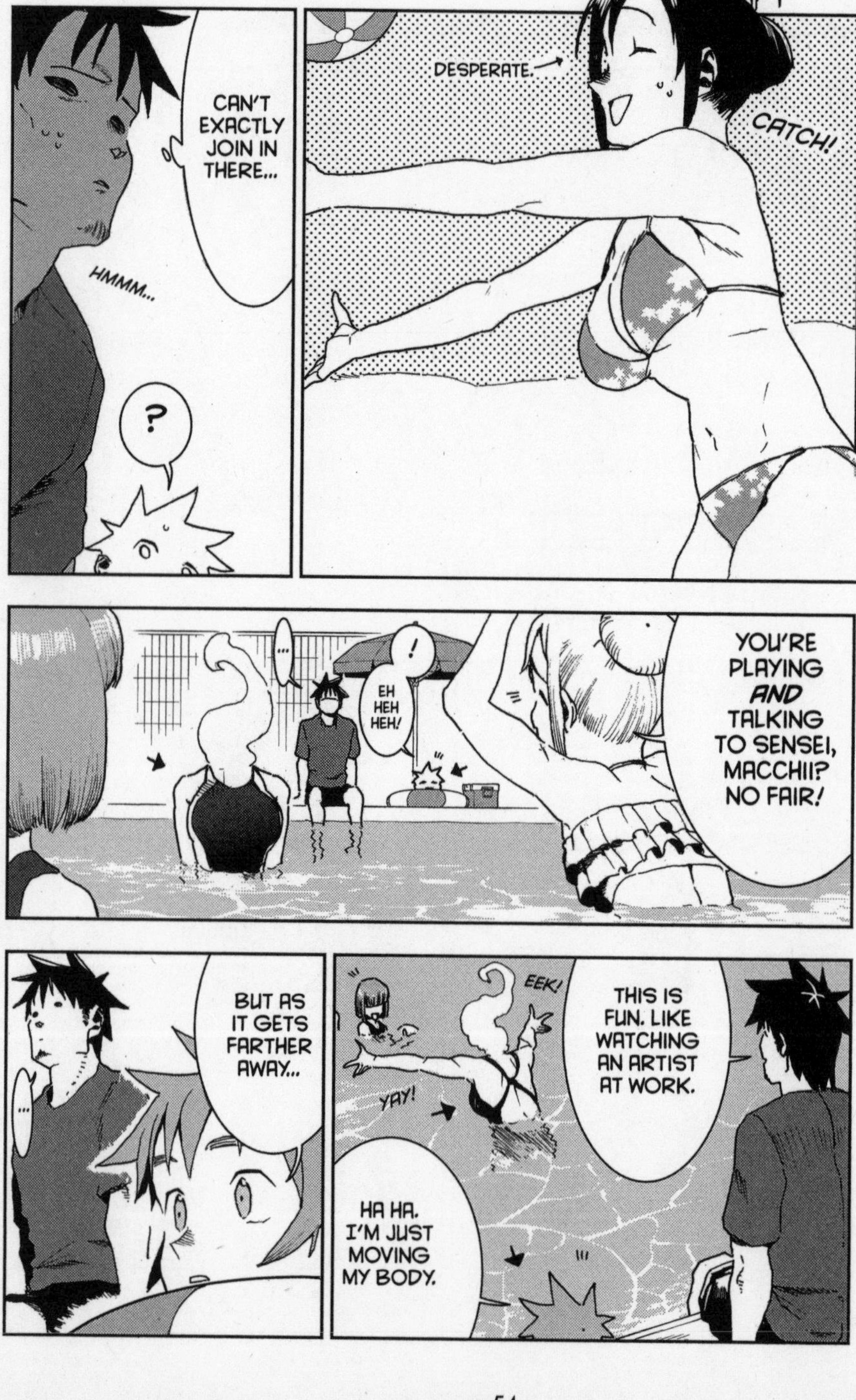
CATCH!
DESPERATE.
CAN'T EXACTLY JOIN IN THERE...
HMMM...
?
YOU'RE PLAYING **AND** TALKING TO SENSEI, MACCHII? NO FAIR!
!
EH HEH HEH!
...
THIS IS FUN. LIKE WATCHING AN ARTIST AT WORK.
EEK!
YAY!
HA HA. I'M JUST MOVING MY BODY.
BUT AS IT GETS FARTHER AWAY...
...

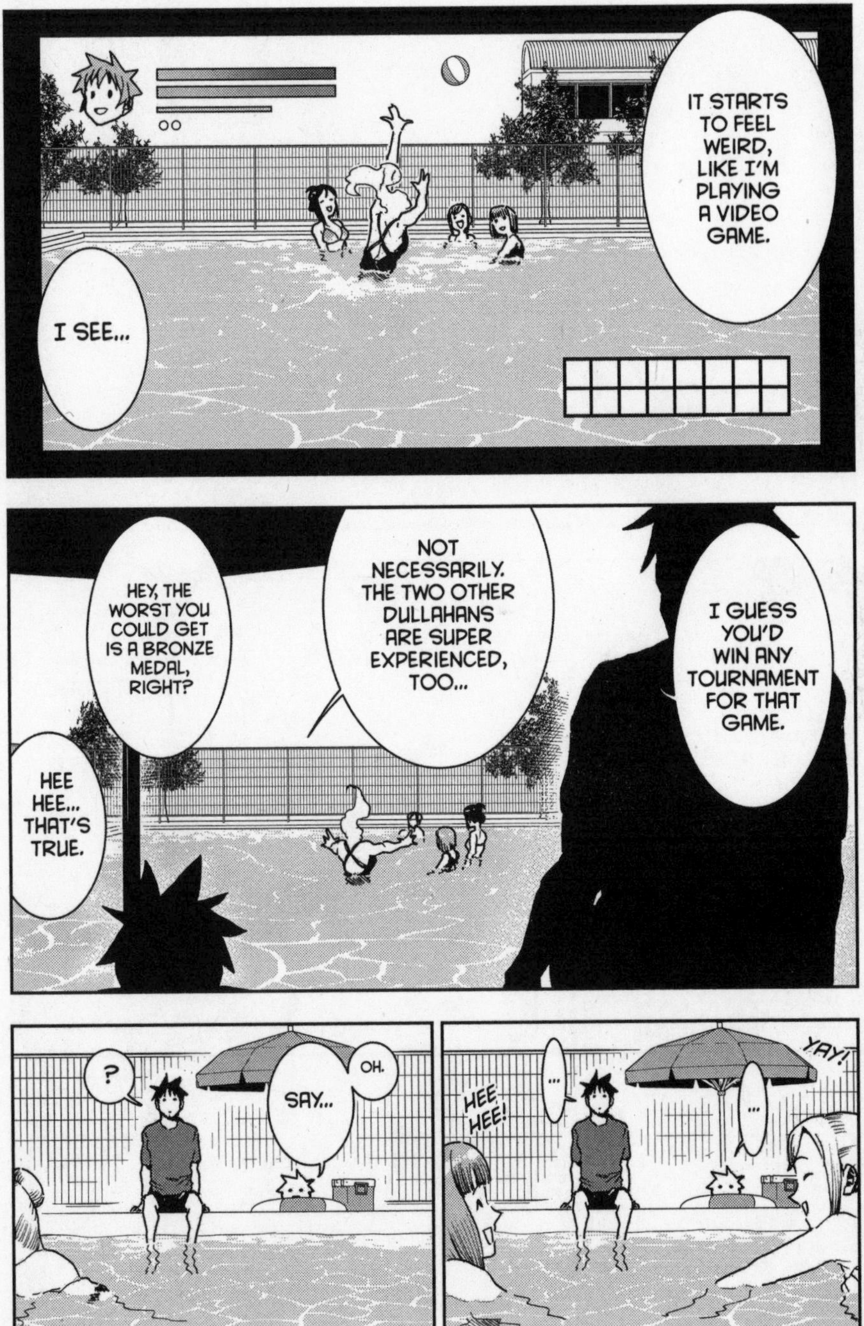
IT STARTS TO FEEL WEIRD, LIKE I'M PLAYING A VIDEO GAME.
I SEE...
I GUESS YOU'D WIN ANY TOURNAMENT FOR THAT GAME.
NOT NECESSARILY. THE TWO OTHER DULLAHANS ARE SUPER EXPERIENCED, TOO...
HEY, THE WORST YOU COULD GET IS A BRONZE MEDAL, RIGHT?
HEE HEE... THAT'S TRUE.
YAY!
...
...
HEE HEE!
OH.
SAY...
?

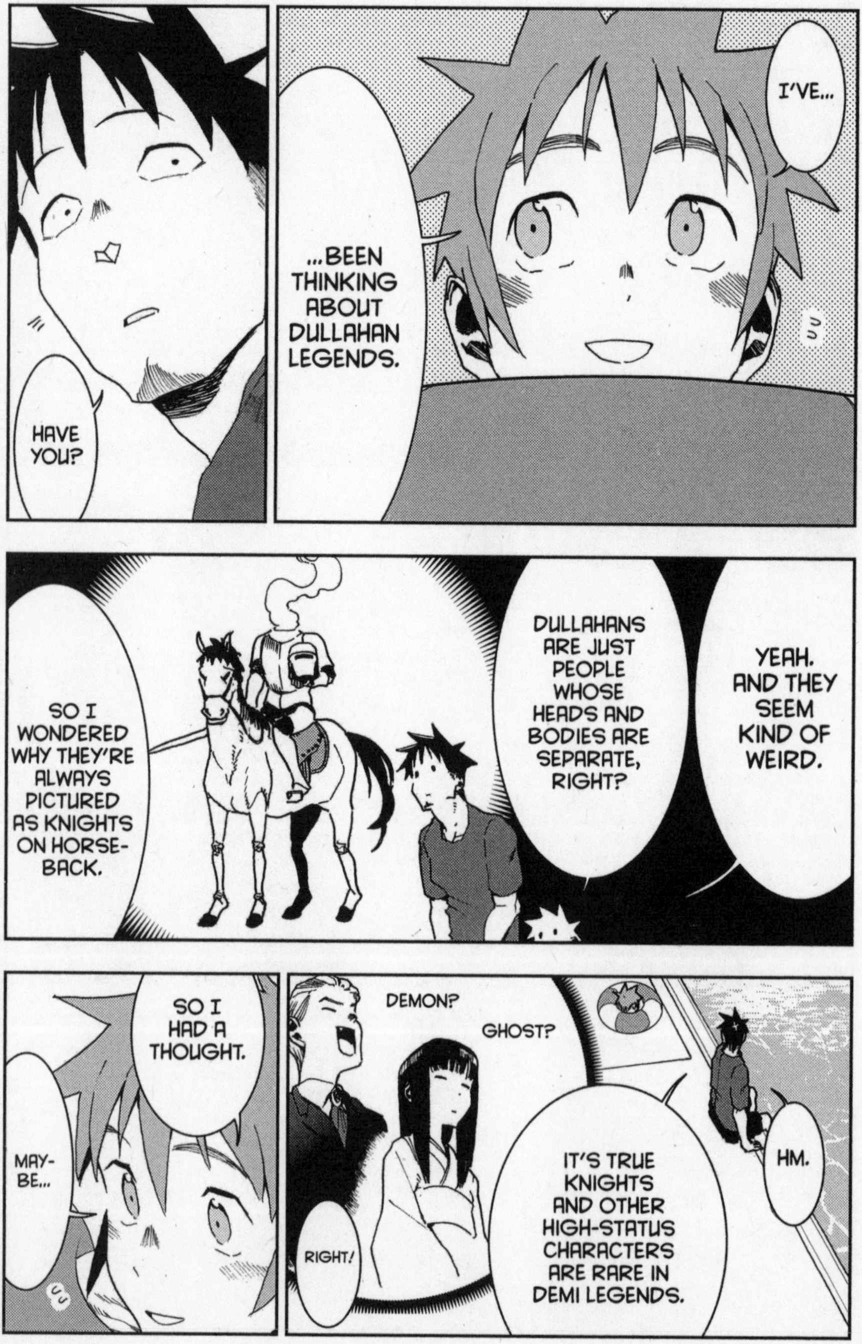
I'VE...
...BEEN THINKING ABOUT DULLAHAN LEGENDS.
HAVE YOU?
YEAH. AND THEY SEEM KIND OF WEIRD.
DULLAHANS ARE JUST PEOPLE WHOSE HEADS AND BODIES ARE SEPARATE, RIGHT?
SO I WONDERED WHY THEY'RE ALWAYS PICTURED AS KNIGHTS ON HORSE-BACK.
HM.
IT'S TRUE KNIGHTS AND OTHER HIGH-STATUS CHARACTERS ARE RARE IN DEMI LEGENDS.
GHOST?
DEMON?
RIGHT!
SO I HAD A THOUGHT.
MAY-BE...

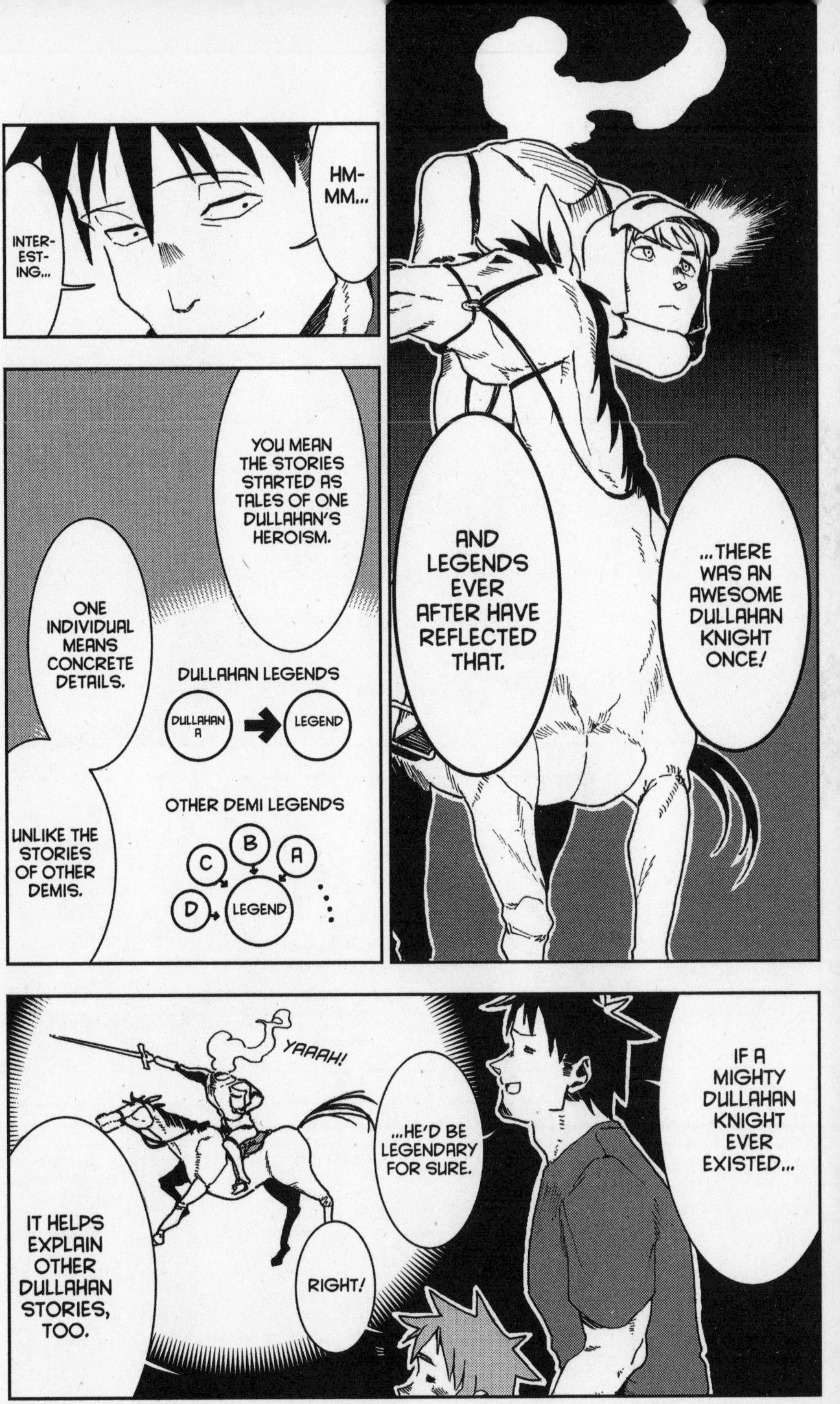
...THERE WAS AN AWESOME DULLAHAN KNIGHT ONCE!
AND LEGENDS EVER AFTER HAVE REFLECTED THAT.
HM-MM...
INTER-EST-ING...
YOU MEAN THE STORIES STARTED AS TALES OF ONE DULLAHAN'S HEROISM.
ONE INDIVIDUAL MEANS CONCRETE DETAILS.
DULLAHAN LEGENDS
DULLAHAN A
LEGEND
OTHER DEMI LEGENDS
B
A
C
D
LEGEND
UNLIKE THE STORIES OF OTHER DEMIS.
IF A MIGHTY DULLAHAN KNIGHT EVER EXISTED...
...HE'D BE LEGENDARY FOR SURE.
YAAAH!
RIGHT!
IT HELPS EXPLAIN OTHER DULLAHAN STORIES, TOO.

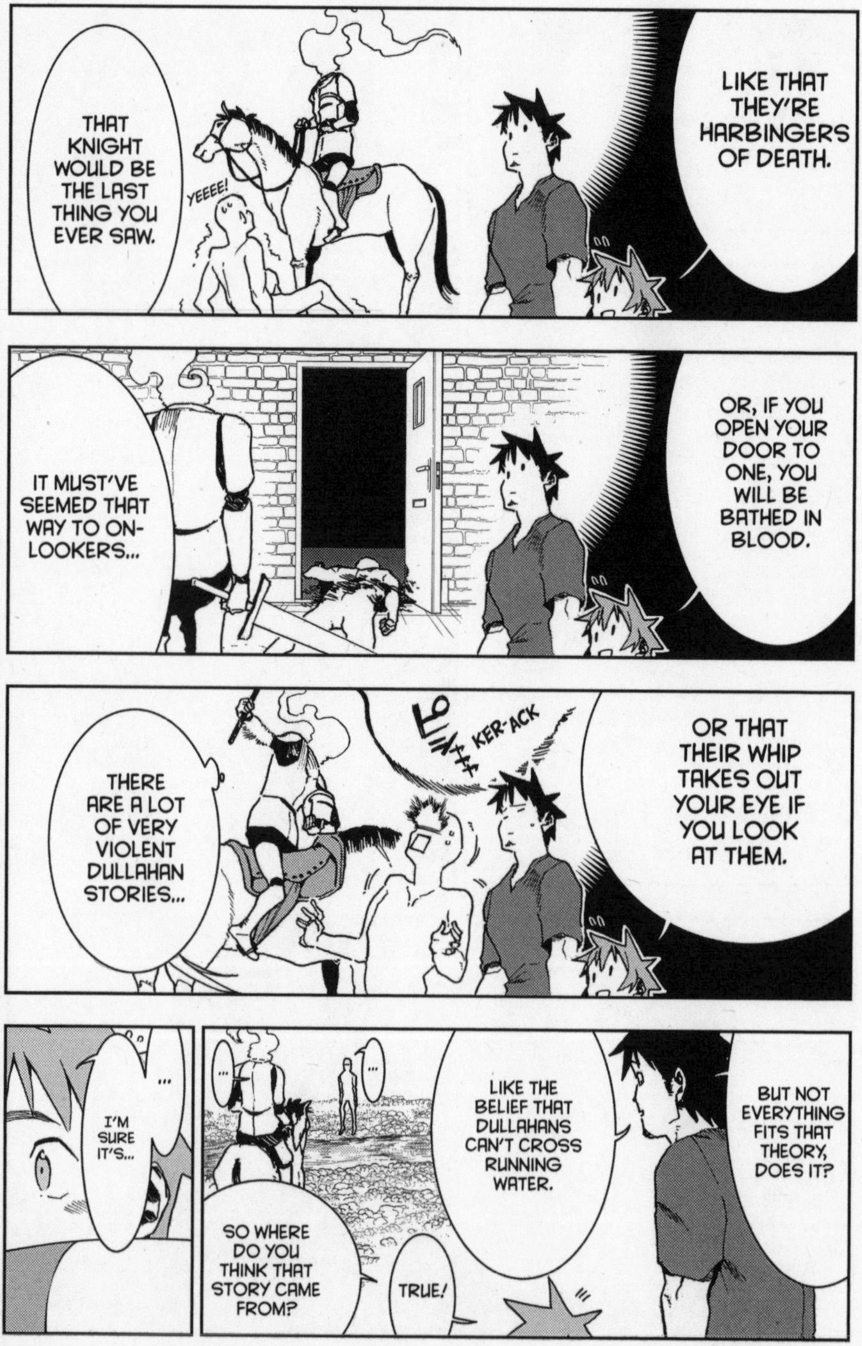
LIKE THAT THEY'RE HARBINGERS OF DEATH.
YEEEE!
THAT KNIGHT WOULD BE THE LAST THING YOU EVER SAW.
OR, IF YOU OPEN YOUR DOOR TO ONE, YOU WILL BE BATHED IN BLOOD.
IT MUST'VE SEEMED THAT WAY TO ON-LOOKERS...
OR THAT THEIR WHIP TAKES OUT YOUR EYE IF YOU LOOK AT THEM.
KER-ACK
THERE ARE A LOT OF VERY VIOLENT DULLAHAN STORIES...
BUT NOT EVERYTHING FITS THAT THEORY, DOES IT?
LIKE THE BELIEF THAT DULLAHANS CAN'T CROSS RUNNING WATER.
...
...
TRUE!
SO WHERE DO YOU THINK THAT STORY CAME FROM?
...
I'M SURE IT'S...

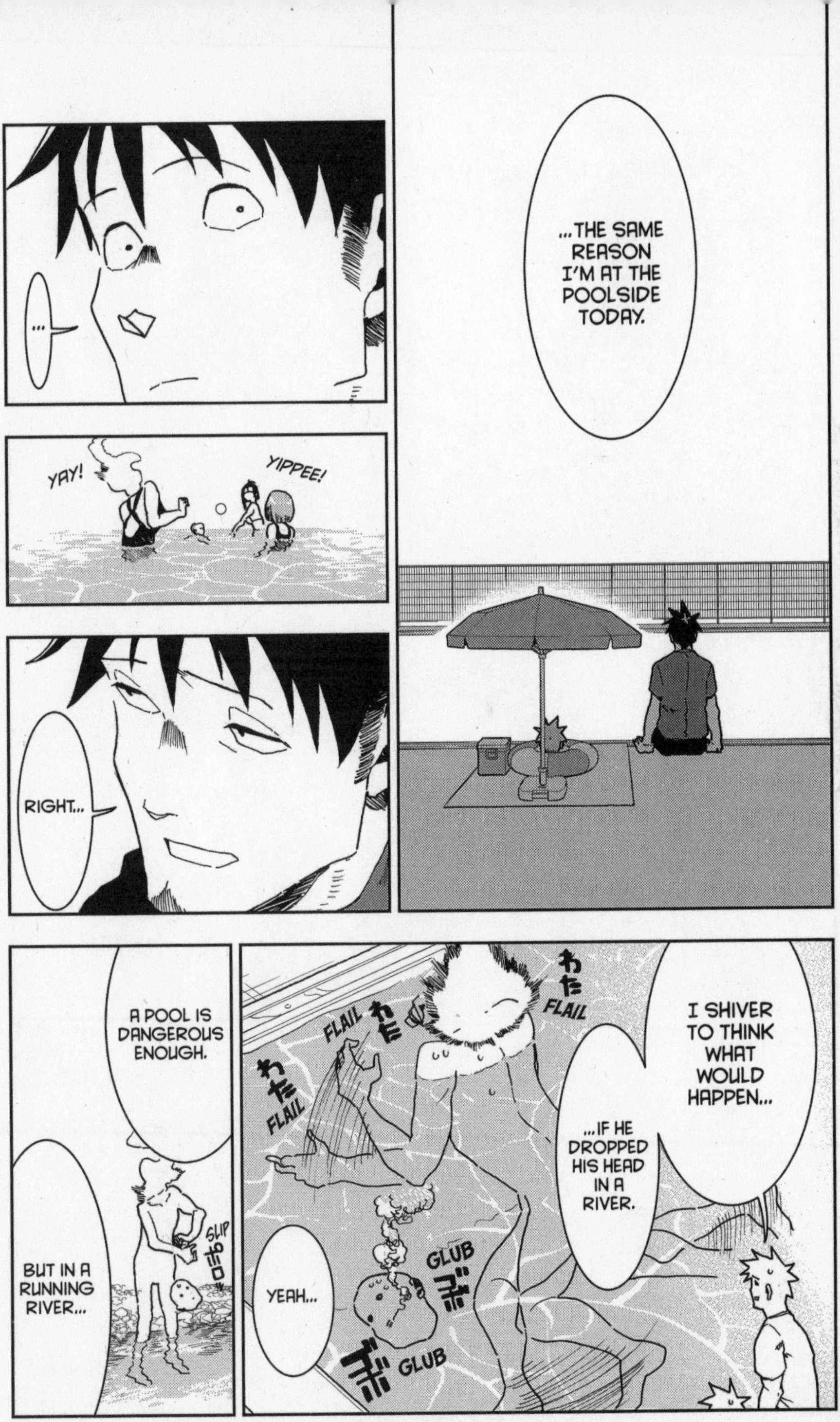
...THE SAME REASON I'M AT THE POOLSIDE TODAY.
...
YAY!
YIPPEE!
RIGHT...
I SHIVER TO THINK WHAT WOULD HAPPEN...
...IF HE DROPPED HIS HEAD IN A RIVER.
わた FLAIL
わた FLAIL
わた FLAIL
GLUB ゴボ
ゴボ GLUB
YEAH...
A POOL IS DANGEROUS ENOUGH.
BUT IN A RUNNING RIVER...
SLIP ポロ

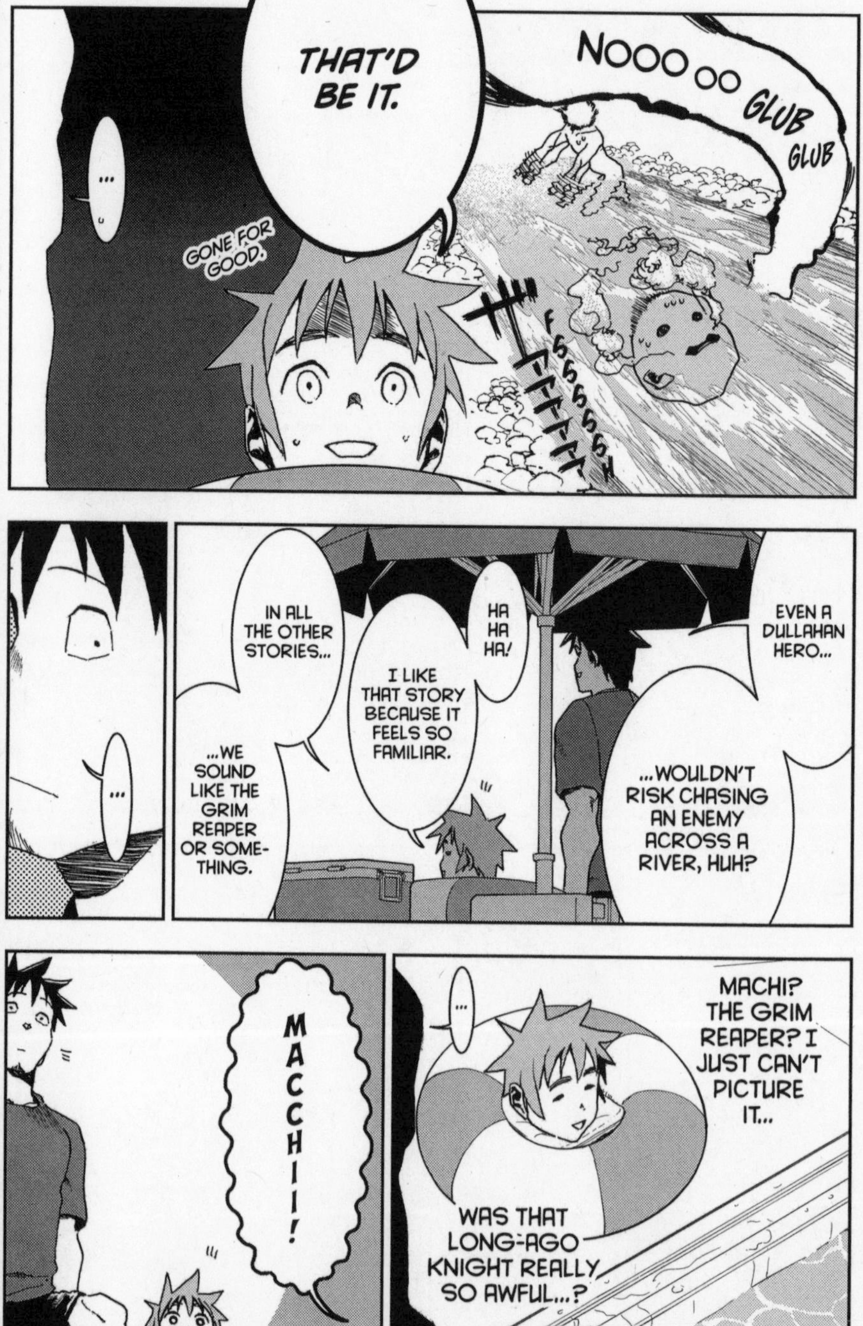
NOOO OO GLUB GLUB
FSSSSSSH
THAT'D BE IT.
GONE FOR GOOD.
...
EVEN A DULLAHAN HERO...
...WOULDN'T RISK CHASING AN ENEMY ACROSS A RIVER, HUH?
HA HA HA!
I LIKE THAT STORY BECAUSE IT FEELS SO FAMILIAR.
IN ALL THE OTHER STORIES...
...WE SOUND LIKE THE GRIM REAPER OR SOME-THING.
...
MACHI? THE GRIM REAPER? I JUST CAN'T PICTURE IT...
...
WAS THAT LONG-AGO KNIGHT REALLY SO AWFUL...?
MACCHI!!

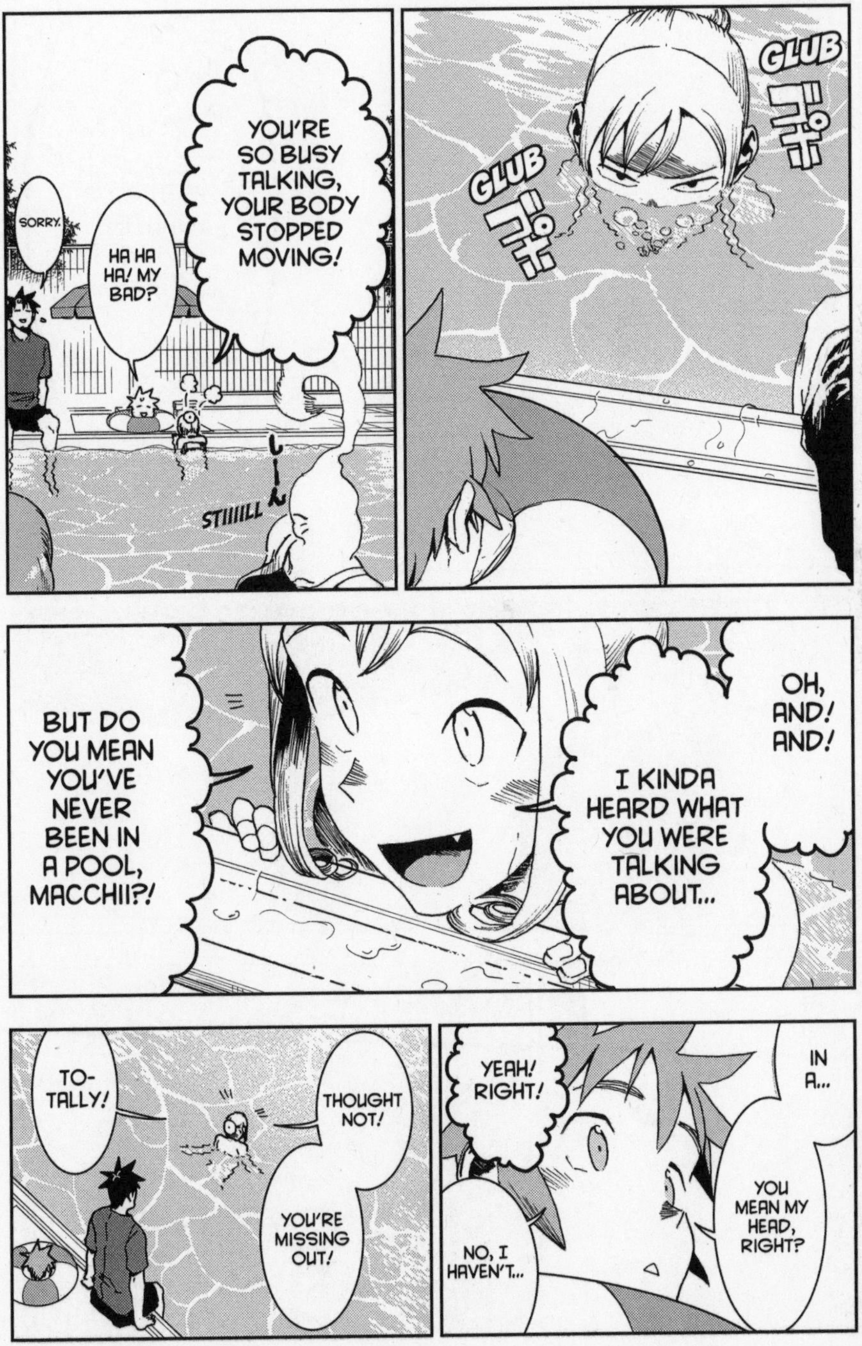
GLUB
ゴポ
GLUB
ゴポ
YOU'RE SO BUSY TALKING, YOUR BODY STOPPED MOVING!
HA HA HA! MY BAD?
SORRY.
しーん
STIIIILL
OH, AND! AND!
I KINDA HEARD WHAT YOU WERE TALKING ABOUT...
BUT DO YOU MEAN YOU'VE NEVER BEEN IN A POOL, MACCHII?!
IN A...
YEAH! RIGHT!
YOU MEAN MY HEAD, RIGHT?
NO, I HAVEN'T...
THOUGHT NOT!
TO-TALLY!
YOU'RE MISSING OUT!

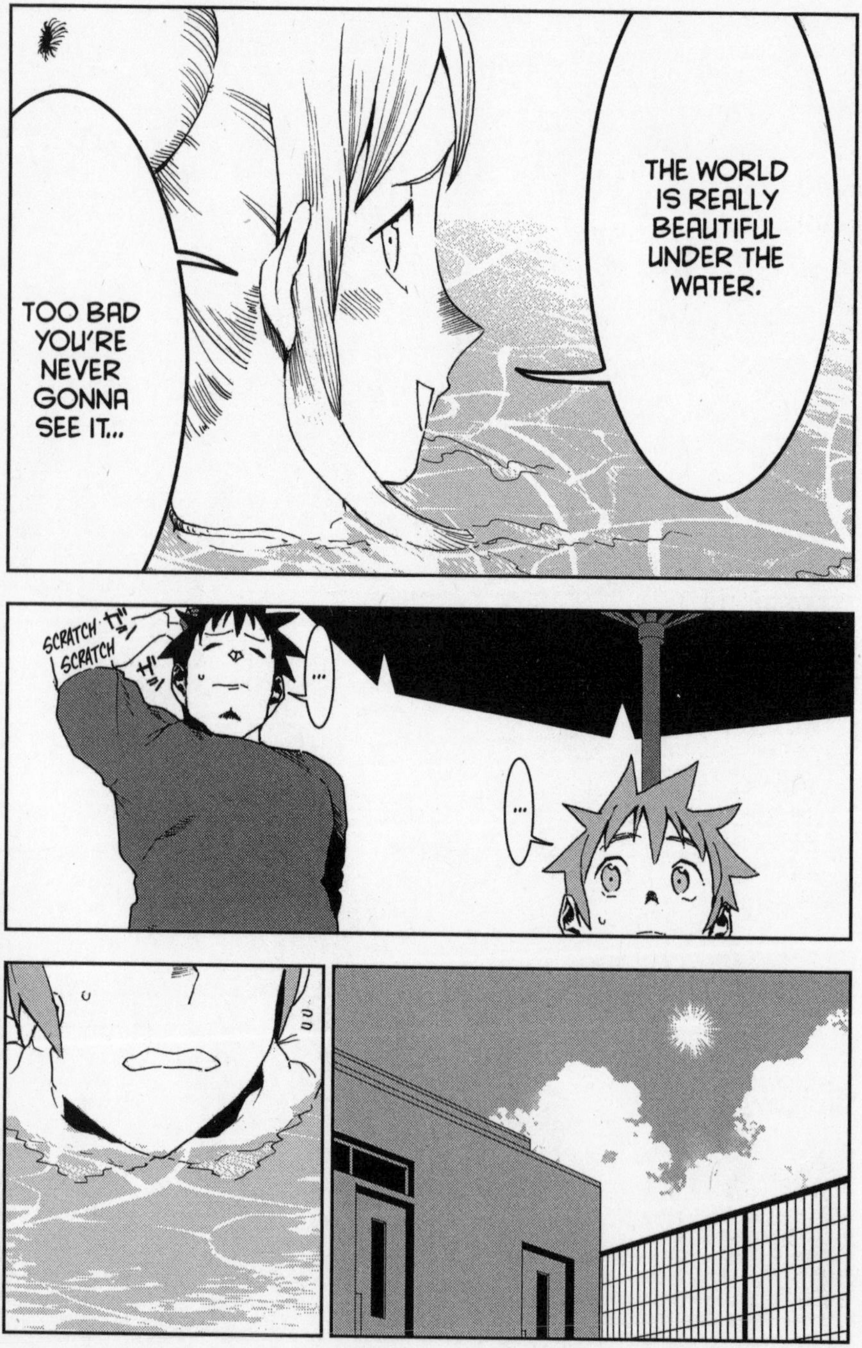
THE WORLD IS REALLY BEAUTIFUL UNDER THE WATER.
TOO BAD YOU'RE NEVER GONNA SEE IT...
...
...
SCRATCH
SCRATCH

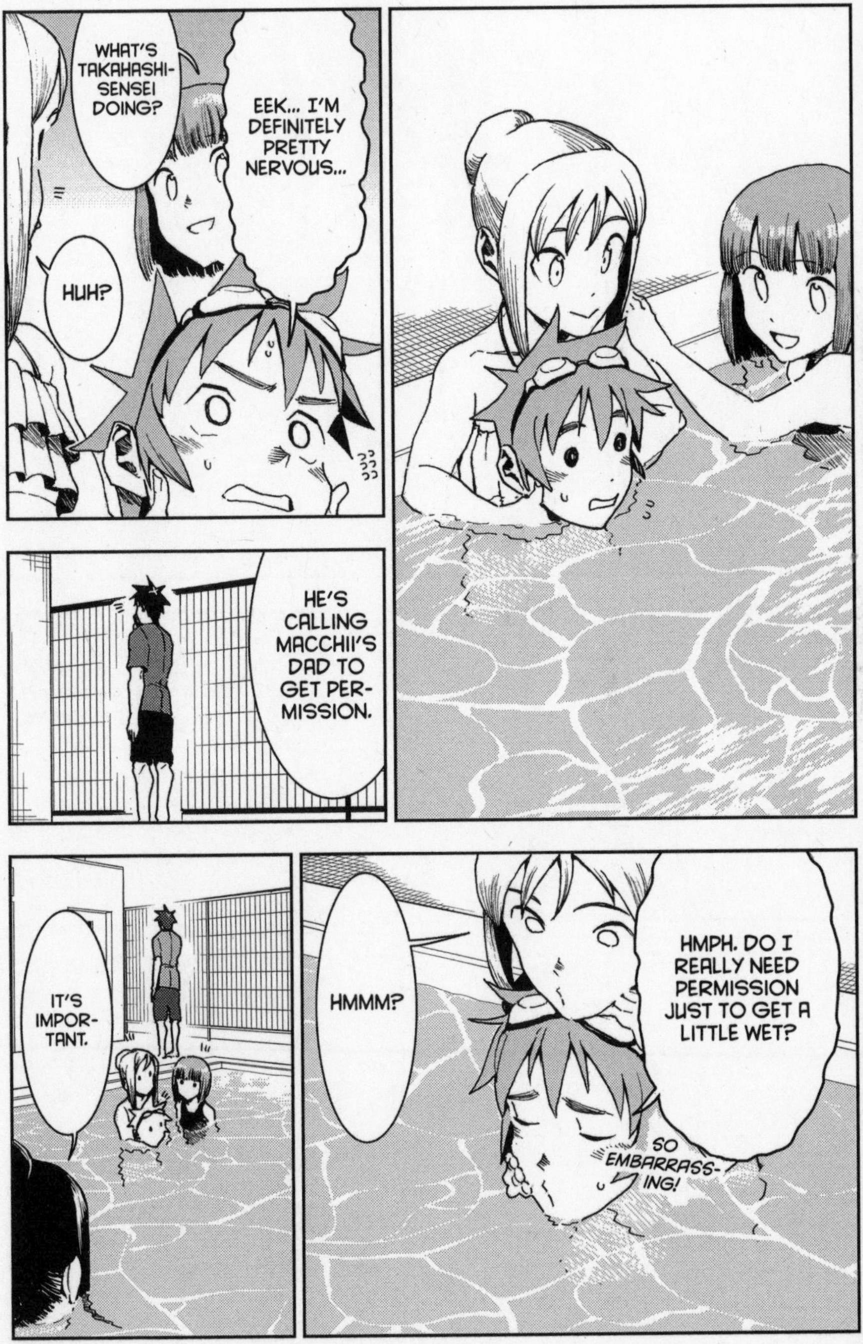
EEK... I'M DEFINITELY PRETTY NERVOUS...
WHAT'S TAKAHASHI-SENSEI DOING?
HUH?
HE'S CALLING MACCHII'S DAD TO GET PERMISSION.
HMPH. DO I REALLY NEED PERMISSION JUST TO GET A LITTLE WET?
HMMM?
SO EMBARRASSING!
IT'S IMPORTANT.

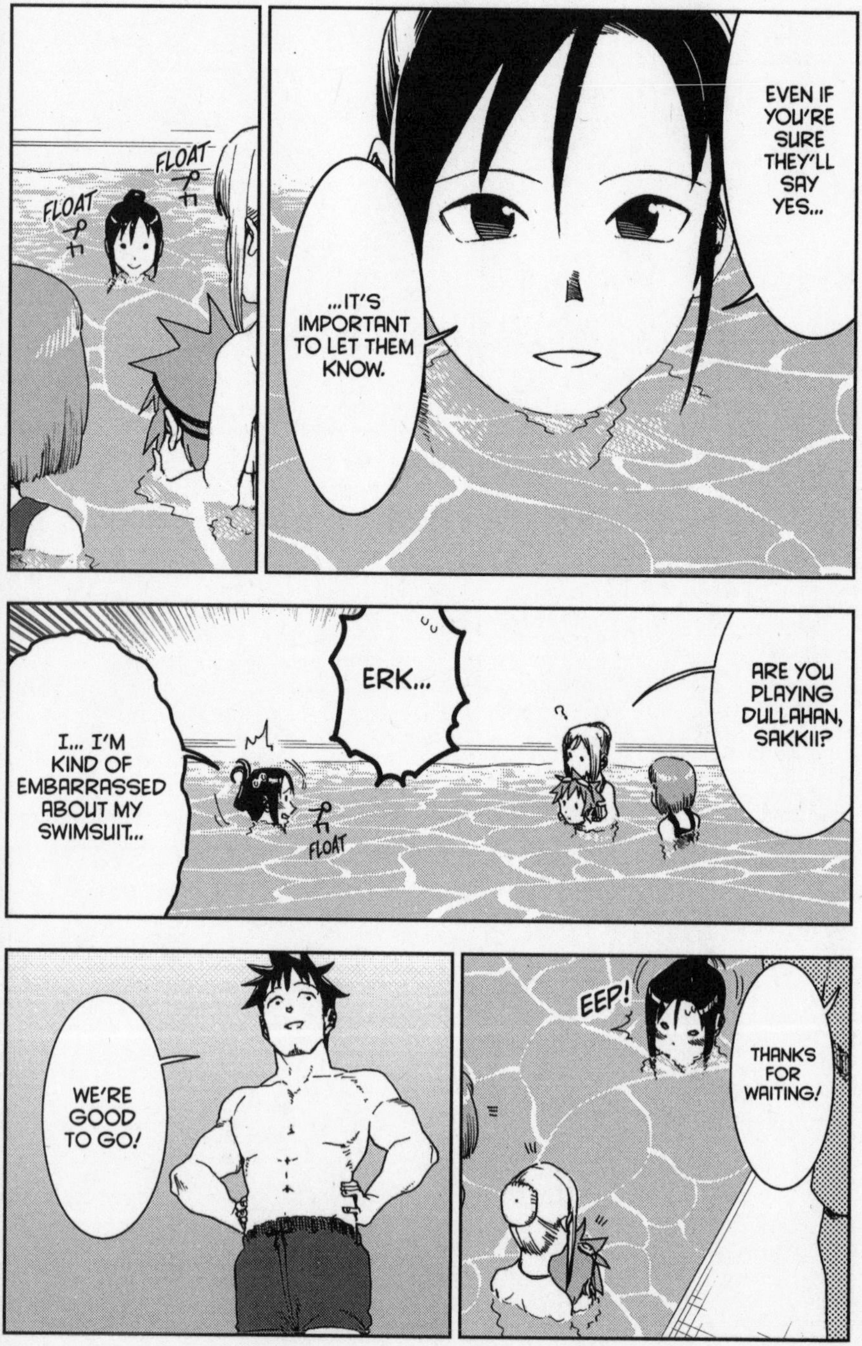
EVEN IF YOU'RE SURE THEY'LL SAY YES...
...IT'S IMPORTANT TO LET THEM KNOW.
FLOAT
FLOAT
ARE YOU PLAYING DULLAHAN, SAKKII?
ERK...
FLOAT
I... I'M KIND OF EMBARRASSED ABOUT MY SWIMSUIT...
THANKS FOR WAITING!
EEP!
WE'RE GOOD TO GO!

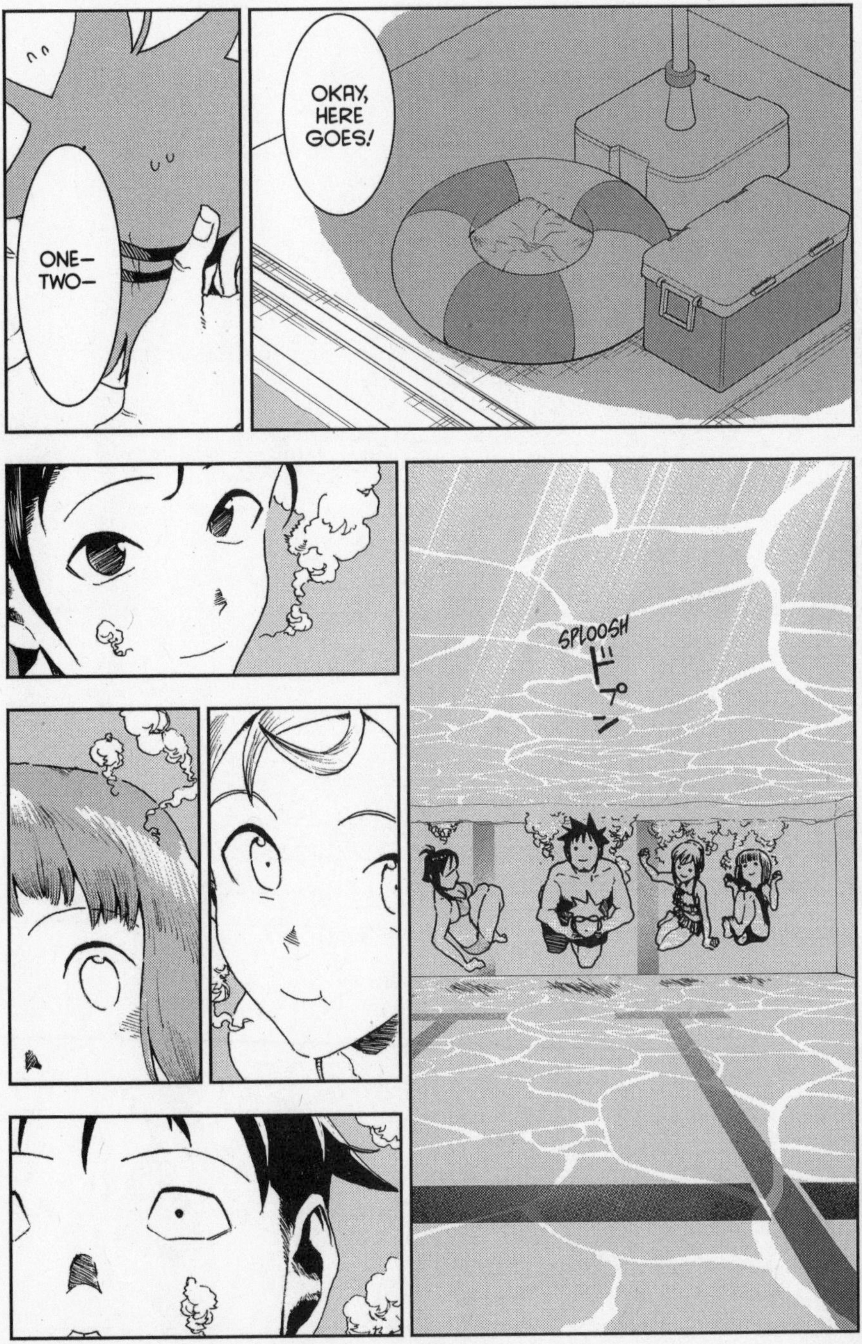
OKAY, HERE GOES!
ONE— TWO—
SPLOOSH
ドプン

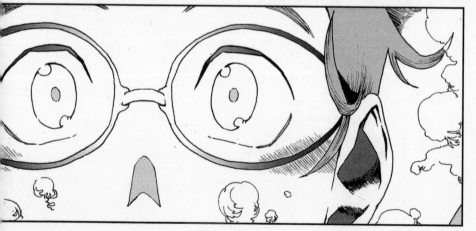

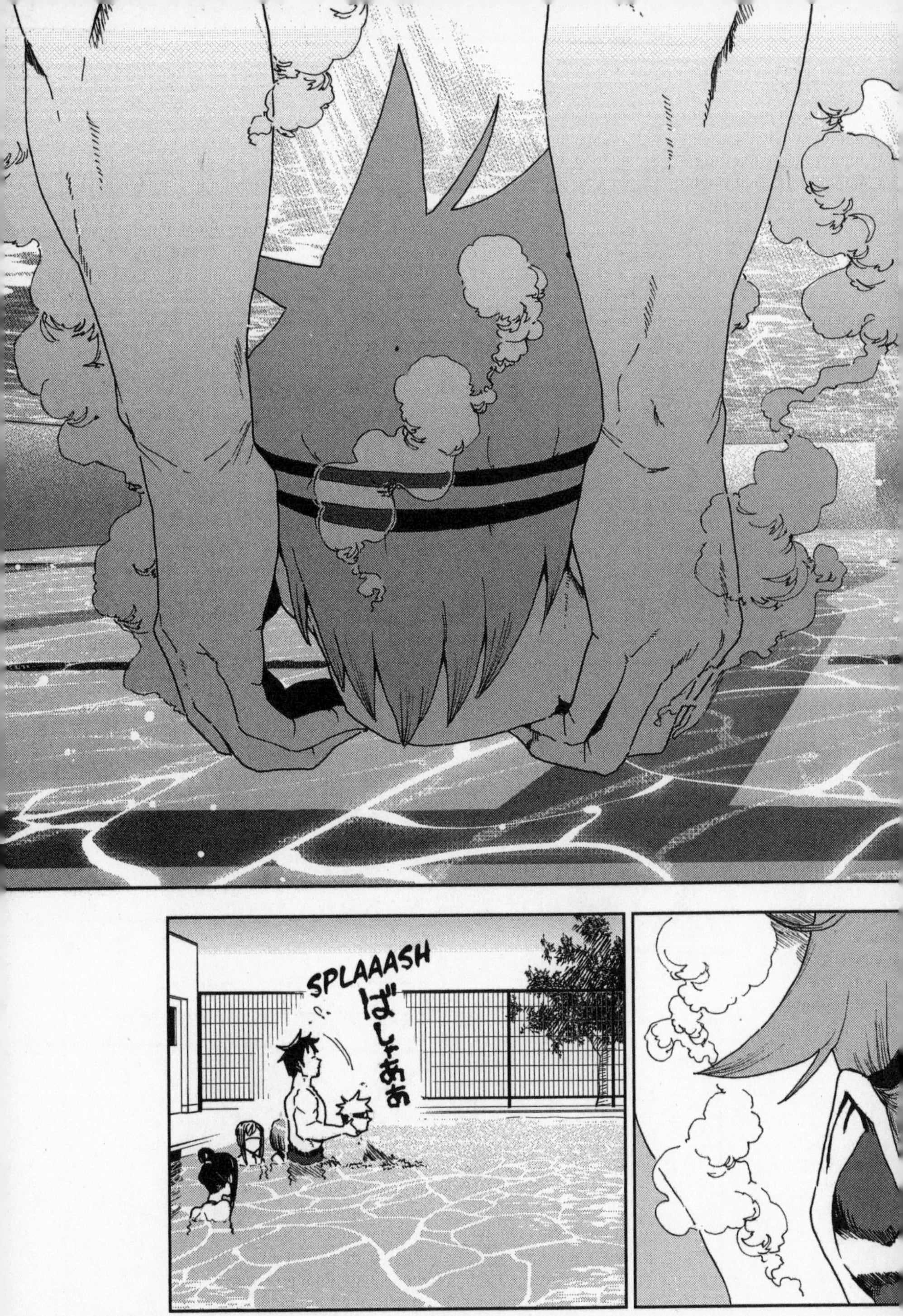
SPLAASH
ばしゃああ

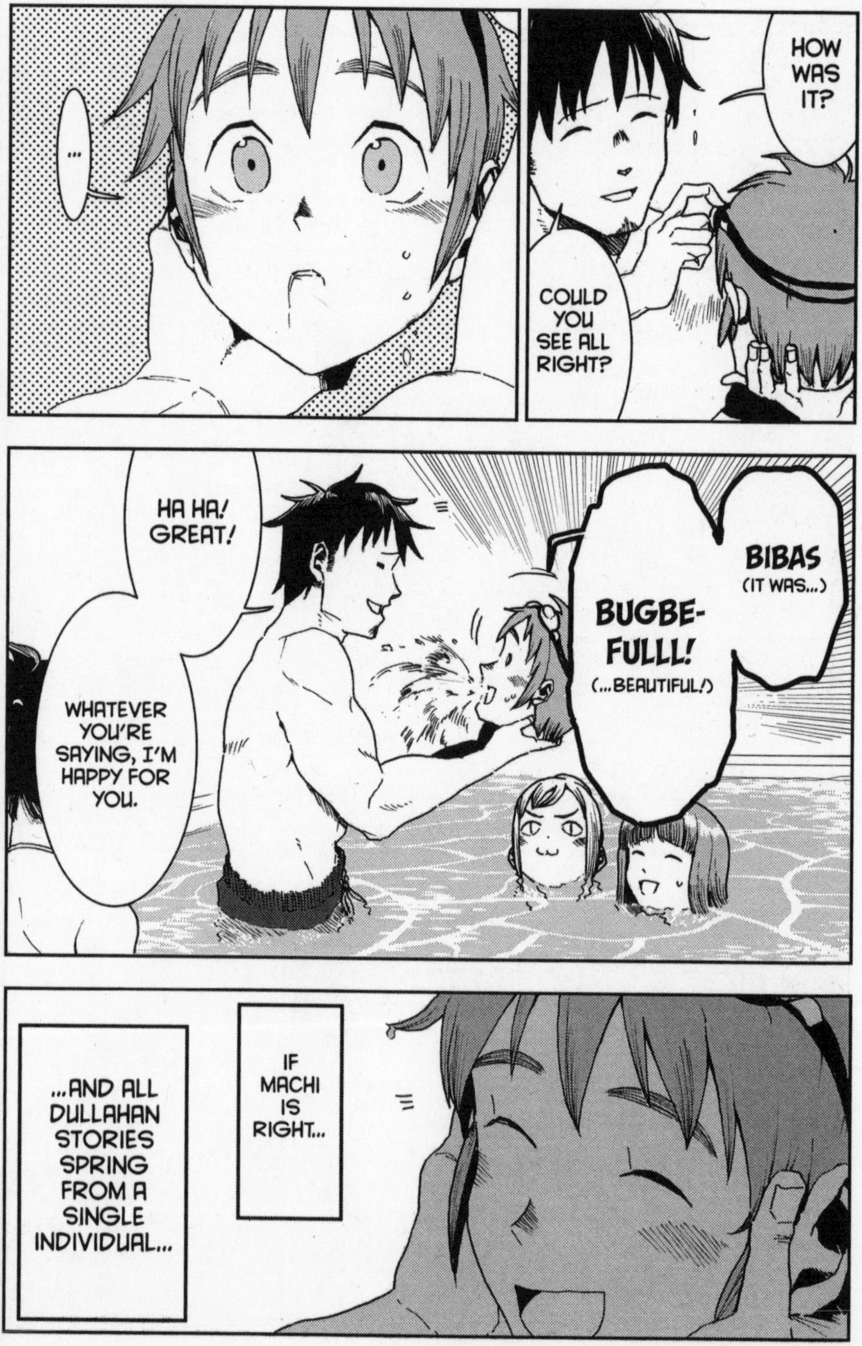
HOW WAS IT?
COULD YOU SEE ALL RIGHT?
...
BIBAS (IT WAS...)
BUGBE-FULLL! (...BEAUTIFUL!)
HA HA! GREAT!
WHATEVER YOU'RE SAYING, I'M HAPPY FOR YOU.
IF MACHI IS RIGHT...
...AND ALL DULLAHAN STORIES SPRING FROM A SINGLE INDIVIDUAL...

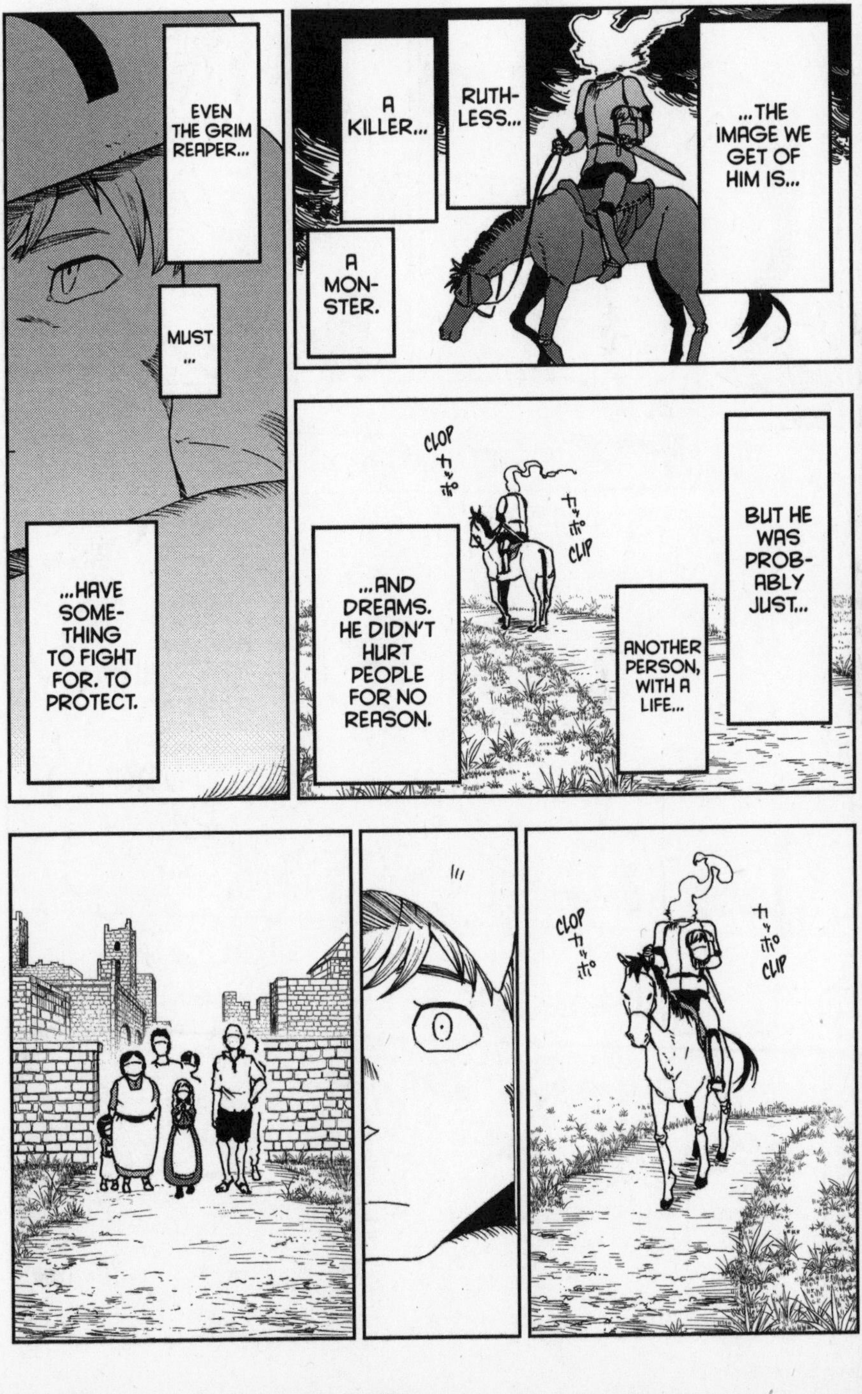
...THE IMAGE WE GET OF HIM IS...
RUTH-LESS...
A KILLER...
A MON-STER.
BUT HE WAS PROB-ABLY JUST...
CLIP カッポ
CLOP カッポ
ANOTHER PERSON, WITH A LIFE...
...AND DREAMS. HE DIDN'T HURT PEOPLE FOR NO REASON.
EVEN THE GRIM REAPER...
MUST ...
...HAVE SOME-THING TO FIGHT FOR. TO PROTECT.
CLIP カッポ
CLOP カッポ

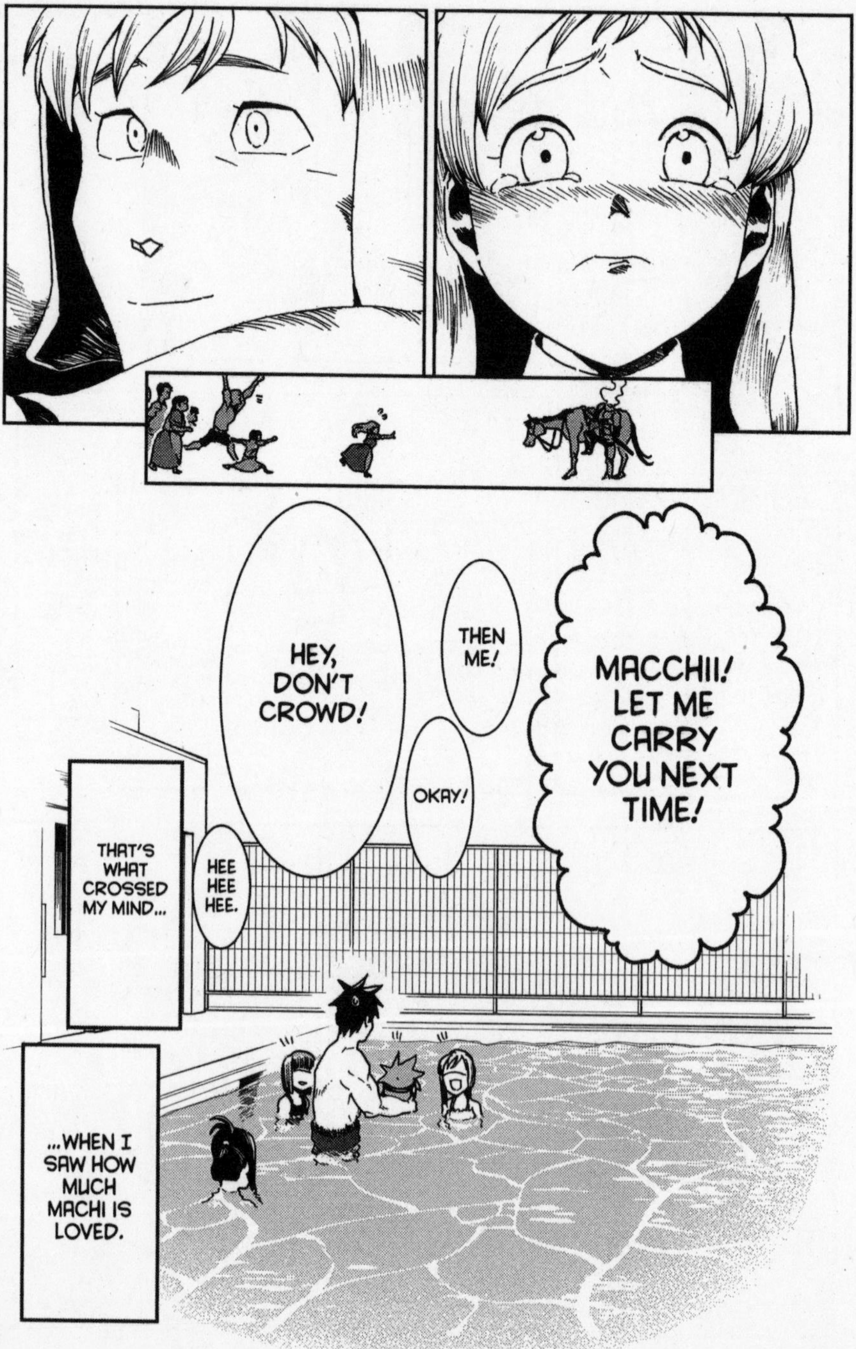
MACCHII! LET ME CARRY YOU NEXT TIME!
THEN ME!
OKAY!
HEY, DON'T CROWD!
HEE HEE HEE.
THAT'S WHAT CROSSED MY MIND...
...WHEN I SAW HOW MUCH MACHI IS LOVED.

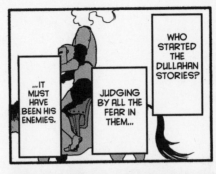

WHO STARTED THE DULLAHAN STORIES?
JUDGING BY ALL THE FEAR IN THEM...
...IT MUST HAVE BEEN HIS ENEMIES.
THE VICTORS WRITE HISTORY.
AND THAT DULLAHAN ISN'T REMEMBERED AS A HERO.
AND ...
THAT
MEANS ...
...
ARE YOU ALL RIGHT, SENSEI?
CAN'T STAND TO SEE US PLAYING IN THE POOL?
THOUGHTS OF LOST YOUTH?
C'MON, NOW, HE'S NOT *THAT* OLD...

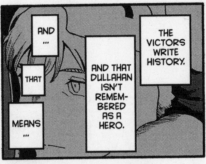

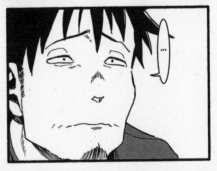

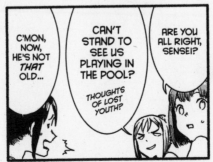

INTERVIEWS WITH MONSTER GIRLS

Chapter 35: Takanashi Talk

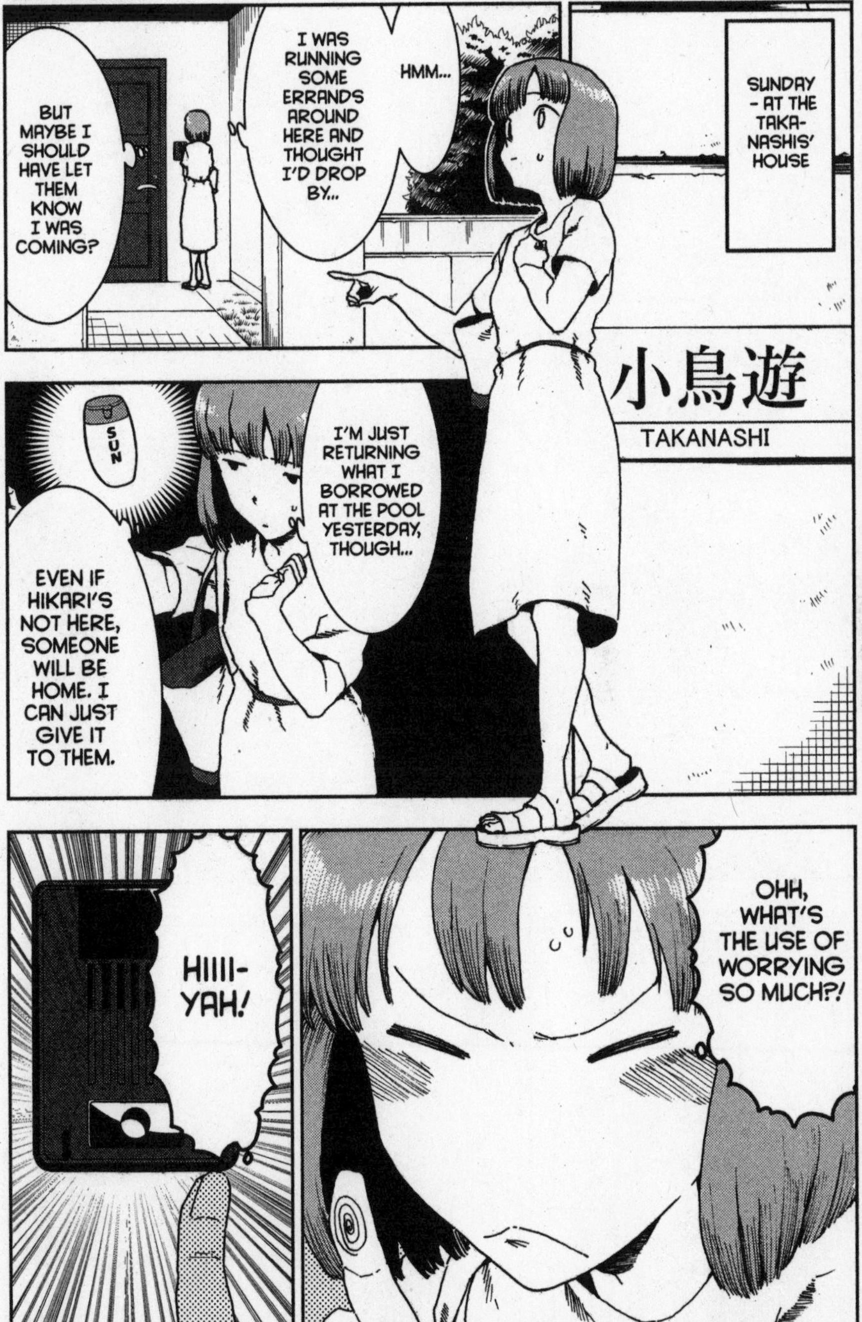
SUNDAY - AT THE TAKA-NASHIS' HOUSE
小鳥遊
TAKANASHI
HMM...
I WAS RUNNING SOME ERRANDS AROUND HERE AND THOUGHT I'D DROP BY...
BUT MAYBE I SHOULD HAVE LET THEM KNOW I WAS COMING?
I'M JUST RETURNING WHAT I BORROWED AT THE POOL YESTERDAY, THOUGH...
SUN
EVEN IF HIKARI'S NOT HERE, SOMEONE WILL BE HOME. I CAN JUST GIVE IT TO THEM.
OHH, WHAT'S THE USE OF WORRYING SO MUCH?!
HIIII-YAH!

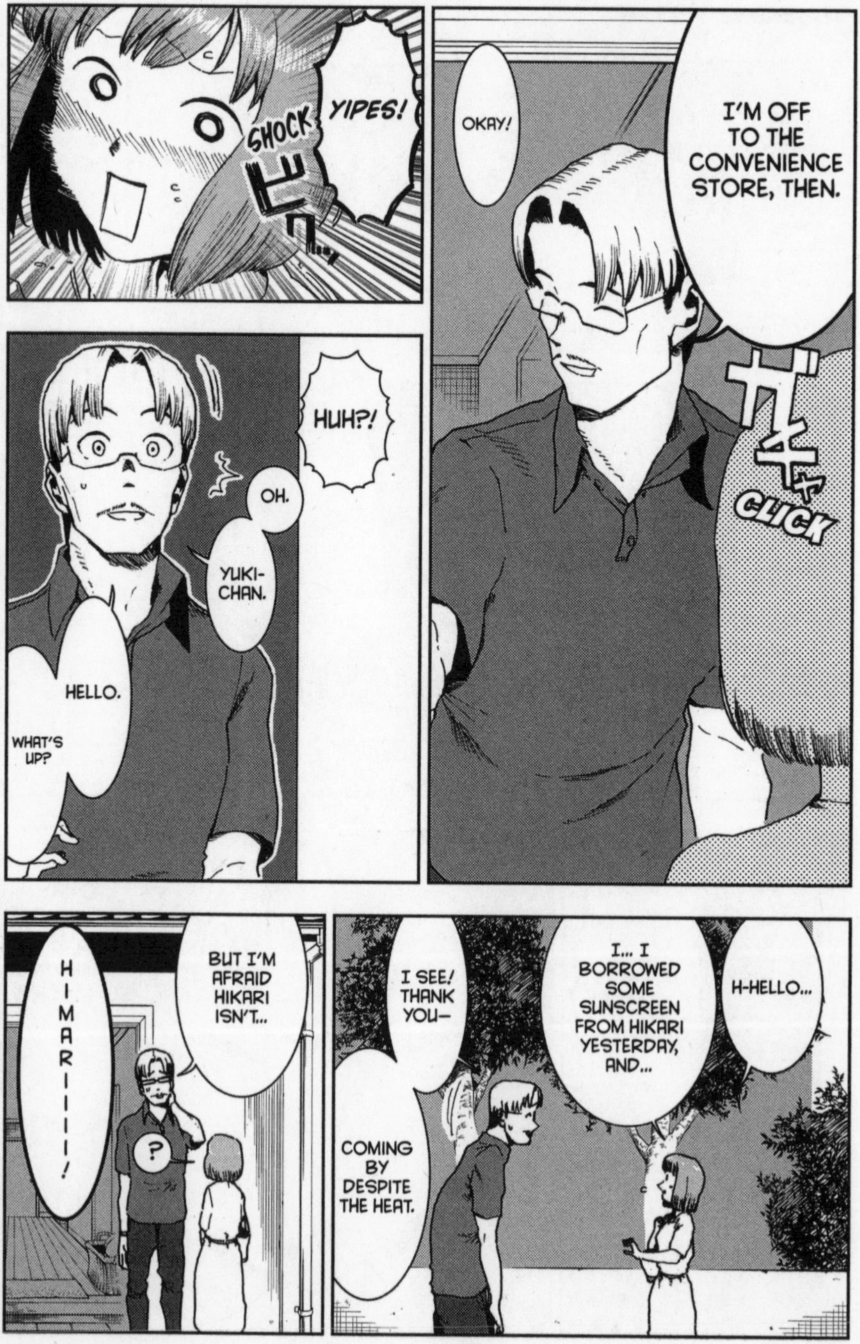
I'M OFF TO THE CONVENIENCE STORE, THEN.
OKAY!
CLICK
YIPES!
SHOCK
HUH?!
OH.
YUKI-CHAN.
HELLO.
WHAT'S UP?
H-HELLO...
I... I BORROWED SOME SUNSCREEN FROM HIKARI YESTERDAY, AND...
I SEE! THANK YOU—
COMING BY DESPITE THE HEAT.
BUT I'M AFRAID HIKARI ISN'T...
HIMARI!!!!!
?

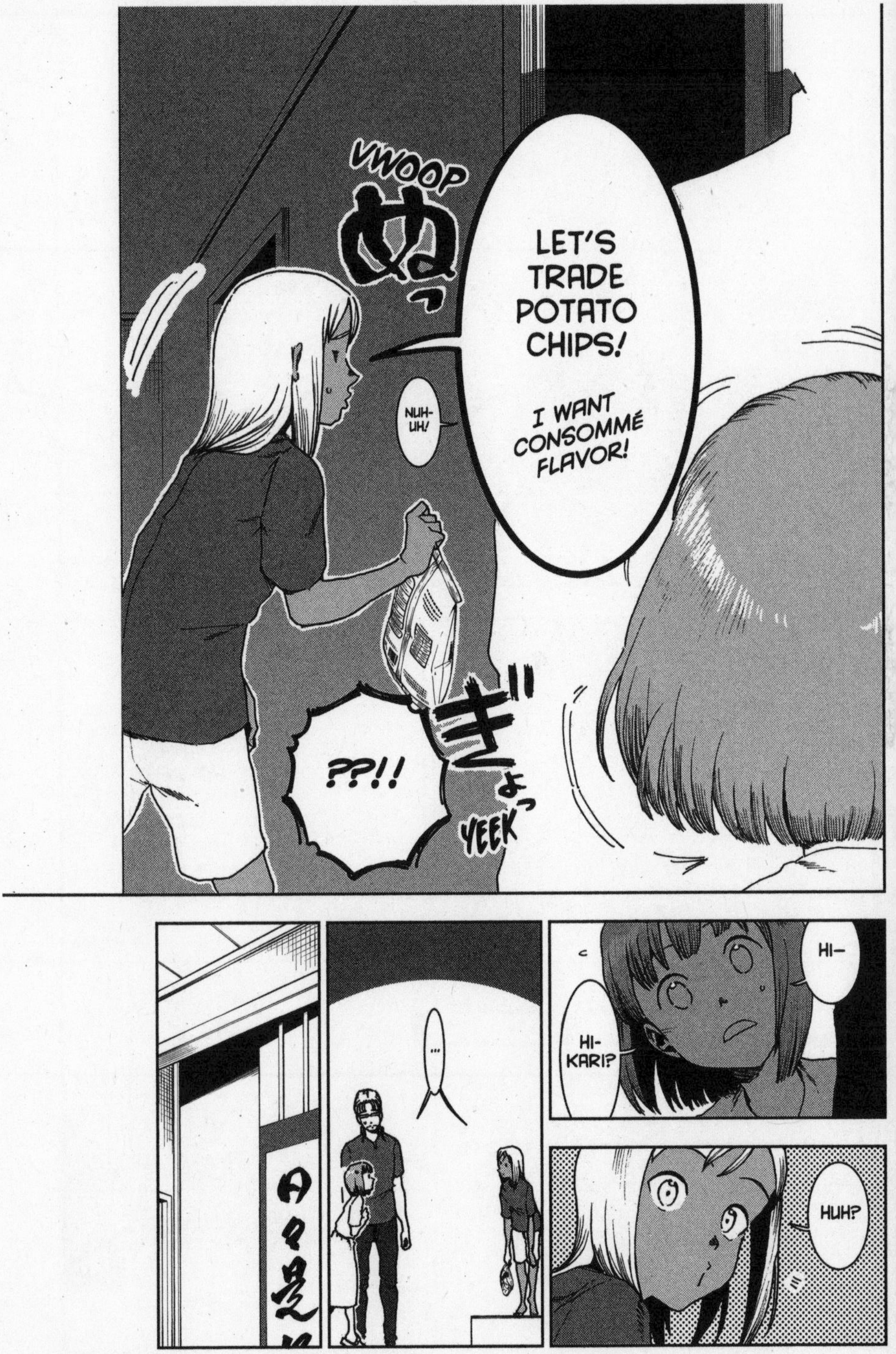
LET'S TRADE POTATO CHIPS!
I WANT CONSOMMÉ FLAVOR!
VWOOP
ぬっ
NUH-UH!
ぎょっ
YEEK
??!!
HI-
HI-KARI?
HUH?
...
日々是

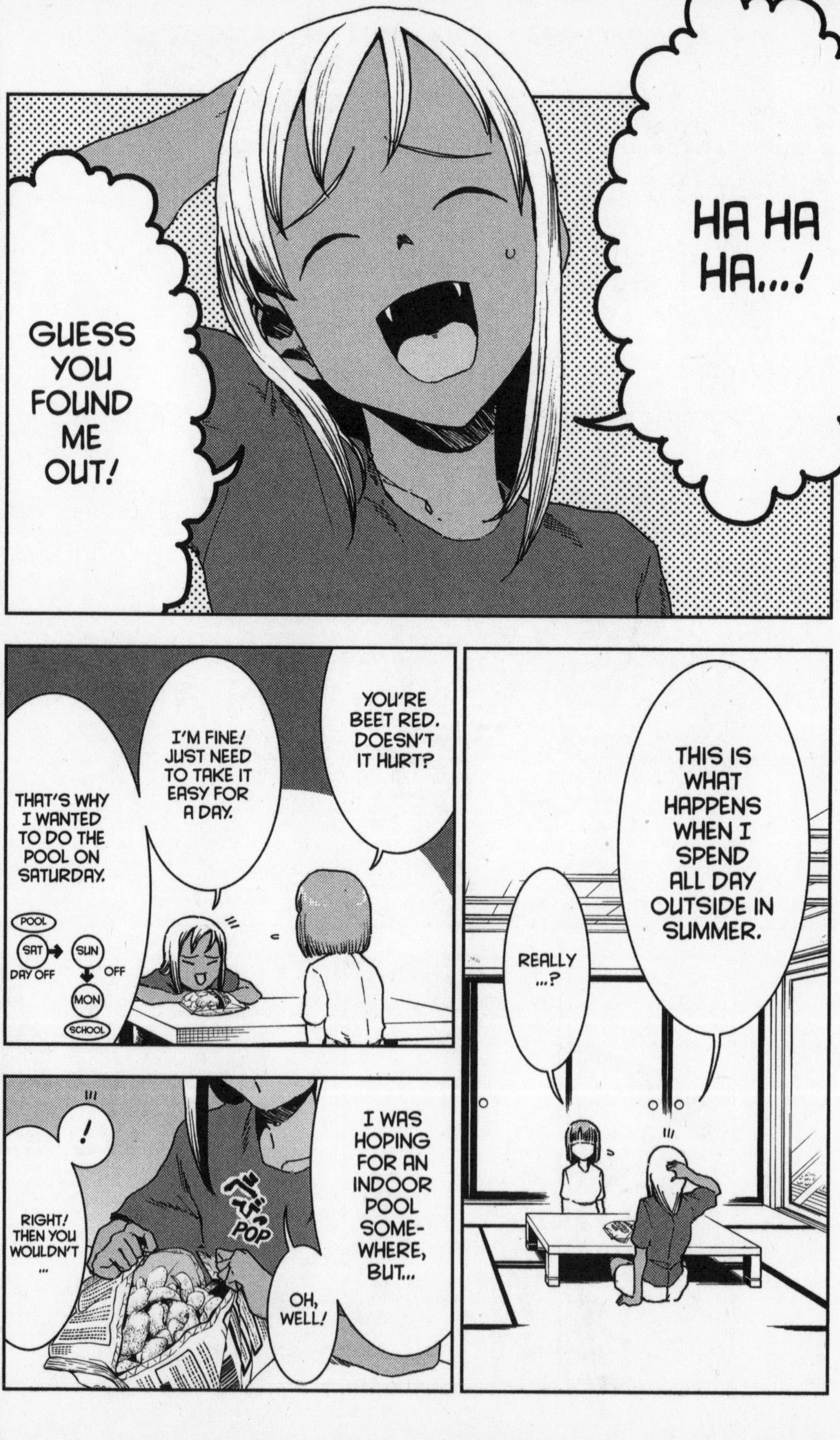
HA HA HA...!
GUESS YOU FOUND ME OUT!
THIS IS WHAT HAPPENS WHEN I SPEND ALL DAY OUTSIDE IN SUMMER.
REALLY ...?
YOU'RE BEET RED. DOESN'T IT HURT?
I'M FINE! JUST NEED TO TAKE IT EASY FOR A DAY.
THAT'S WHY I WANTED TO DO THE POOL ON SATURDAY.
POOL
SAT
DAY OFF
SUN
OFF
MON
SCHOOL
I WAS HOPING FOR AN INDOOR POOL SOME-WHERE, BUT...
OH, WELL!
POP
!
RIGHT! THEN YOU WOULDN'T ...

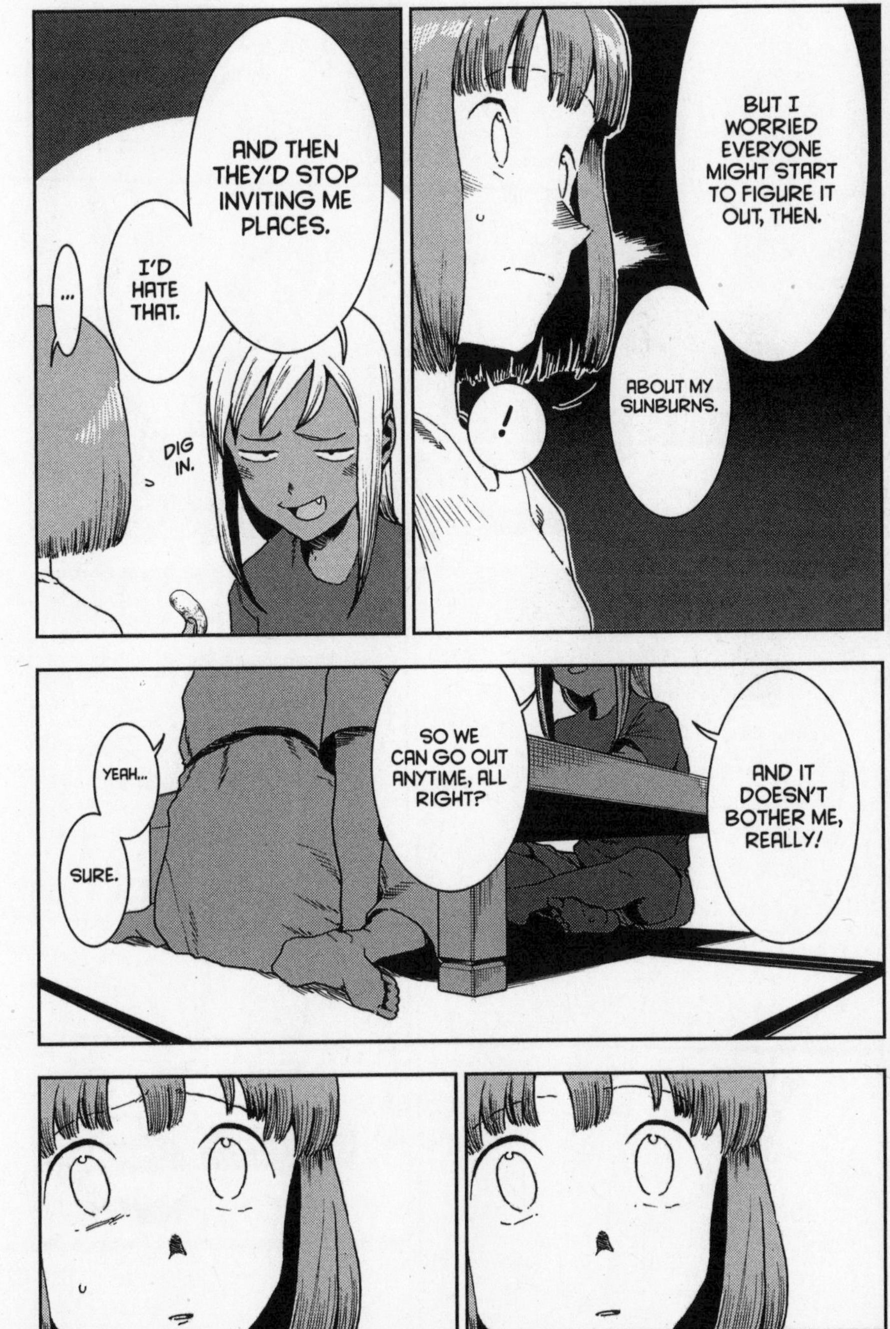
BUT I WORRIED EVERYONE MIGHT START TO FIGURE IT OUT, THEN.
ABOUT MY SUNBURNS.
!
AND THEN THEY'D STOP INVITING ME PLACES.
I'D HATE THAT.
...
DIG IN.
AND IT DOESN'T BOTHER ME, REALLY!
SO WE CAN GO OUT ANYTIME, ALL RIGHT?
YEAH...
SURE.

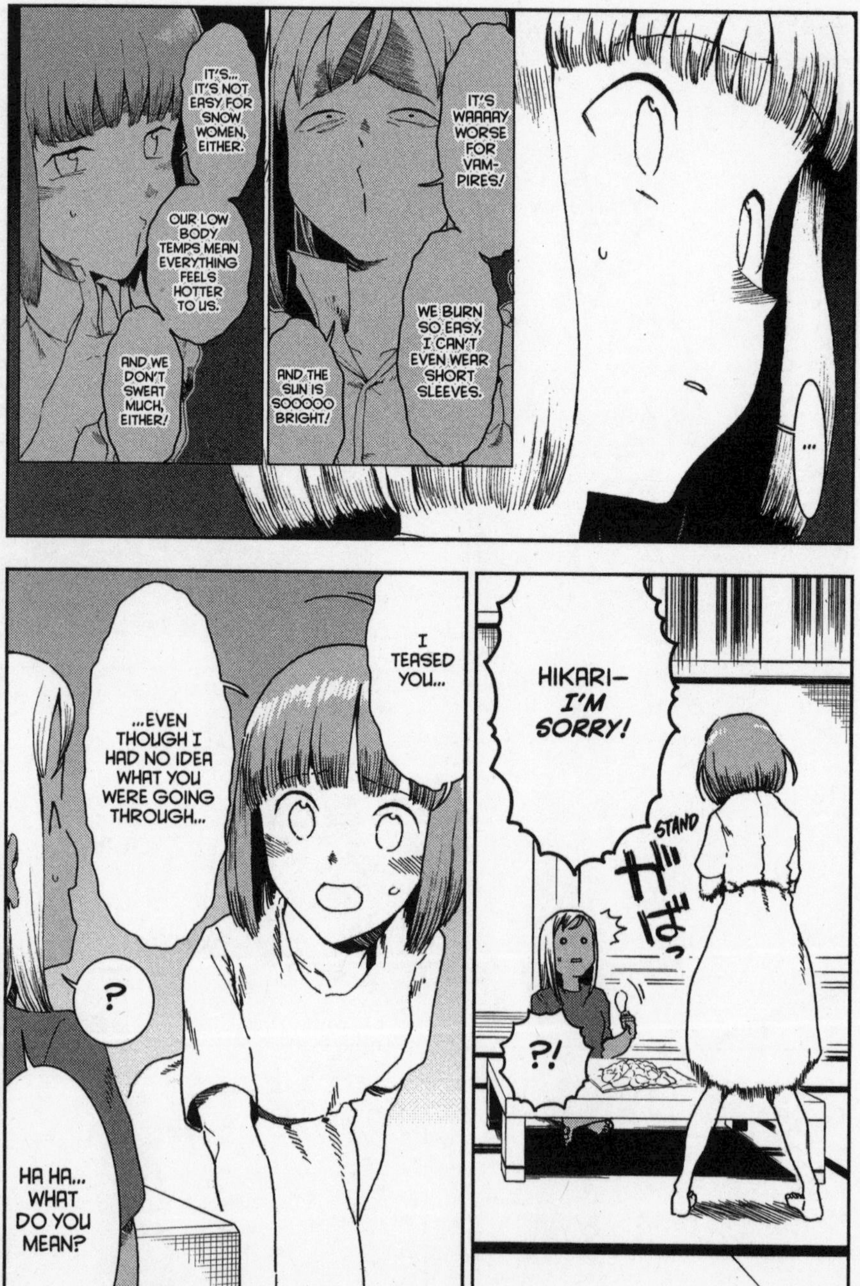
...
IT'S WAAAAY WORSE FOR VAMPIRES!
WE BURN SO EASY, I CAN'T EVEN WEAR SHORT SLEEVES.
AND THE SUN IS SOOOOO BRIGHT!
IT'S... IT'S NOT EASY FOR SNOW WOMEN, EITHER.
OUR LOW BODY TEMPS MEAN EVERYTHING FEELS HOTTER TO US.
AND WE DON'T SWEAT MUCH, EITHER!
HIKARI— *I'M SORRY!*
STAND
ガばっ
?!
I TEASED YOU...
...EVEN THOUGH I HAD NO IDEA WHAT YOU WERE GOING THROUGH...
?
HA HA... WHAT DO YOU MEAN?

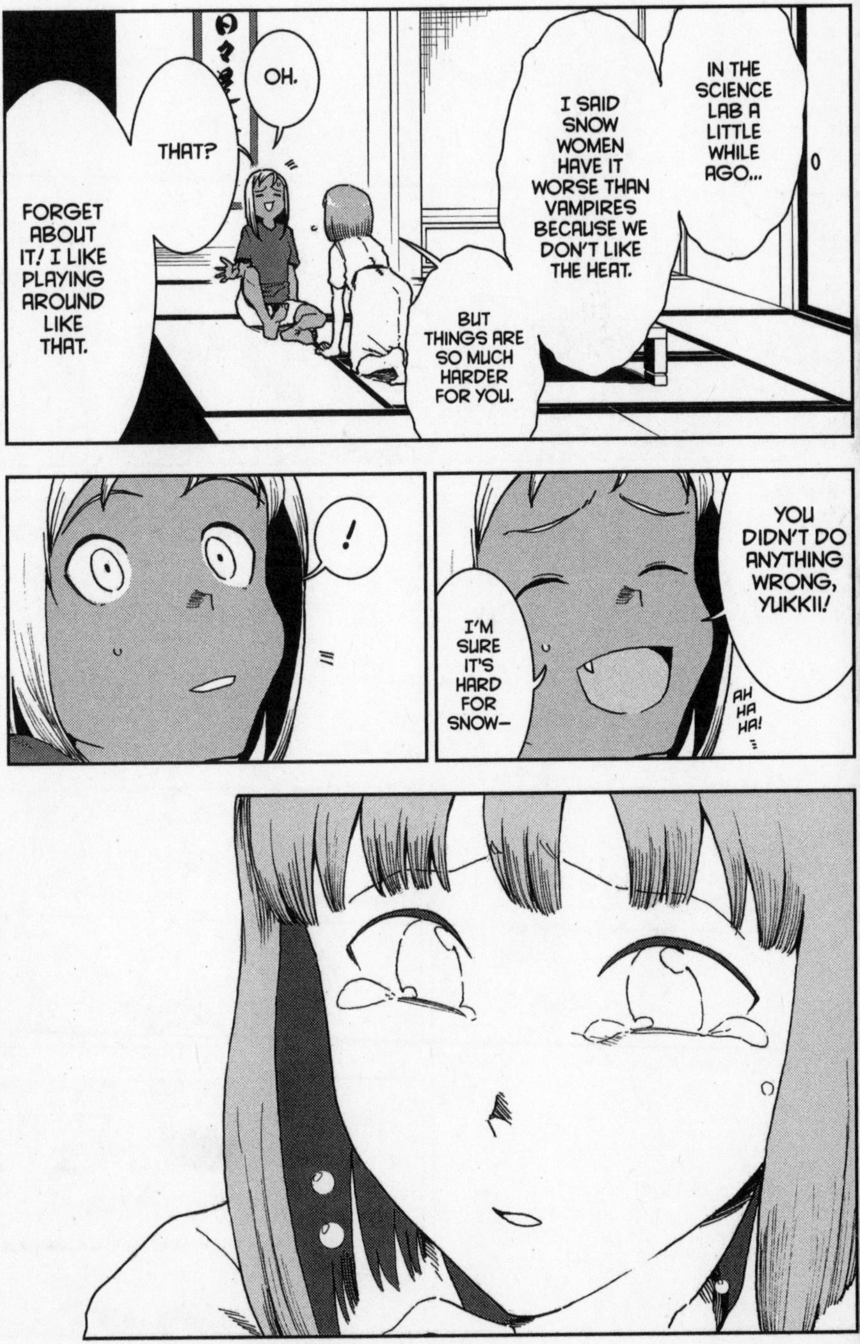
IN THE SCIENCE LAB A LITTLE WHILE AGO...
I SAID SNOW WOMEN HAVE IT WORSE THAN VAMPIRES BECAUSE WE DON'T LIKE THE HEAT.
BUT THINGS ARE SO MUCH HARDER FOR YOU.
OH.
THAT?
FORGET ABOUT IT! I LIKE PLAYING AROUND LIKE THAT.
YOU DIDN'T DO ANYTHING WRONG, YUKKII!
AH HA HA!
I'M SURE IT'S HARD FOR SNOW–
!

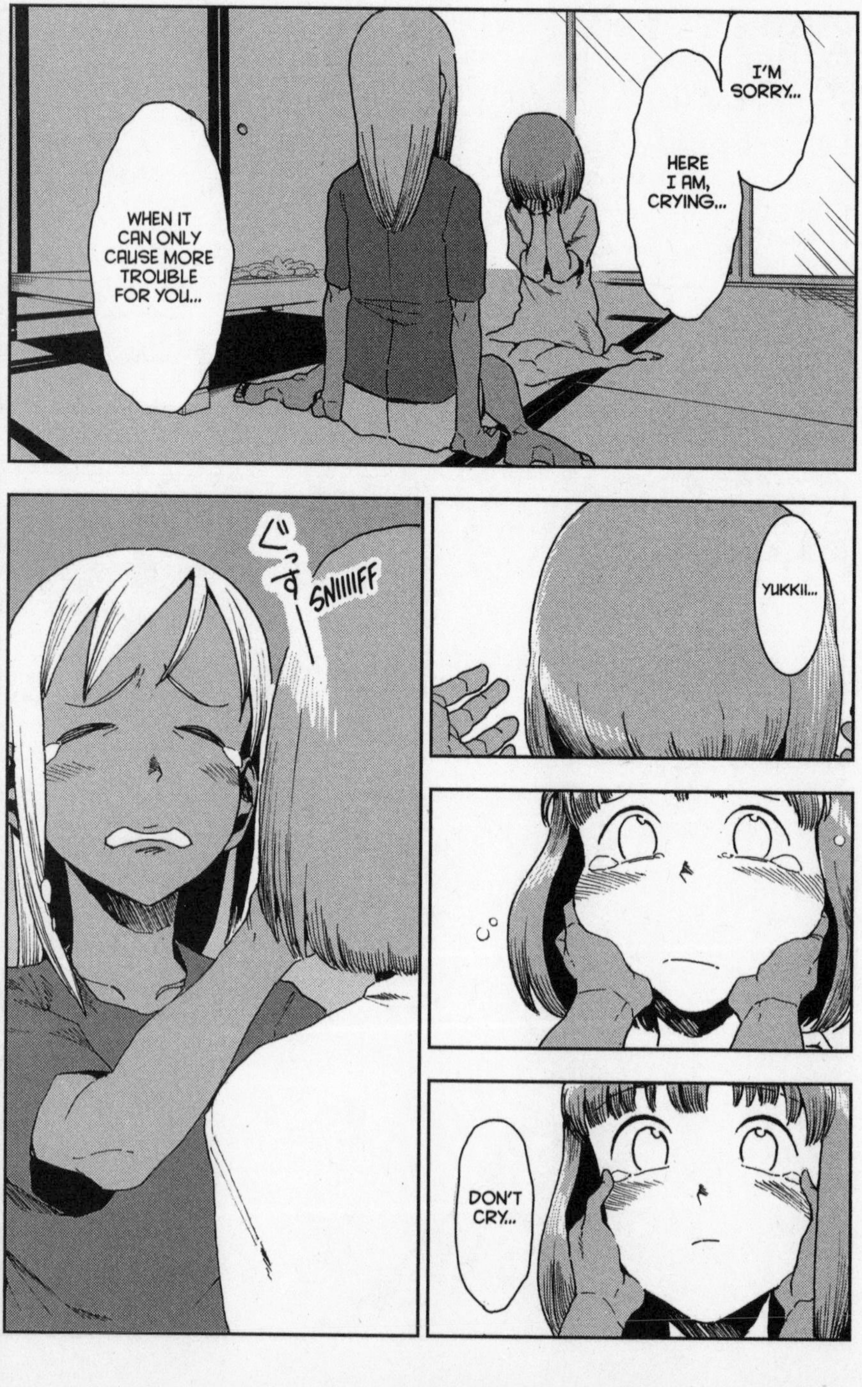
I'M SORRY...
HERE I AM, CRYING...
WHEN IT CAN ONLY CAUSE MORE TROUBLE FOR YOU...
YUKKII...
DON'T CRY...
ぐっす
SNIIIIFF

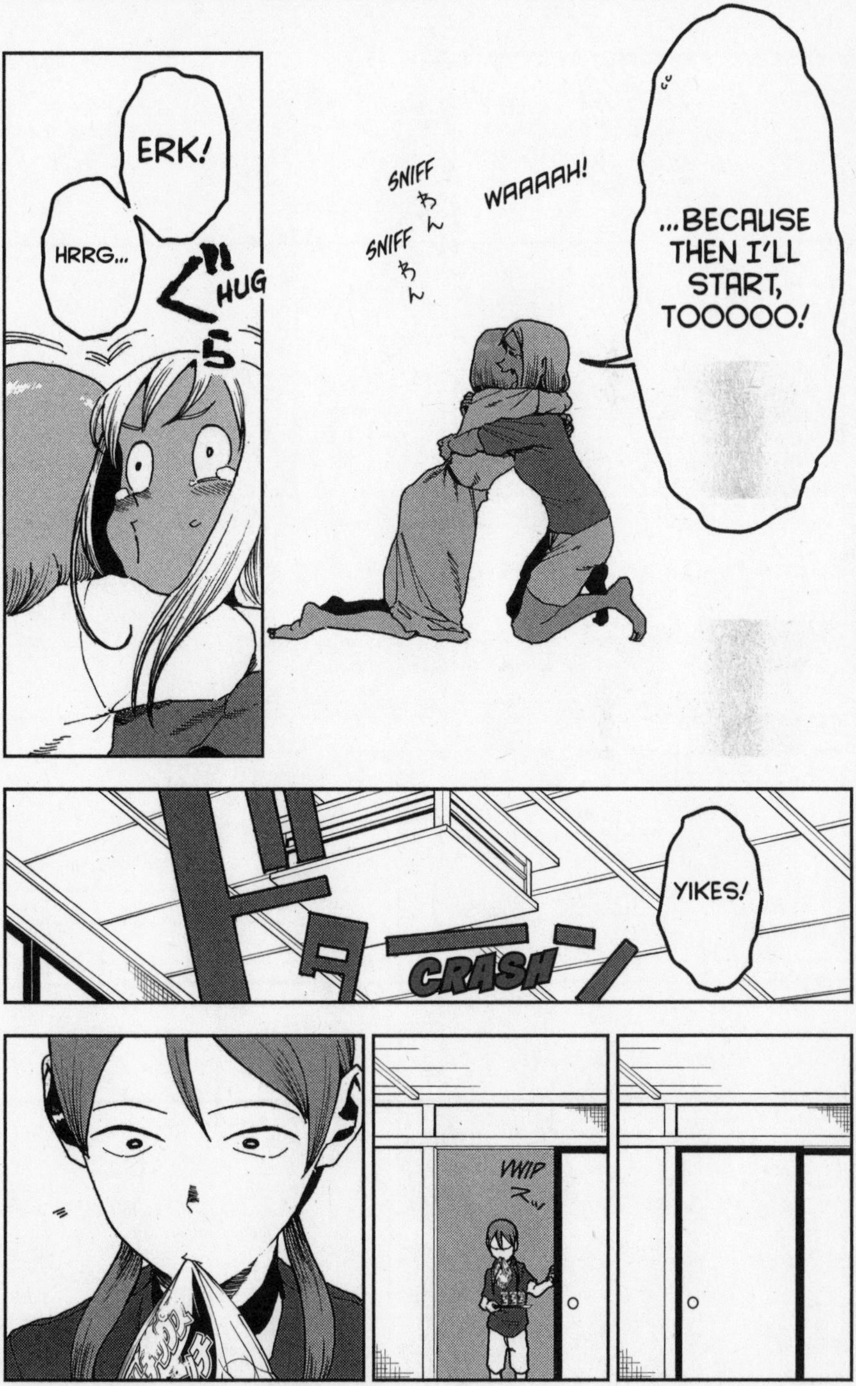
...BECAUSE THEN I'LL START, TOOOOO!
WAAAAH!
SNIFF わん
SNIFF わん
ERK!
HRRG...
HUG
YIKES!
CRASH
VWIP

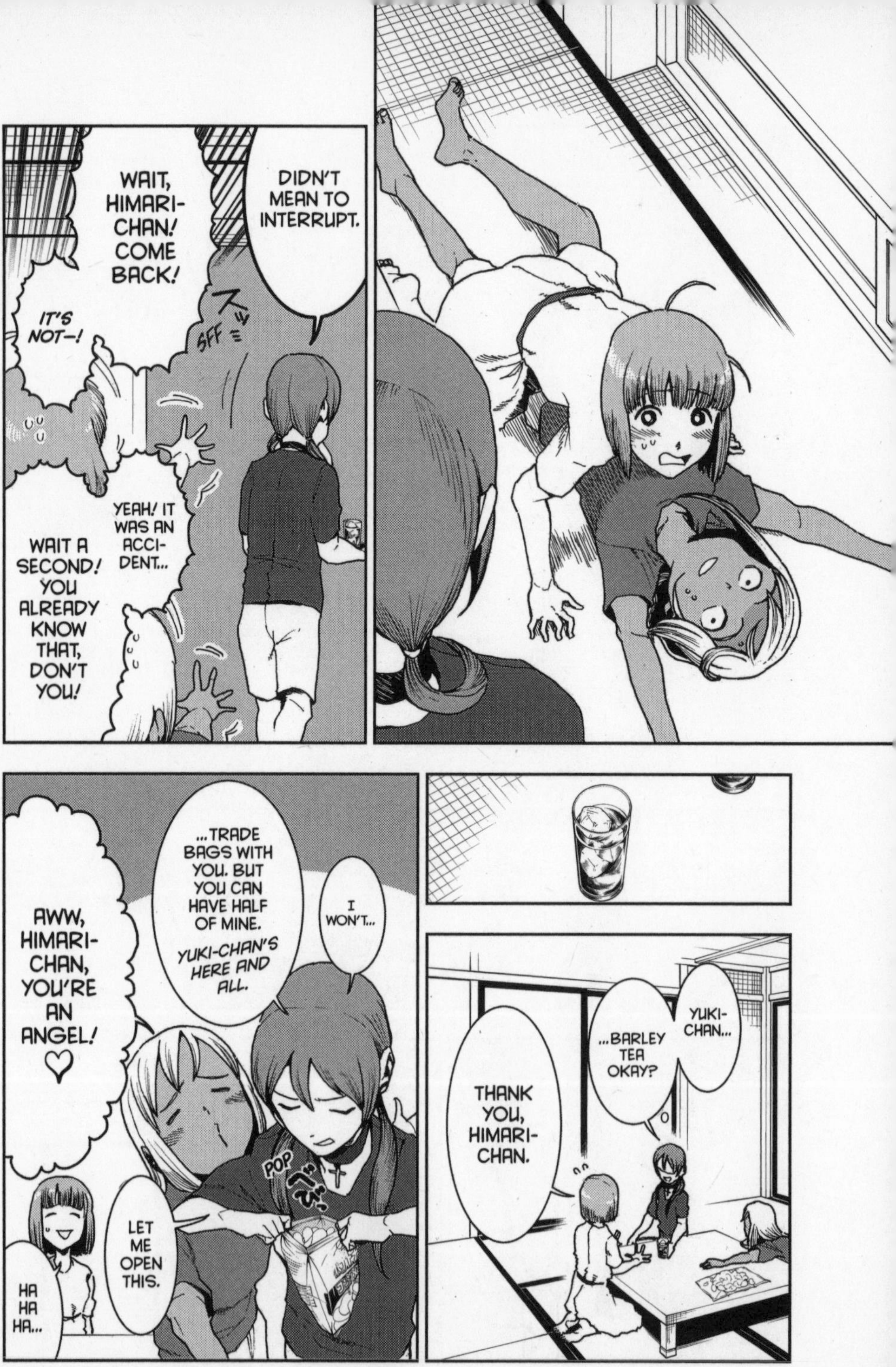
DIDN'T MEAN TO INTERRUPT.
WAIT, HIMARI-CHAN! COME BACK!
IT'S NOT—!
スッ
SFF
YEAH! IT WAS AN ACCI-DENT...
WAIT A SECOND! YOU ALREADY KNOW THAT, DON'T YOU!
YUKI-CHAN...
...BARLEY TEA OKAY?
THANK YOU, HIMARI-CHAN.
I WON'T...
...TRADE BAGS WITH YOU. BUT YOU CAN HAVE HALF OF MINE.
YUKI-CHAN'S HERE AND ALL.
AWW, HIMARI-CHAN, YOU'RE AN ANGEL! ♡
POP
LET ME OPEN THIS.
HA HA HA HA...

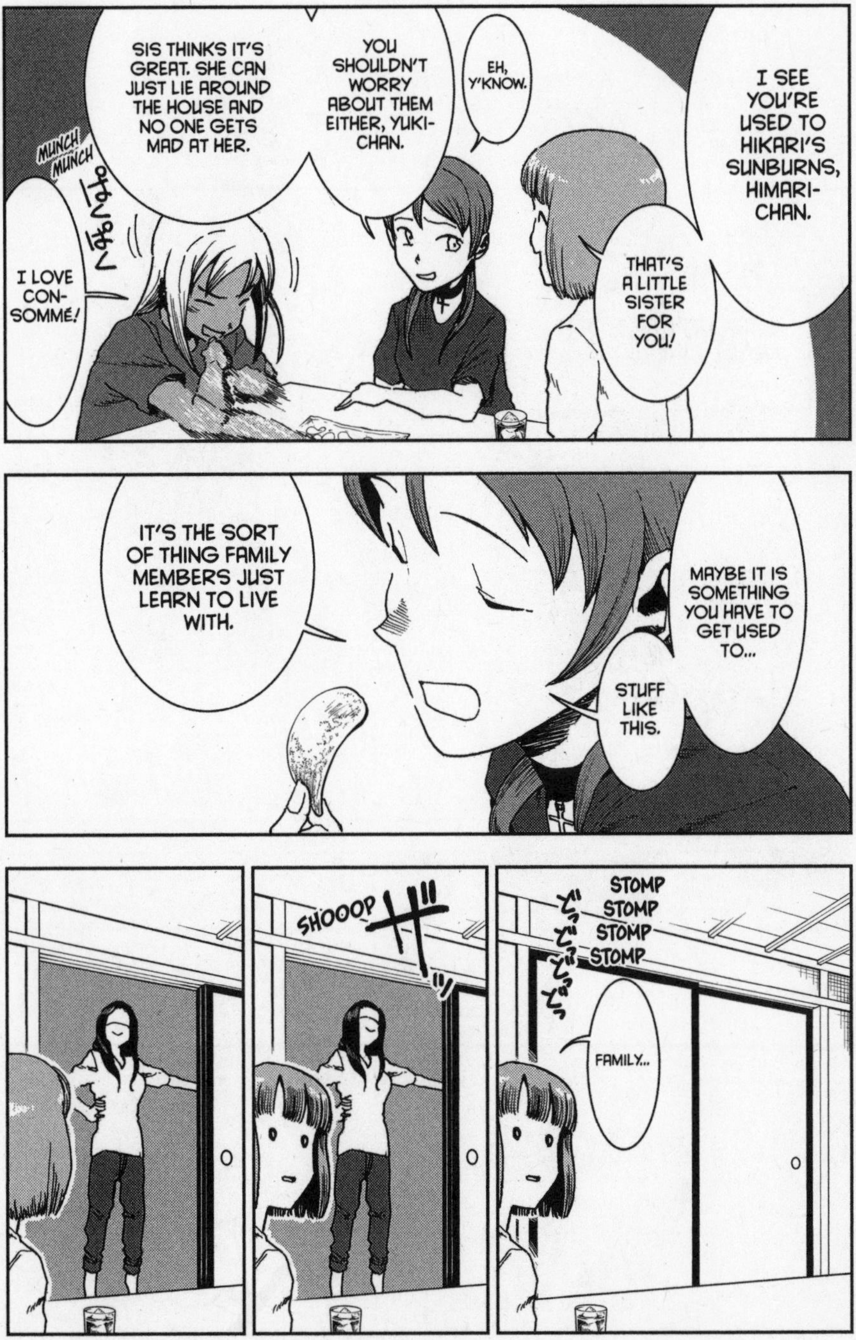
I SEE YOU'RE USED TO HIKARI'S SUNBURNS, HIMARI-CHAN.
THAT'S A LITTLE SISTER FOR YOU!
EH, Y'KNOW.
YOU SHOULDN'T WORRY ABOUT THEM EITHER, YUKI-CHAN.
SIS THINKS IT'S GREAT. SHE CAN JUST LIE AROUND THE HOUSE AND NO ONE GETS MAD AT HER.
MUNCH MUNCH
I LOVE CON-SOMMÉ!
MAYBE IT IS SOMETHING YOU HAVE TO GET USED TO...
STUFF LIKE THIS.
IT'S THE SORT OF THING FAMILY MEMBERS JUST LEARN TO LIVE WITH.
STOMP STOMP STOMP STOMP
FAMILY...
SHOOOP

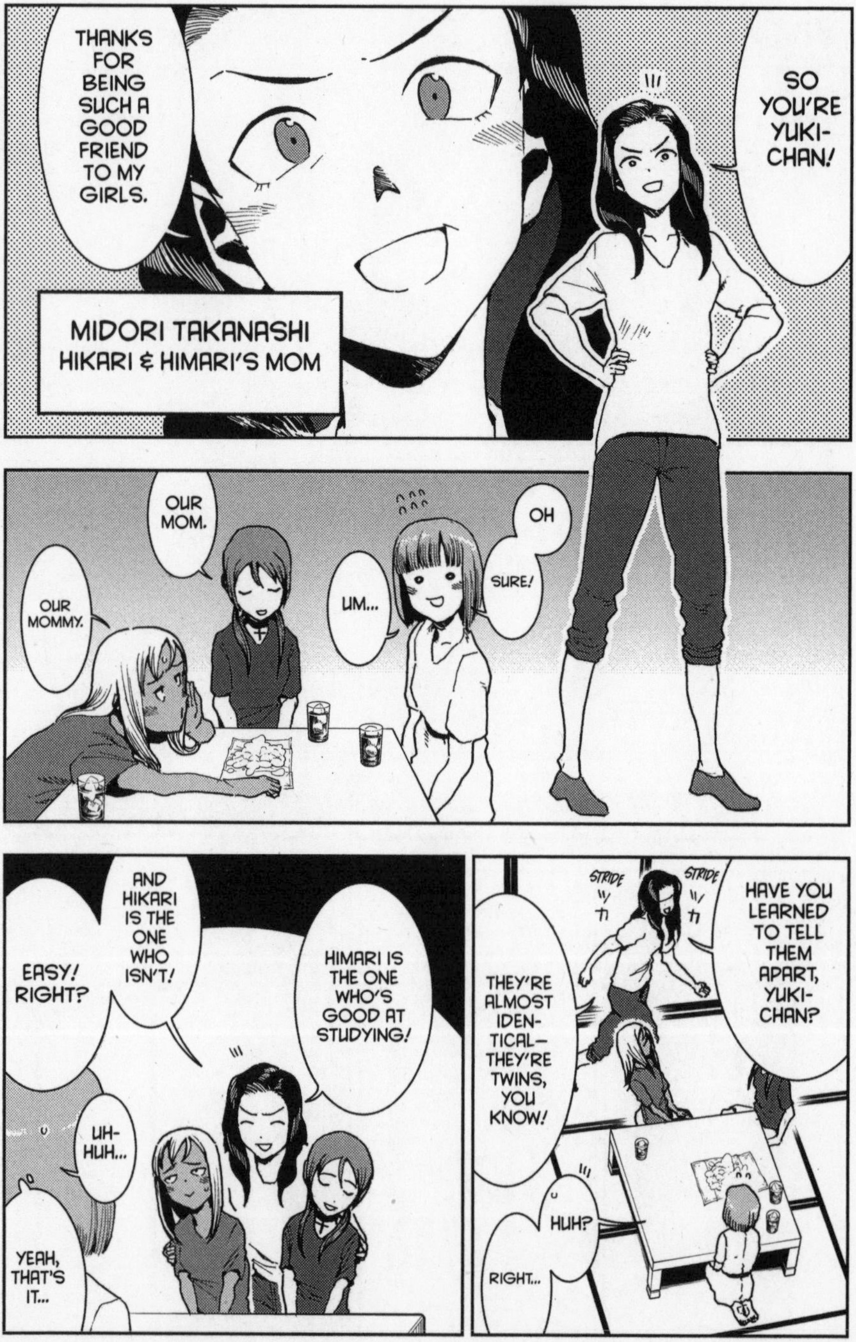
SO YOU'RE YUKI-CHAN!
THANKS FOR BEING SUCH A GOOD FRIEND TO MY GIRLS.
MIDORI TAKANASHI HIKARI & HIMARI'S MOM
OH SURE!
UM...
OUR MOM.
OUR MOMMY.
STRIDE ツカ
STRIDE ツカ
HAVE YOU LEARNED TO TELL THEM APART, YUKI-CHAN?
THEY'RE ALMOST IDENTICAL—THEY'RE TWINS, YOU KNOW!
HUH?
RIGHT...
HIMARI IS THE ONE WHO'S GOOD AT STUDYING!
AND HIKARI IS THE ONE WHO ISN'T!
EASY! RIGHT?
UH-HUH...
YEAH, THAT'S IT...

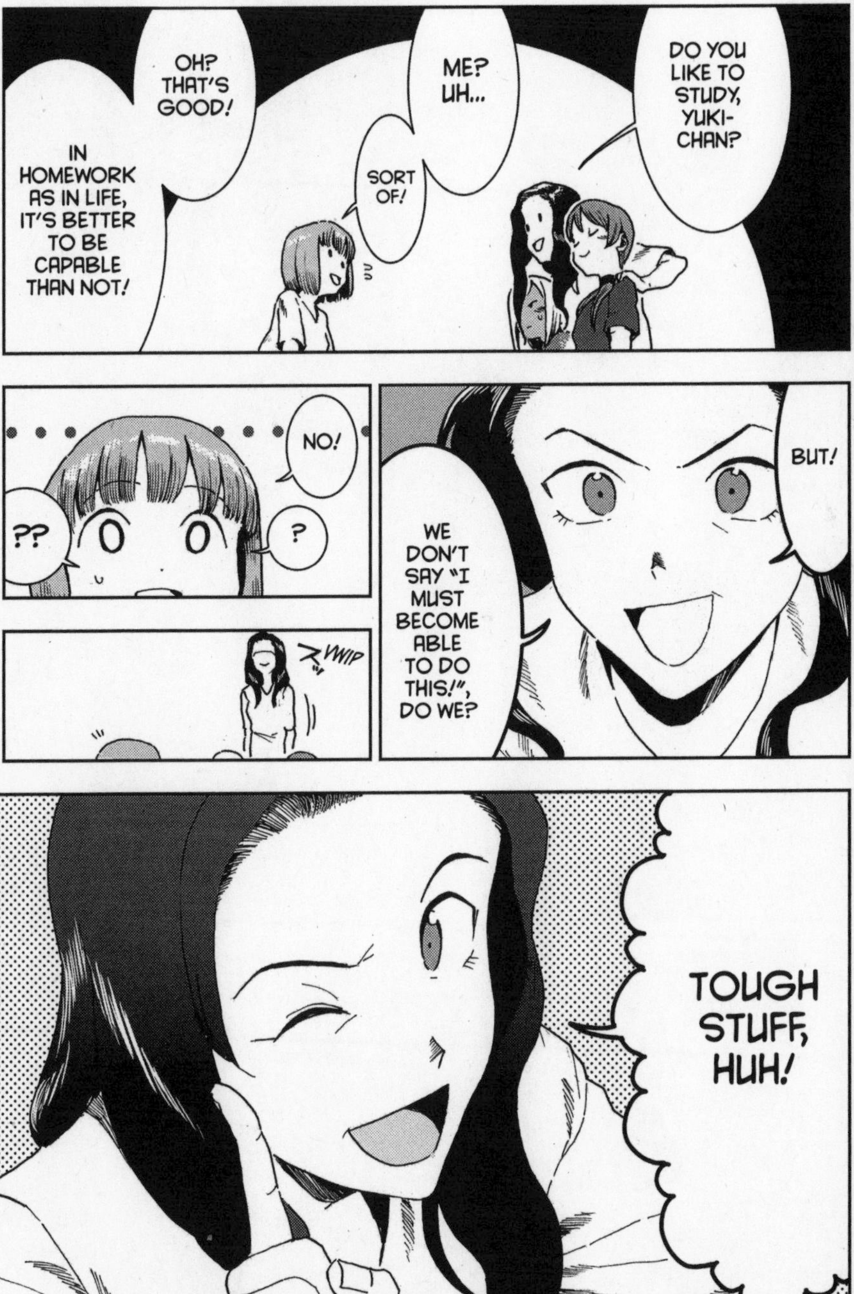
DO YOU LIKE TO STUDY, YUKI-CHAN?
ME? UH...
SORT OF!
OH? THAT'S GOOD!
IN HOMEWORK AS IN LIFE, IT'S BETTER TO BE CAPABLE THAN NOT!
BUT!
WE DON'T SAY "I MUST BECOME ABLE TO DO THIS!", DO WE?
NO!
?
??
WHIP
TOUGH STUFF, HUH!

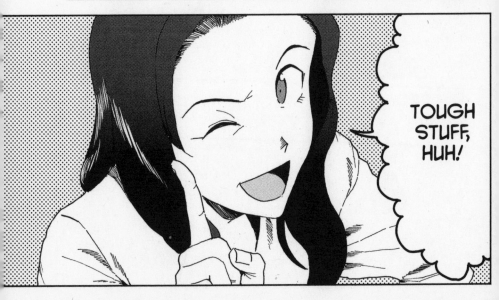

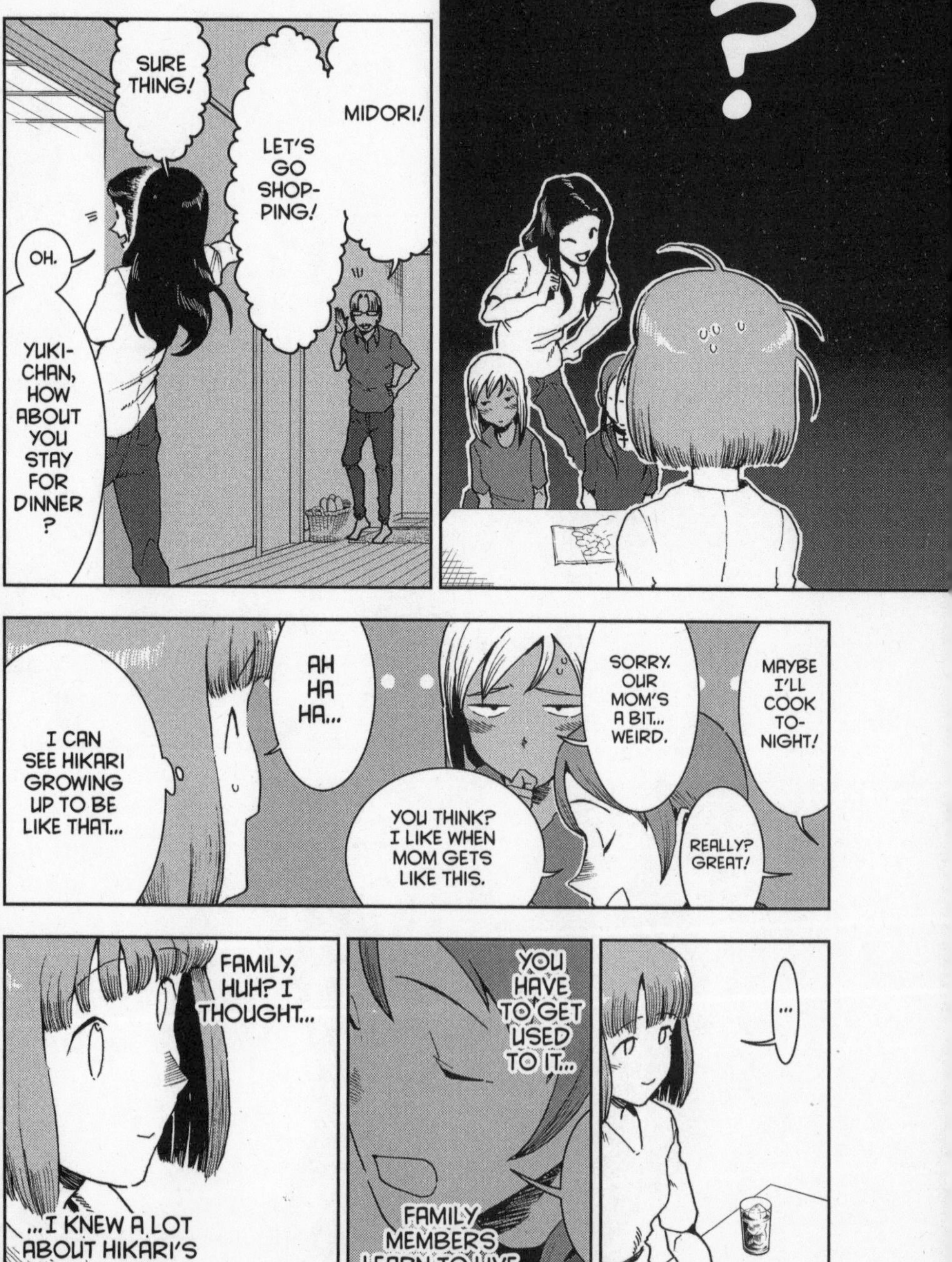
?
MIDORI! LET'S GO SHOPPING!
SURE THING!
OH.
YUKI-CHAN, HOW ABOUT YOU STAY FOR DINNER?
MAYBE I'LL COOK TONIGHT!
REALLY? GREAT!
SORRY. OUR MOM'S A BIT... WEIRD.
YOU THINK? I LIKE WHEN MOM GETS LIKE THIS.
AH HA HA...
I CAN SEE HIKARI GROWING UP TO BE LIKE THAT...
...
YOU HAVE TO GET USED TO IT...
FAMILY MEMBERS LEARN TO LIVE WITH IT.
FAMILY, HUH? I THOUGHT...
...I KNEW A LOT ABOUT HIKARI'S GOOD SIDE.

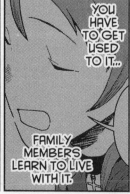

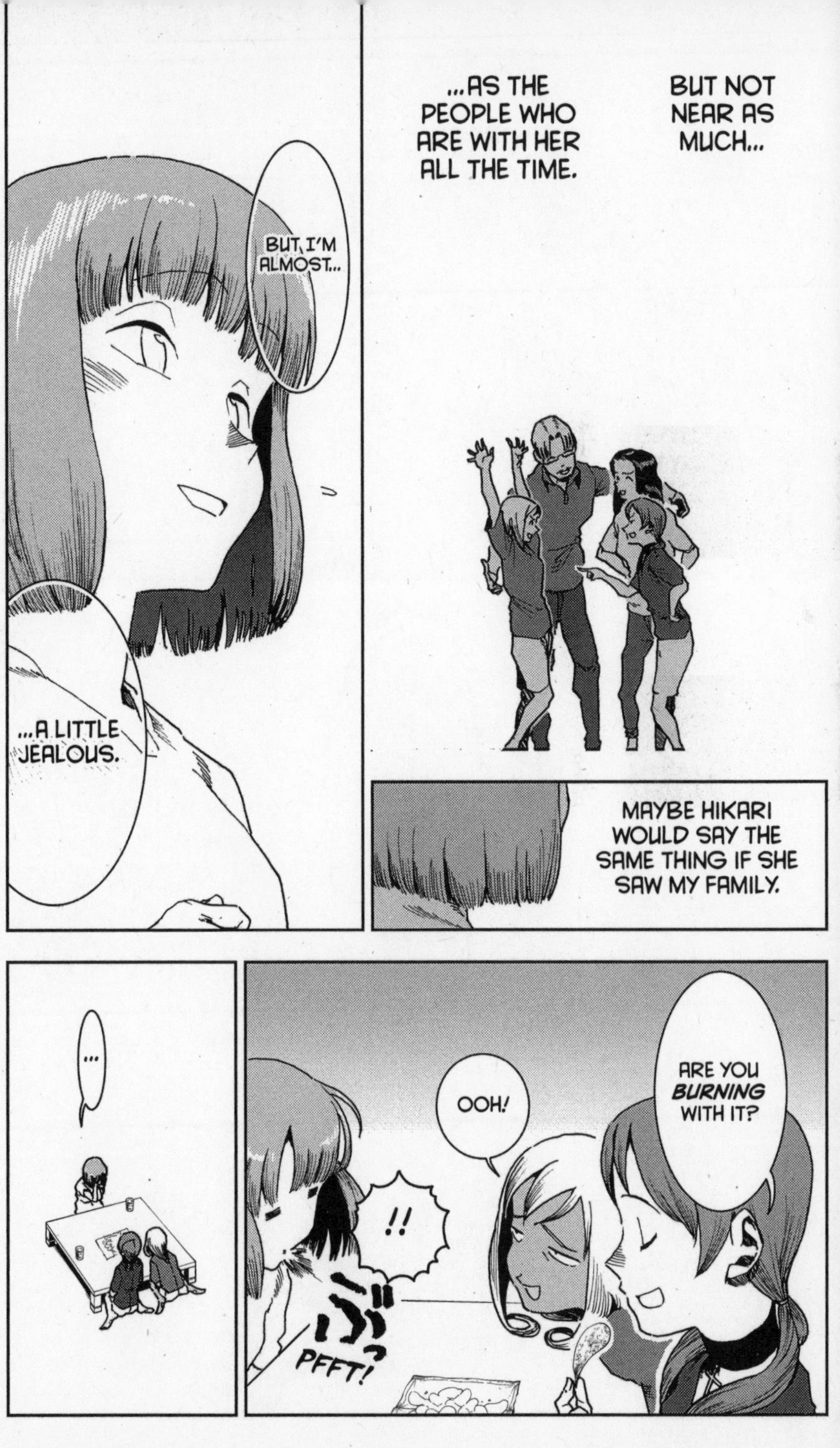
BUT NOT NEAR AS MUCH...
...AS THE PEOPLE WHO ARE WITH HER ALL THE TIME.
MAYBE HIKARI WOULD SAY THE SAME THING IF SHE SAW MY FAMILY.
BUT, I'M ALMOST...
...A LITTLE JEALOUS.
ARE YOU *BURNING* WITH IT?
OOH!
!!
PFFT!
...

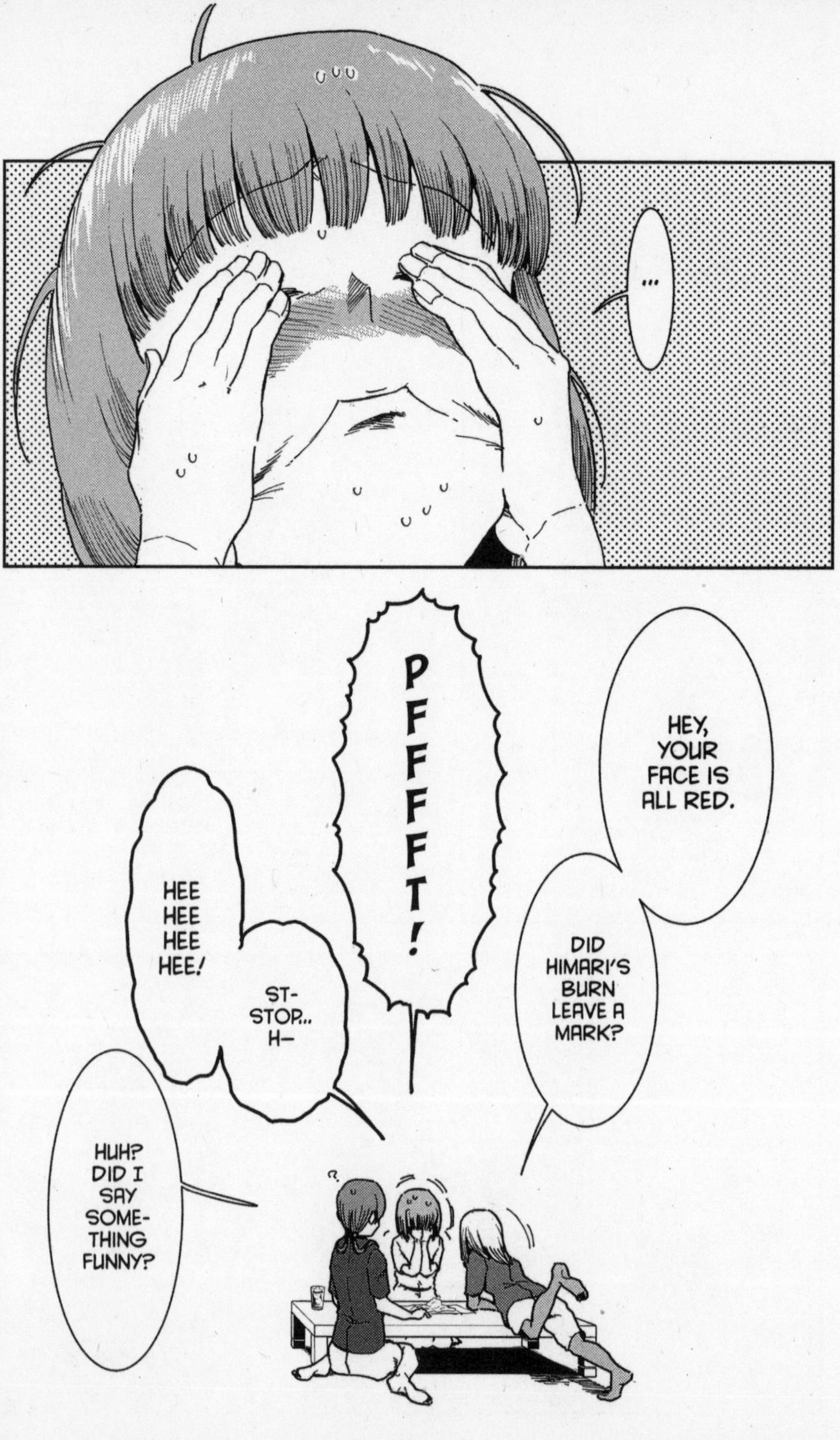
...
HEY, YOUR FACE IS ALL RED.
DID HIMARI'S BURN LEAVE A MARK?
PFFFFT!
HEE HEE HEE HEE!
ST- STOP... H–
HUH? DID I SAY SOME-THING FUNNY?

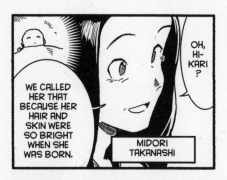

OH, HI-KARI?
MIDORI TAKANASHI
WE CALLED HER THAT BECAUSE HER HAIR AND SKIN WERE SO BRIGHT WHEN SHE WAS BORN.
AND HIMARI-CHAN?
OH!
THEY WERE TWINS, SO WE WANTED SIMILAR NAMES. AND "HIMARI" SOUNDS SO WARM, SOMEHOW.
KOJI AND I HAVE TRIED HARD TO RAISE THEM RIGHT...
...BUT I THINK WE'VE LEARNED EVEN MORE THAN WE TAUGHT.
"GREEN" GROWS IN THE WARM LIGHT...
LIGHT (HIKARI)
WARMTH
GREEN (MIDORI)
AND WHERE DO I COME IN...?
HA HA HA...

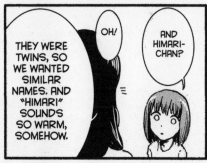

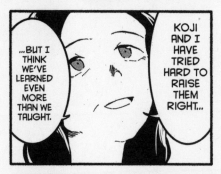

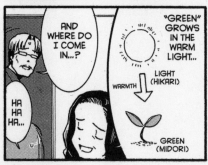

INTERVIEWS WITH
MONSTER GIRLS

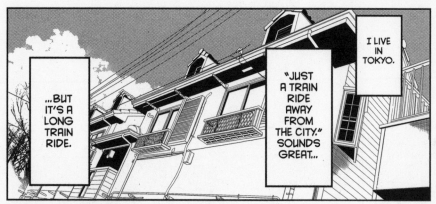

I LIVE IN TOKYO.
"JUST A TRAIN RIDE AWAY FROM THE CITY." SOUNDS GREAT...
...BUT IT'S A LONG TRAIN RIDE.
OUT HERE, THOUGH, YOU CAN GET PRETTY GOOD DIGS.
I PAY 32,000 YEN A MONTH.
I'VE GOT A BATH, OF COURSE, AN ELECTRIC STOVETOP, AND A NICE, BIG LOFT.
AND...
BOING
バイーン
GAH!
THUMP
どた
THUMP
どた
YIKES!

32,000 YEN IS APPROXIMATELY 320 USD.

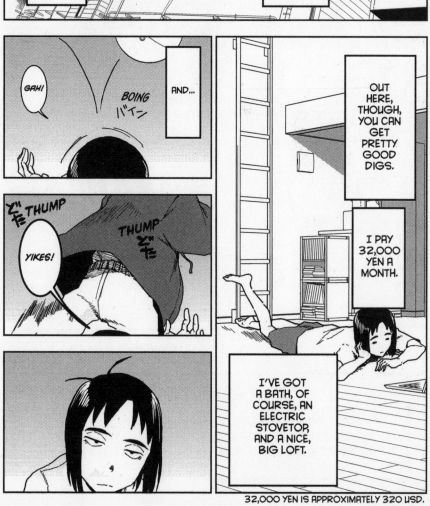

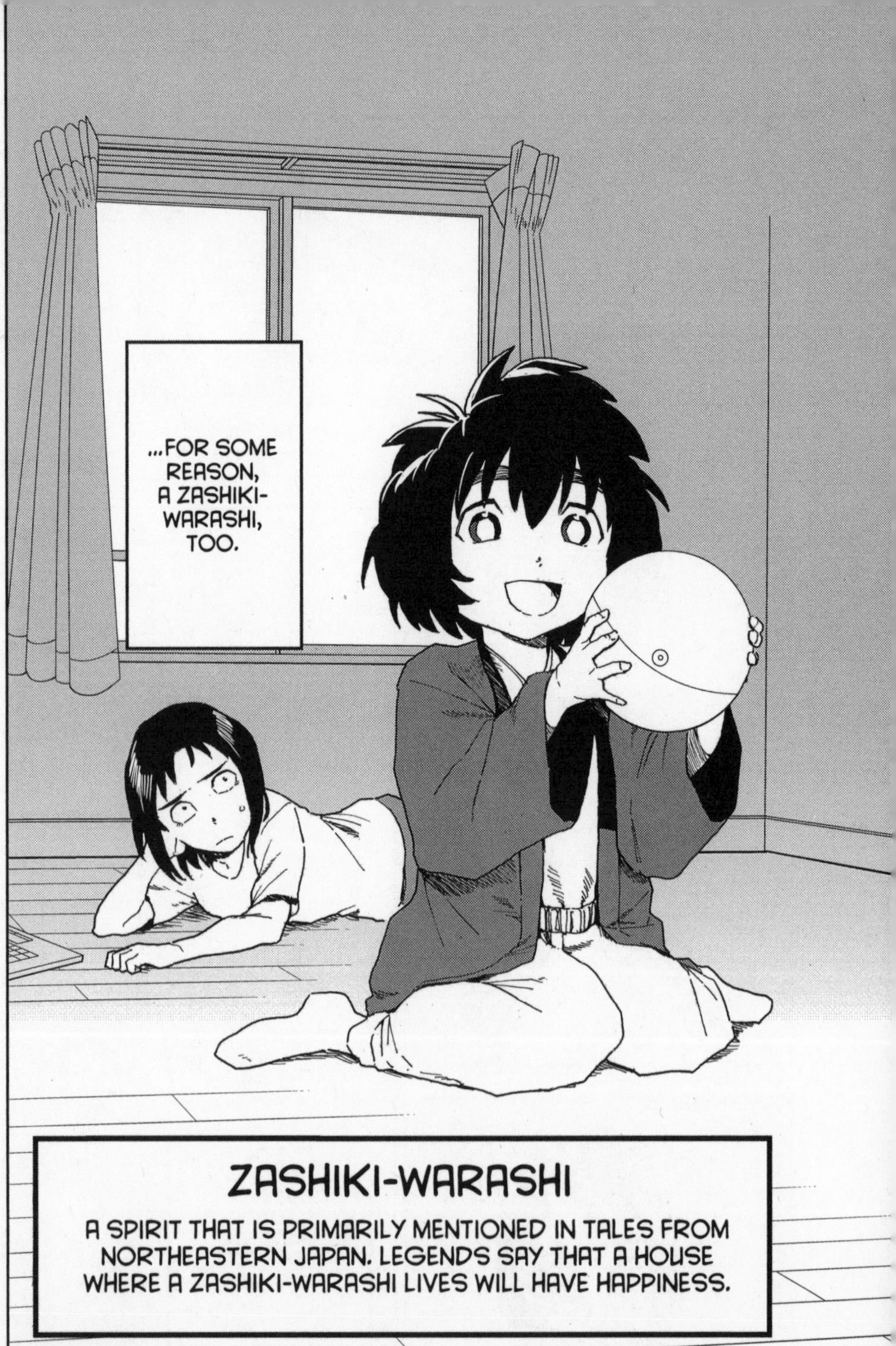
...FOR SOME REASON, A ZASHIKI-WARASHI, TOO.
ZASHIKI-WARASHI
A SPIRIT THAT IS PRIMARILY MENTIONED IN TALES FROM NORTHEASTERN JAPAN. LEGENDS SAY THAT A HOUSE WHERE A ZASHIKI-WARASHI LIVES WILL HAVE HAPPINESS.

CHAPTER 36: A ZASHIKI-WARASHI'S HAPPINESS (PART 1)

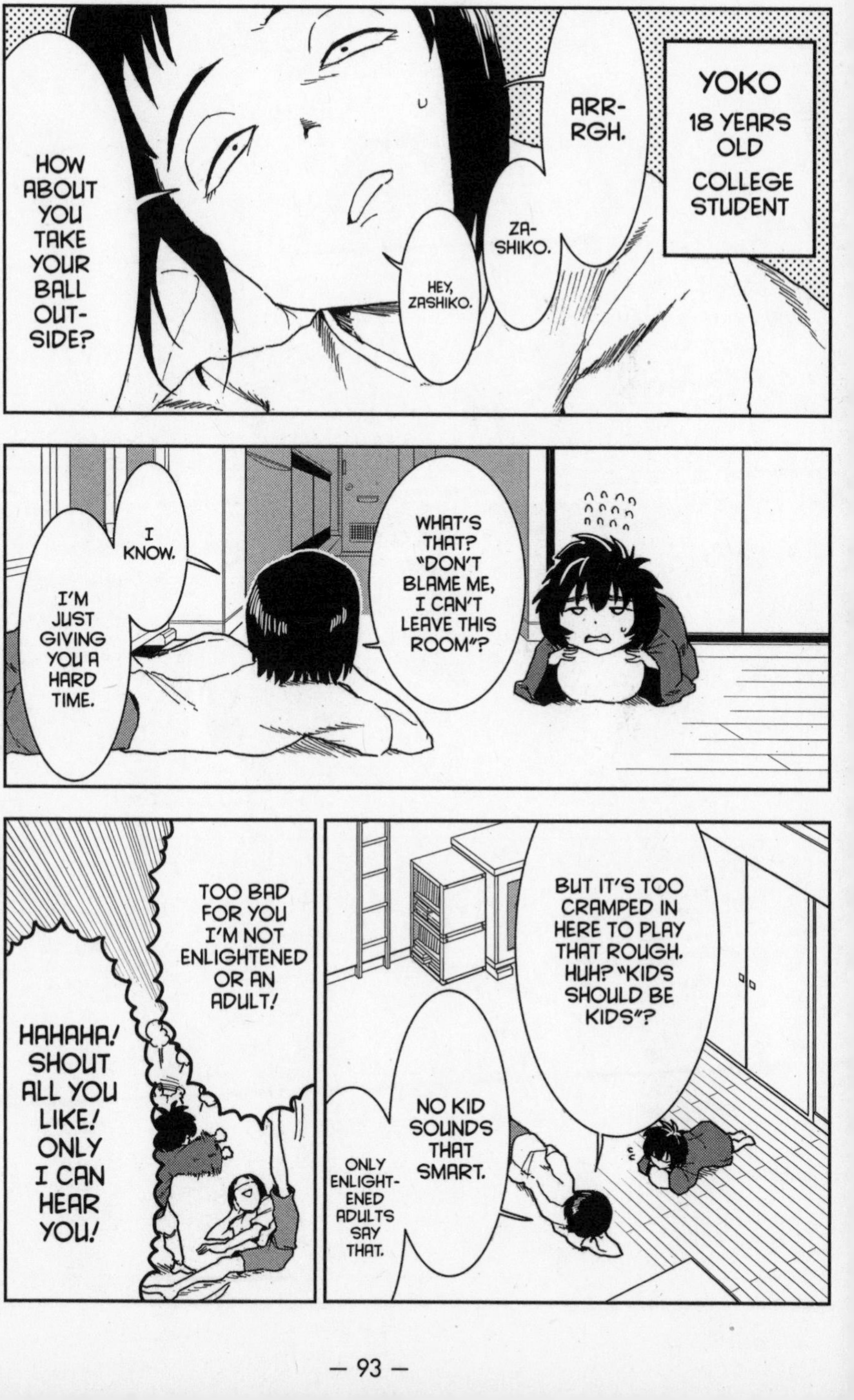
YOKO 18 YEARS OLD COLLEGE STUDENT
ARR-RGH.
ZA-SHIKO.
HEY, ZASHIKO.
HOW ABOUT YOU TAKE YOUR BALL OUT-SIDE?
WHAT'S THAT? "DON'T BLAME ME, I CAN'T LEAVE THIS ROOM"?
I KNOW.
I'M JUST GIVING YOU A HARD TIME.
BUT IT'S TOO CRAMPED IN HERE TO PLAY THAT ROUGH. HUH? "KIDS SHOULD BE KIDS"?
NO KID SOUNDS THAT SMART.
ONLY ENLIGHT-ENED ADULTS SAY THAT.
TOO BAD FOR YOU I'M NOT ENLIGHTENED OR AN ADULT!
HAHAHA! SHOUT ALL YOU LIKE! ONLY I CAN HEAR YOU!

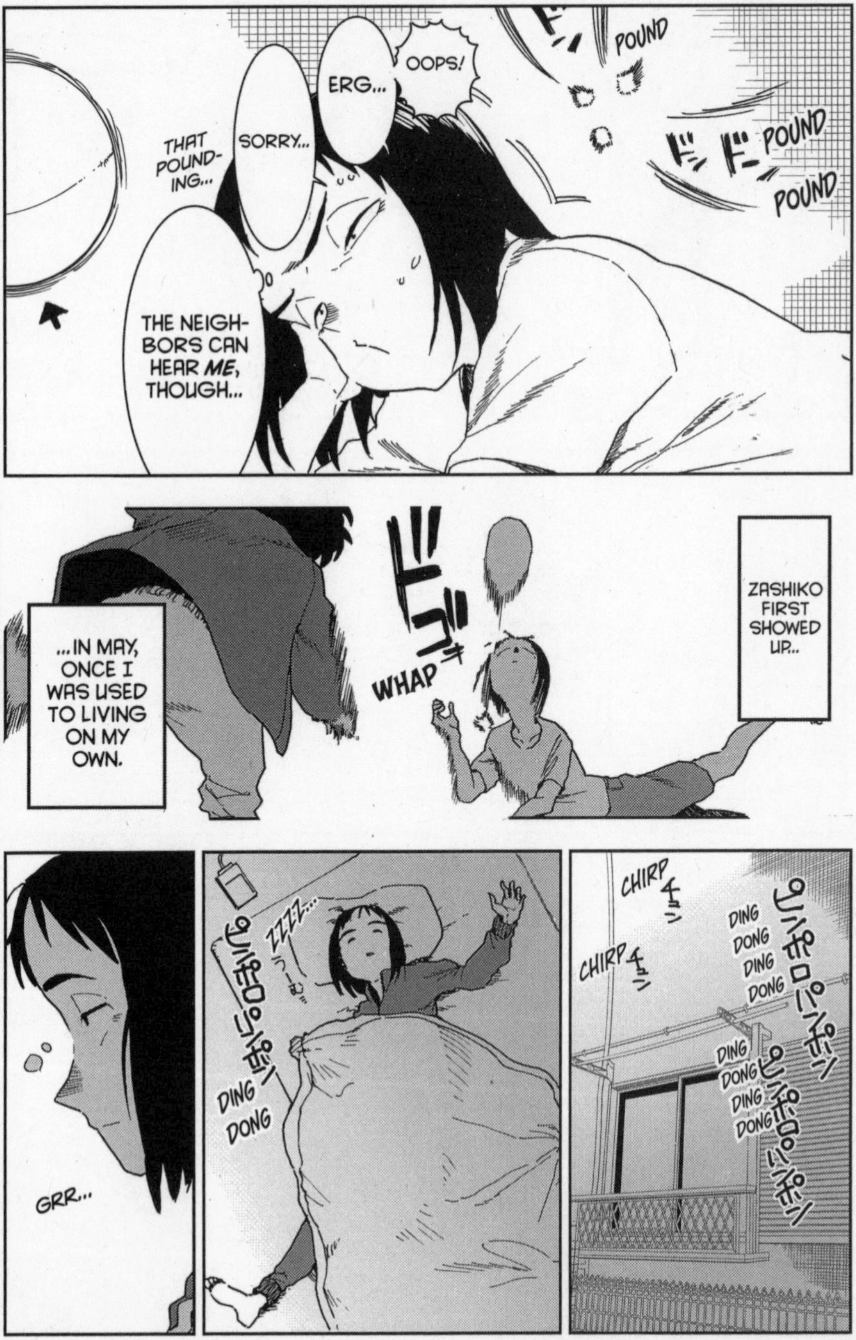
POUND
POUND
POUND
OOPS!
ERG...
SORRY...
THAT POUNDING...
THE NEIGHBORS CAN HEAR *ME*, THOUGH...
ZASHIKO FIRST SHOWED UP...
WHAP
...IN MAY, ONCE I WAS USED TO LIVING ON MY OWN.
CHIRP
CHIRP
DING DONG DING DONG
DING DONG DING DONG
ZZZZ...
DING DONG
GRR...

I WOKE UP, AND THERE SHE WAS.

...BUT SHE FOUGHT HARD AT THE FRONT DOOR.

I TRIED TO TAKE HER TO THE POLICE BOX....

HER CLOTHES MADE ME THINK "ZASHIKI-WARASHI."

THE SHORT COAT AND ALL.

I'M SORRY!

BUT I AM THROWING YOU—

BUT I WASN'T SURE.

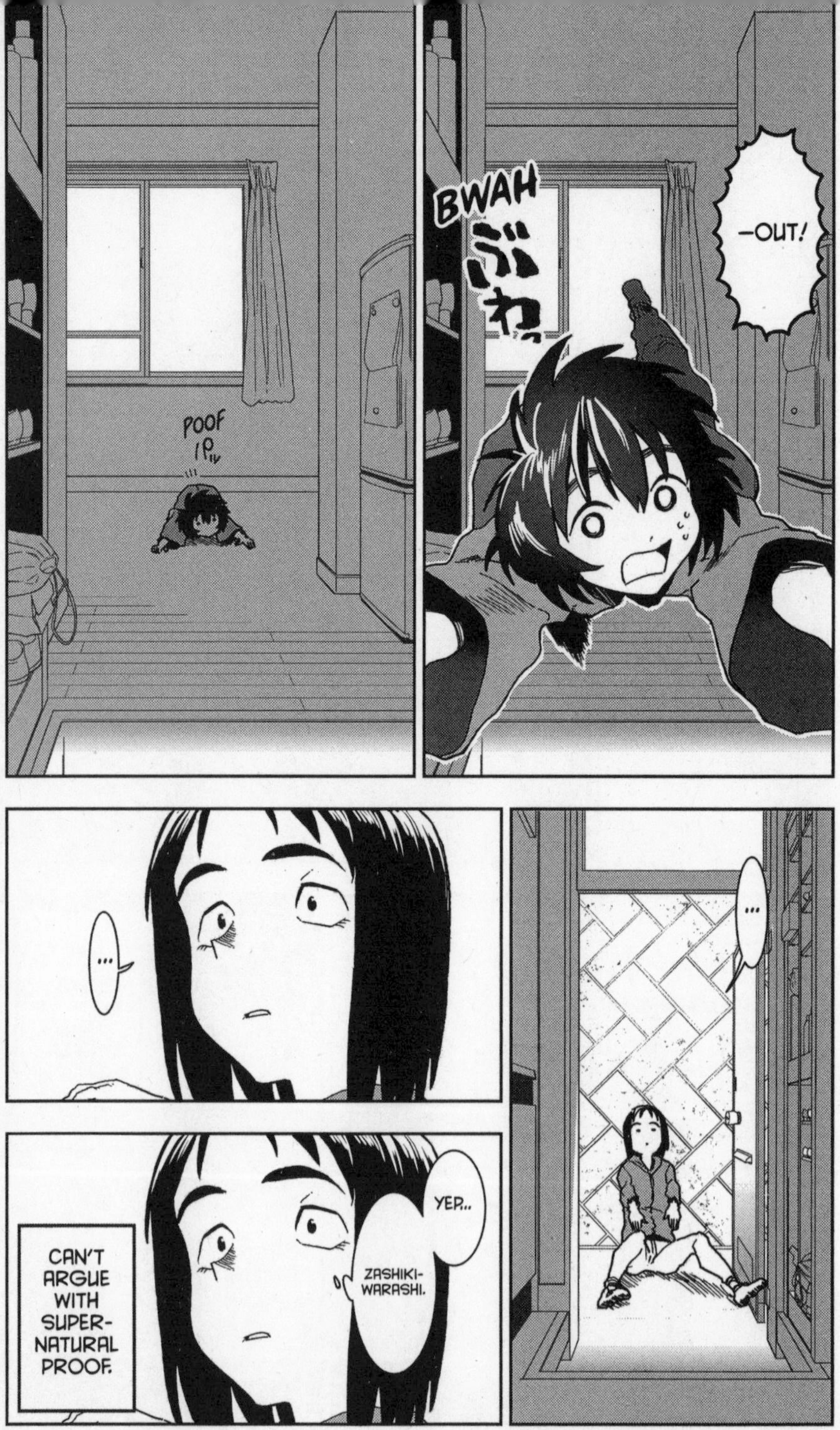
—OUT!
BWAH
ぶわっ
POOF
...
...
YEP...
ZASHIKI-WARASHI.
CAN'T ARGUE WITH SUPER-NATURAL PROOF.

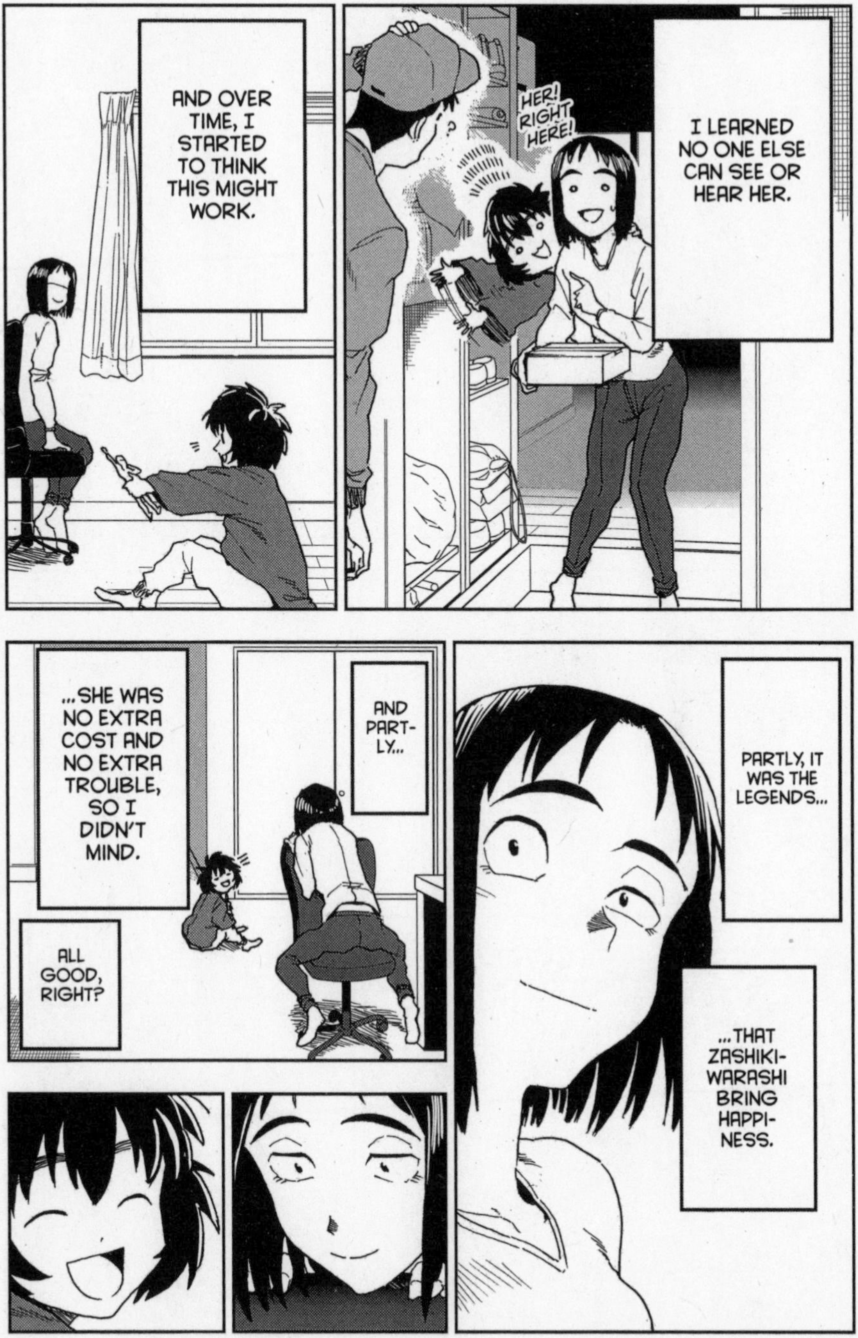
HER! RIGHT HERE!
I LEARNED NO ONE ELSE CAN SEE OR HEAR HER.
AND OVER TIME, I STARTED TO THINK THIS MIGHT WORK.
PARTLY, IT WAS THE LEGENDS...
...THAT ZASHIKI-WARASHI BRING HAPPINESS.
AND PART-LY...
...SHE WAS NO EXTRA COST AND NO EXTRA TROUBLE, SO I DIDN'T MIND.
ALL GOOD, RIGHT?

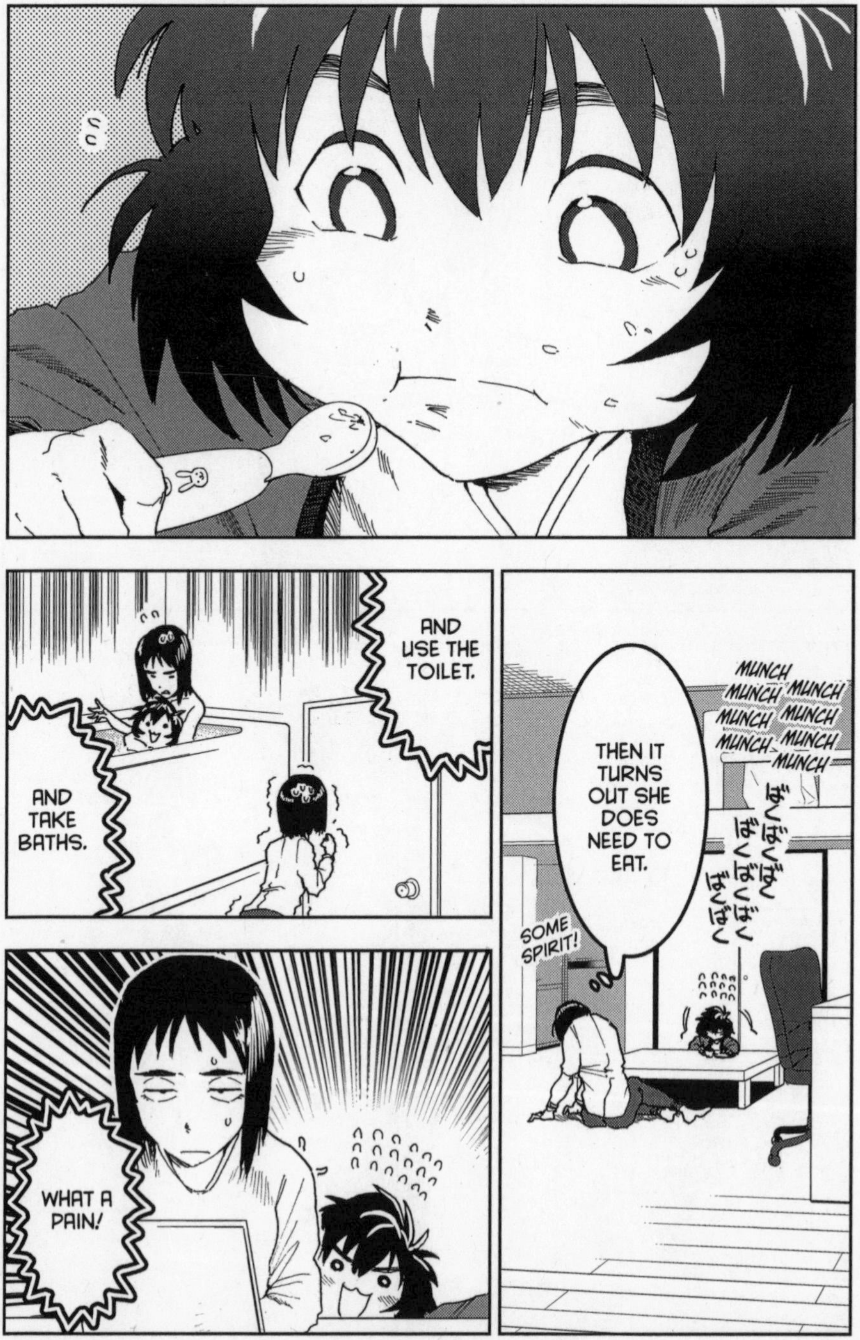
MUNCH MUNCH MUNCH MUNCH MUNCH MUNCH MUNCH MUNCH
ばくばくばく ばくばくばく ばくばく
THEN IT TURNS OUT SHE DOES NEED TO EAT.
SOME SPIRIT!
AND USE THE TOILET.
AND TAKE BATHS.
WHAT A PAIN!

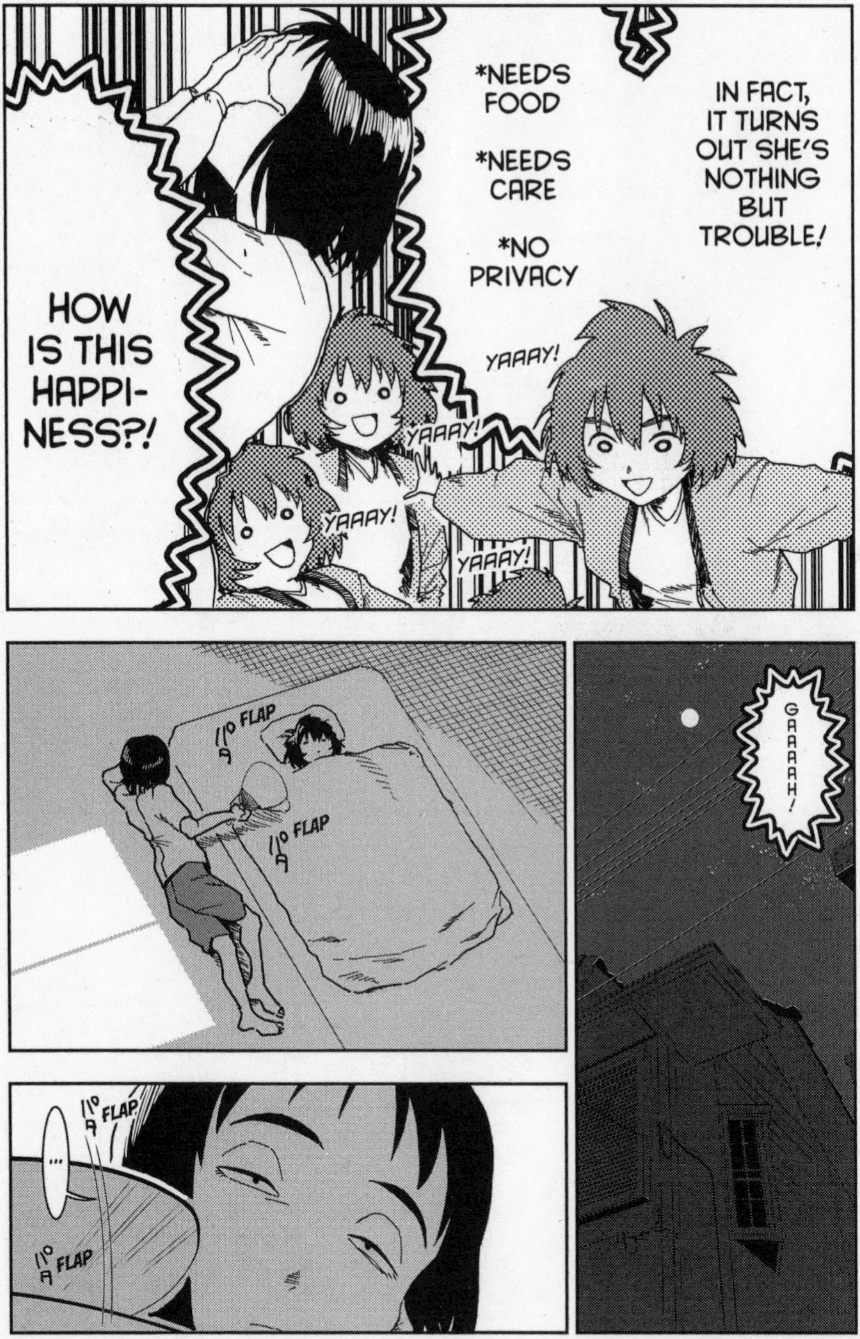
IN FACT, IT TURNS OUT SHE'S NOTHING BUT TROUBLE!
*NEEDS FOOD
*NEEDS CARE
*NO PRIVACY
YAAAY!
YAAAY!
YAAAY!
YAAAY!
HOW IS THIS HAPPI-NESS?!
GAAAAH!
FLAP
FLAP
FLAP
...
FLAP

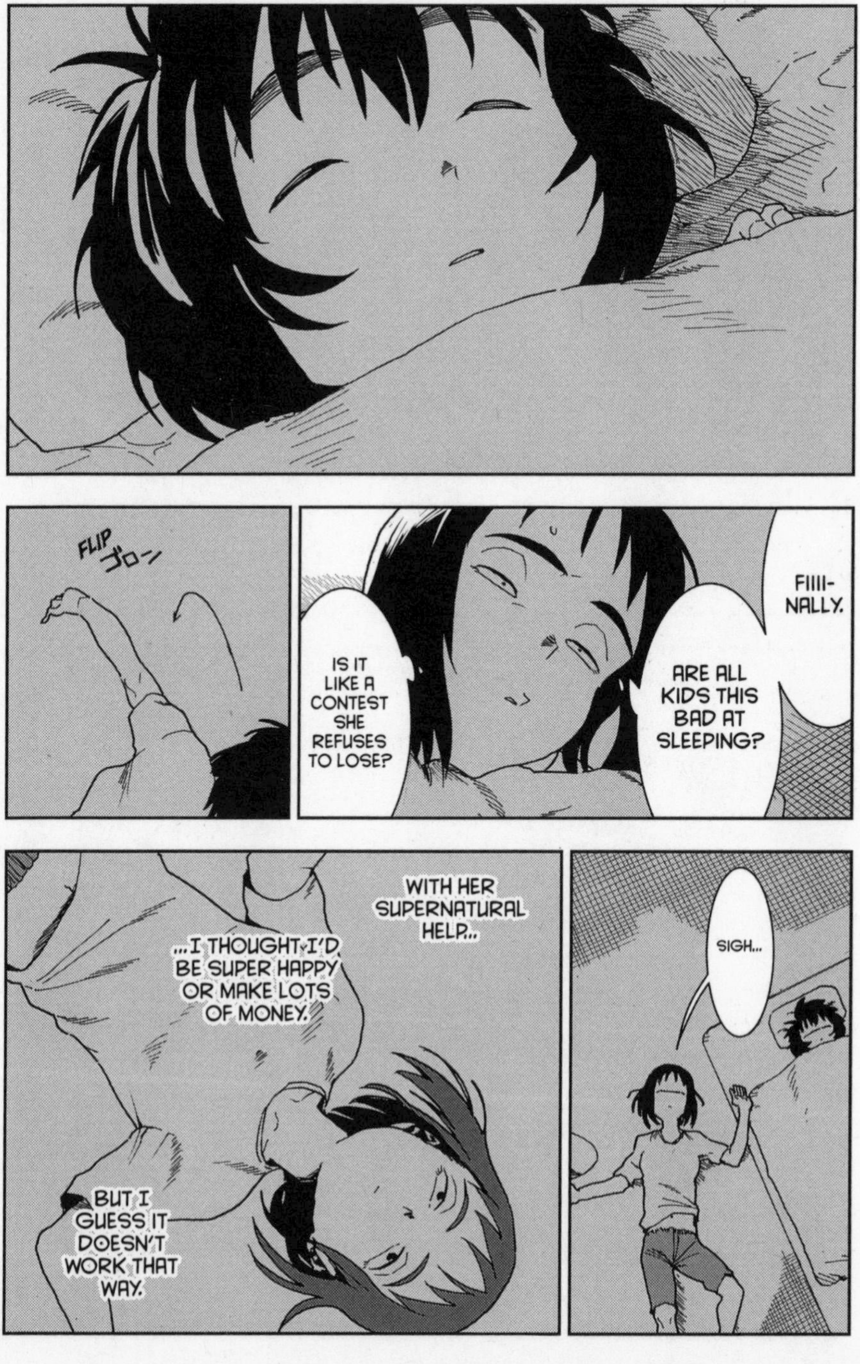
FIIII-NALLY.
ARE ALL KIDS THIS BAD AT SLEEPING?
IS IT LIKE A CONTEST SHE REFUSES TO LOSE?
FLIP
SIGH...
WITH HER SUPERNATURAL HELP...
...I THOUGHT I'D BE SUPER HAPPY OR MAKE LOTS OF MONEY.
BUT I GUESS IT DOESN'T WORK THAT WAY.

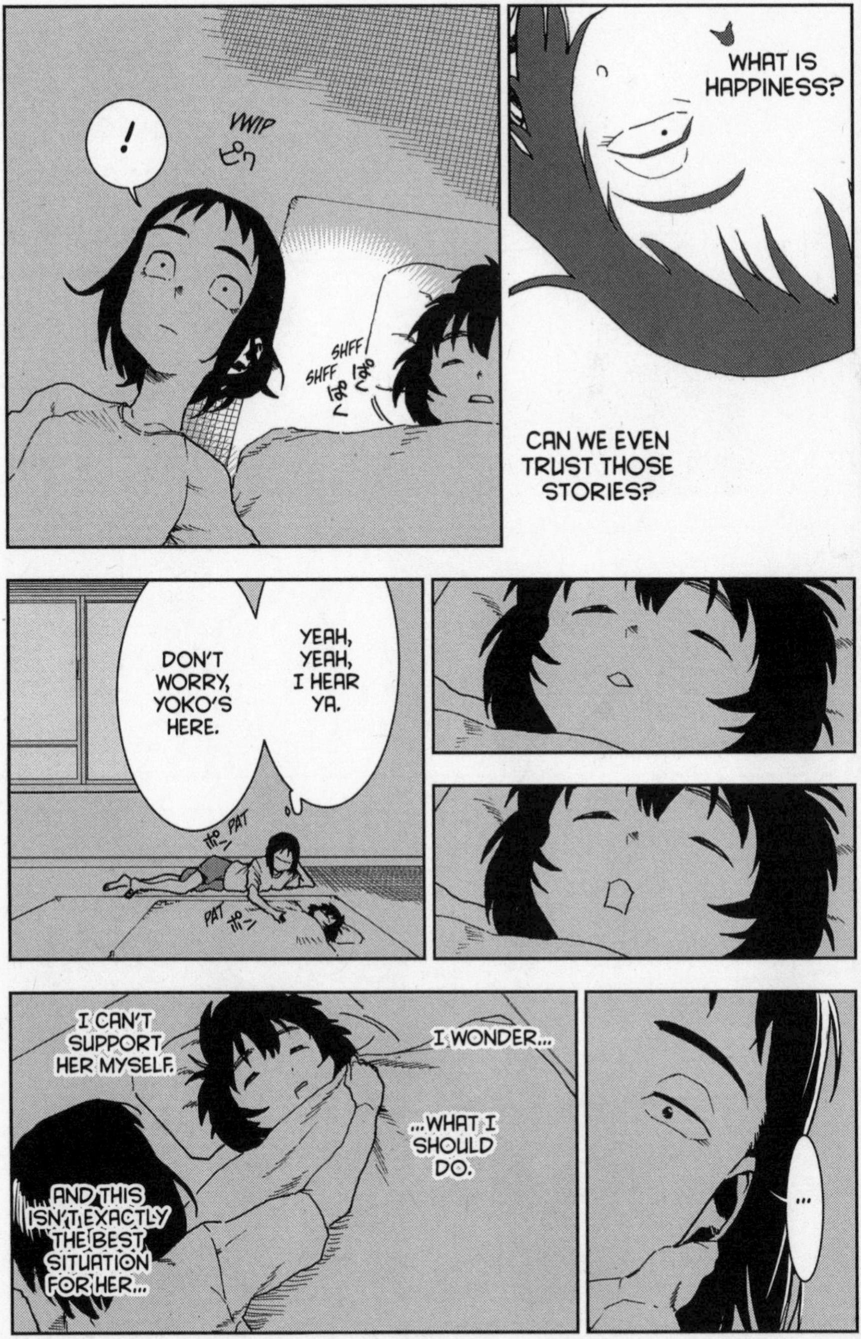
WHAT IS HAPPINESS?
CAN WE EVEN TRUST THOSE STORIES?
!
VWIP
ピク
SHFF SHFF
ぱくぱく
YEAH, YEAH, I HEAR YA.
DON'T WORRY, YOKO'S HERE.
PAT
ポン
PAT
ポン
...
I WONDER...
I CAN'T SUPPORT HER MYSELF.
...WHAT I SHOULD DO.
AND THIS ISN'T EXACTLY THE BEST SITUATION FOR HER...

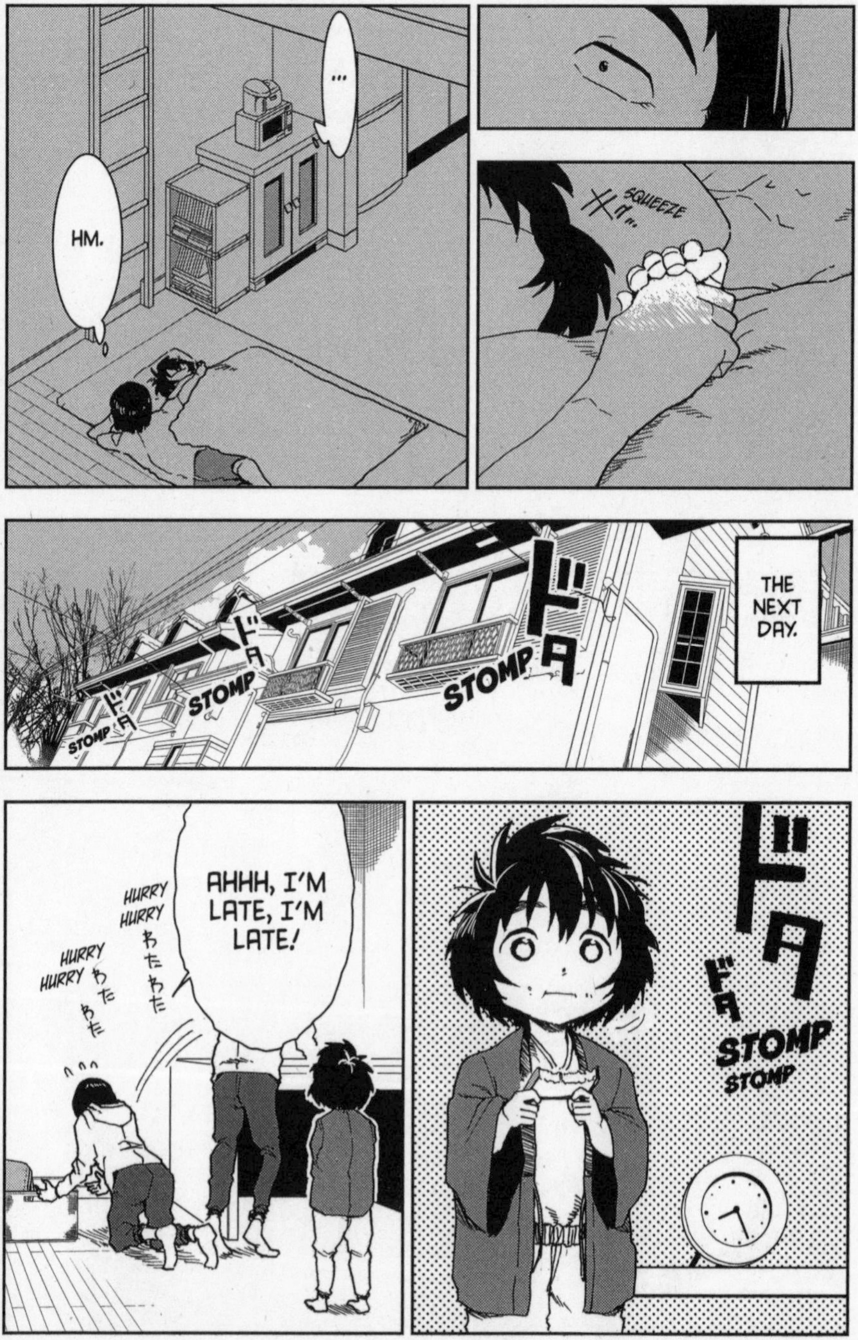
SQUEEZE
...
HM.
THE NEXT DAY.
ドタ
STOMP
ドタ
STOMP
ドタ
STOMP
ドタ
STOMP
ドタ
ドタ
STOMP
STOMP
AHHH, I'M LATE, I'M LATE!
HURRY HURRY わたわた
HURRY HURRY わたわた

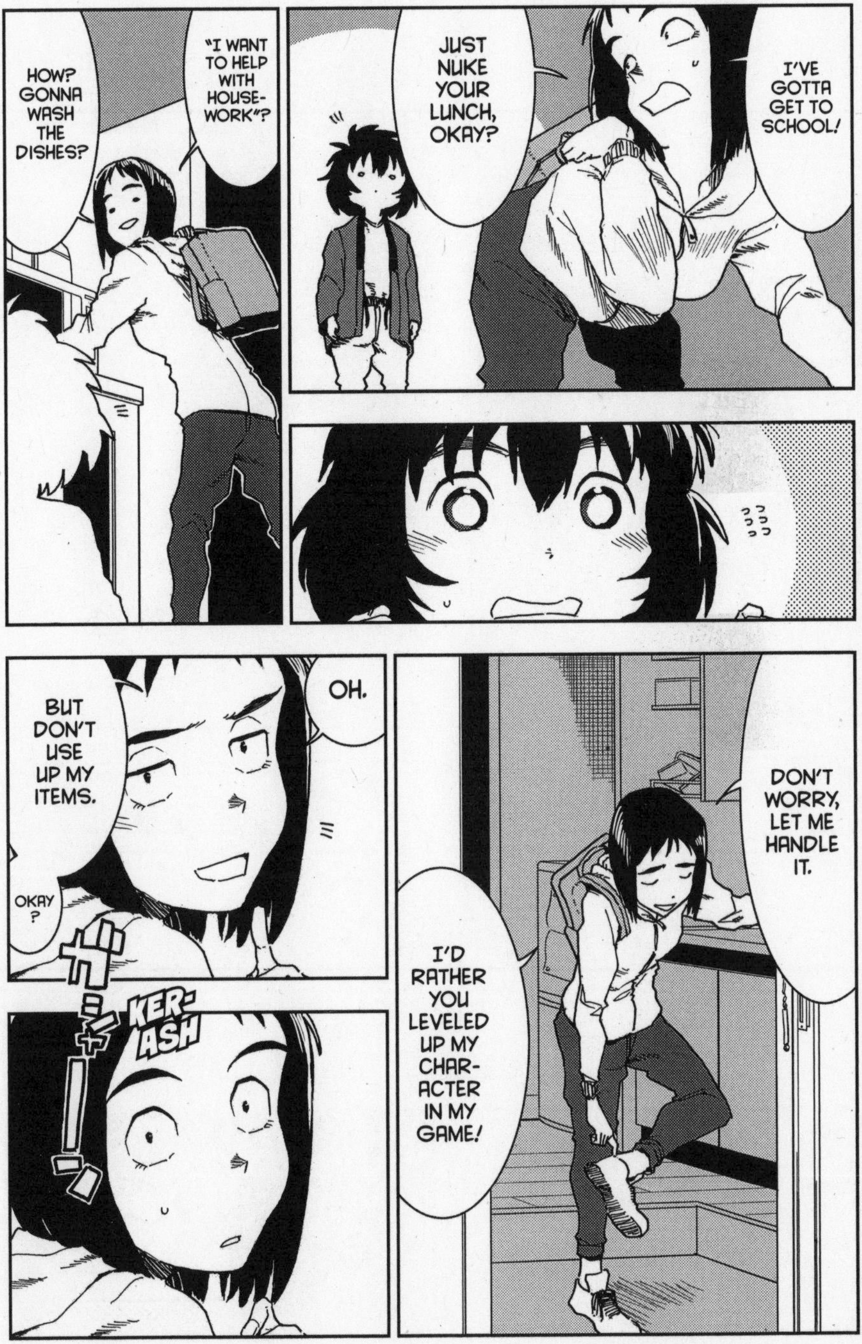
I'VE GOTTA GET TO SCHOOL!
JUST NUKE YOUR LUNCH, OKAY?
"I WANT TO HELP WITH HOUSE-WORK"?
HOW? GONNA WASH THE DISHES?
DON'T WORRY, LET ME HANDLE IT.
I'D RATHER YOU LEVELED UP MY CHAR-ACTER IN MY GAME!
OH.
BUT DON'T USE UP MY ITEMS.
OKAY?
KER-ASH

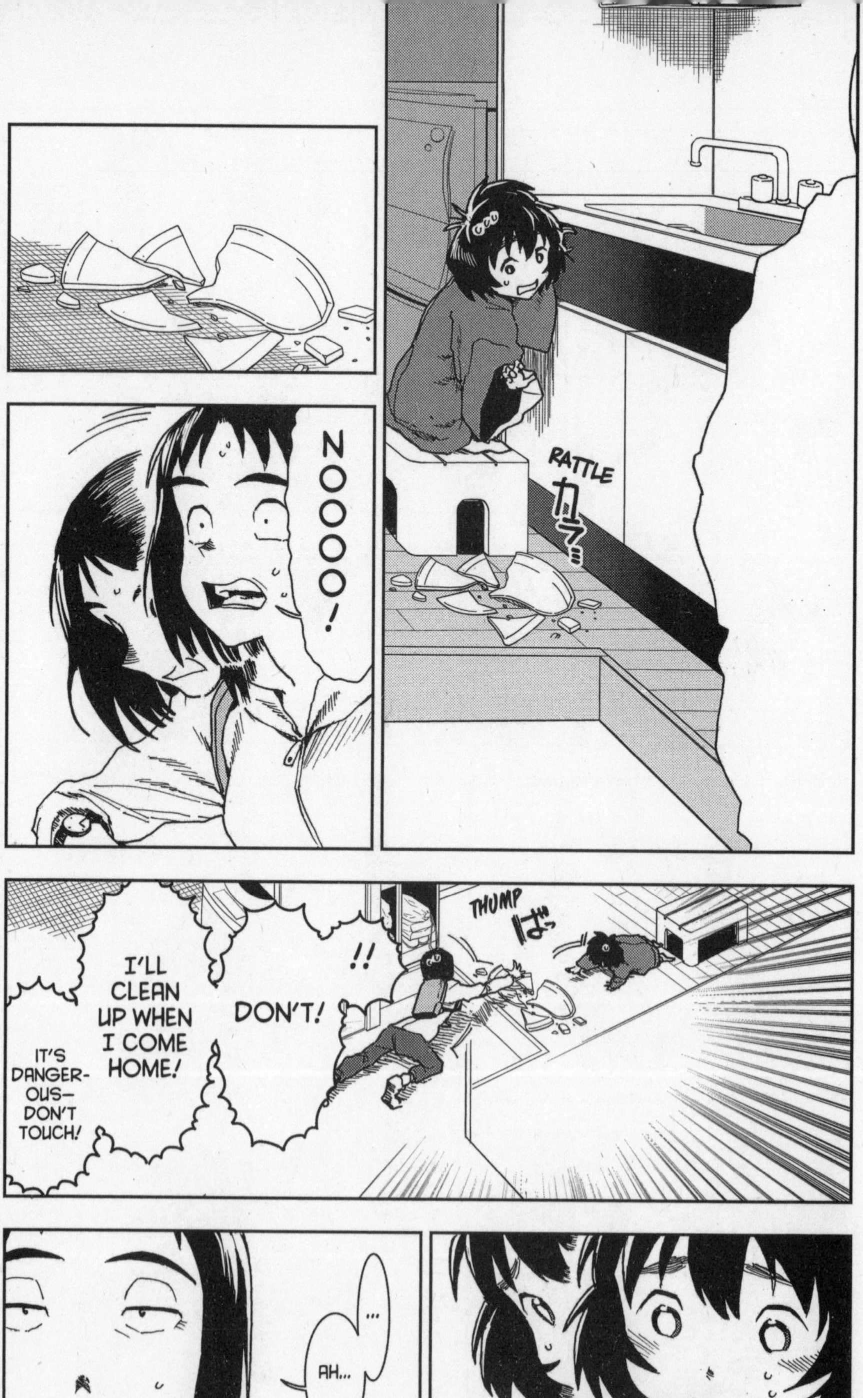
RATTLE
カラ…
NOOOO!
THUMP
ばっ
!!
DON'T!
I'LL CLEAN UP WHEN I COME HOME!
IT'S DANGER-OUS—DON'T TOUCH!
??
...
AH...

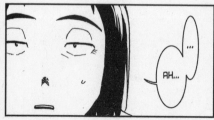

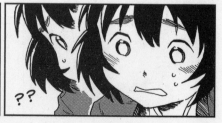

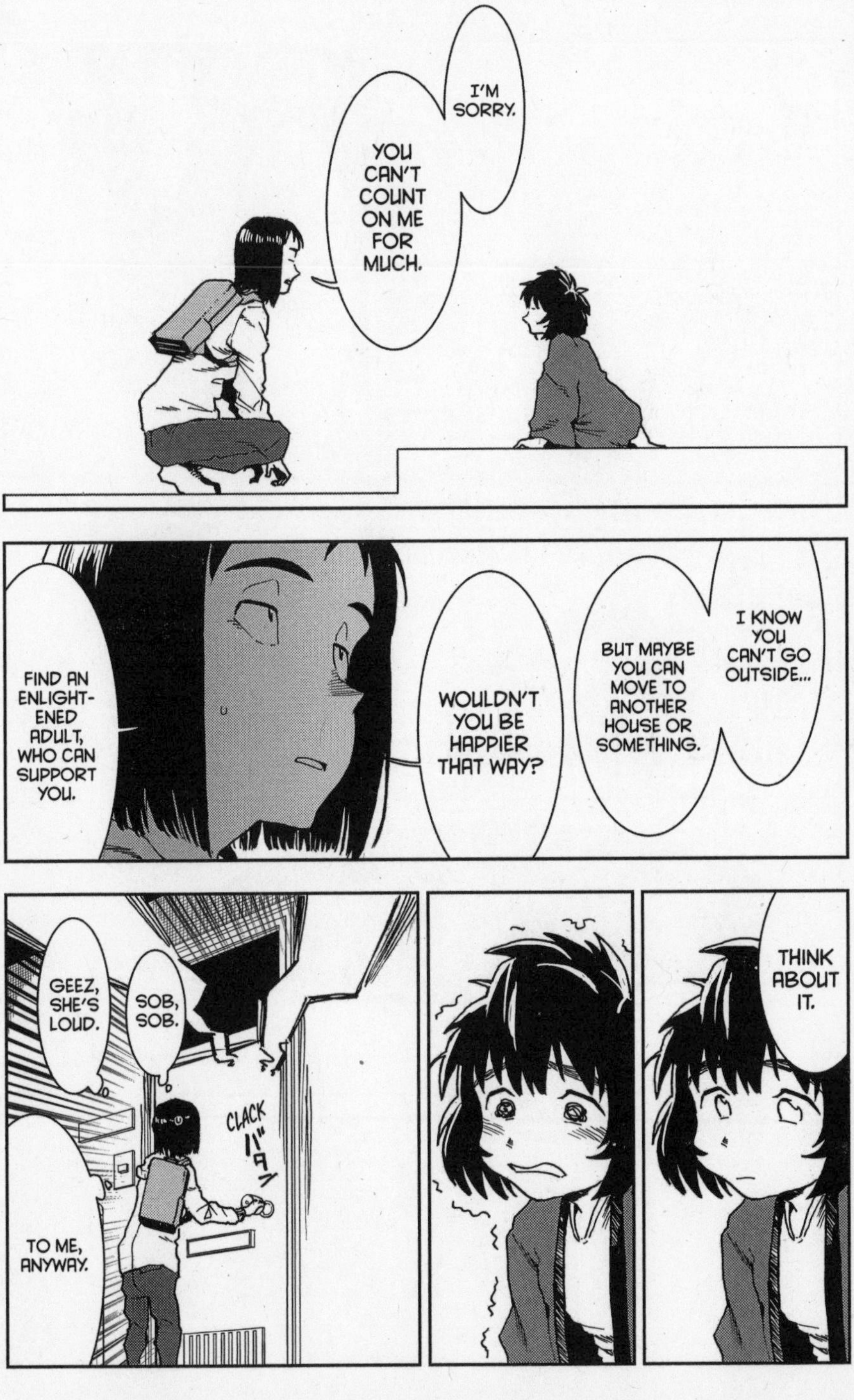
I'M SORRY.
YOU CAN'T COUNT ON ME FOR MUCH.
I KNOW YOU CAN'T GO OUTSIDE...
BUT MAYBE YOU CAN MOVE TO ANOTHER HOUSE OR SOMETHING.
WOULDN'T YOU BE HAPPIER THAT WAY?
FIND AN ENLIGHTENED ADULT, WHO CAN SUPPORT YOU.
THINK ABOUT IT.
SOB, SOB.
GEEZ, SHE'S LOUD.
CLACK
バタン
TO ME, ANYWAY.

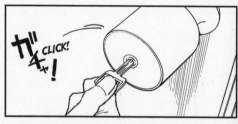

GAB GAB

...

NO ONE ELSE CAN HEAR HER...

GAB GAB

MUSASHINO UNIVERSITY OF SCIENCE

PHY- SICS.

WITH SOMA.

WHAT'VE YOU GOT THIRD PERIOD?

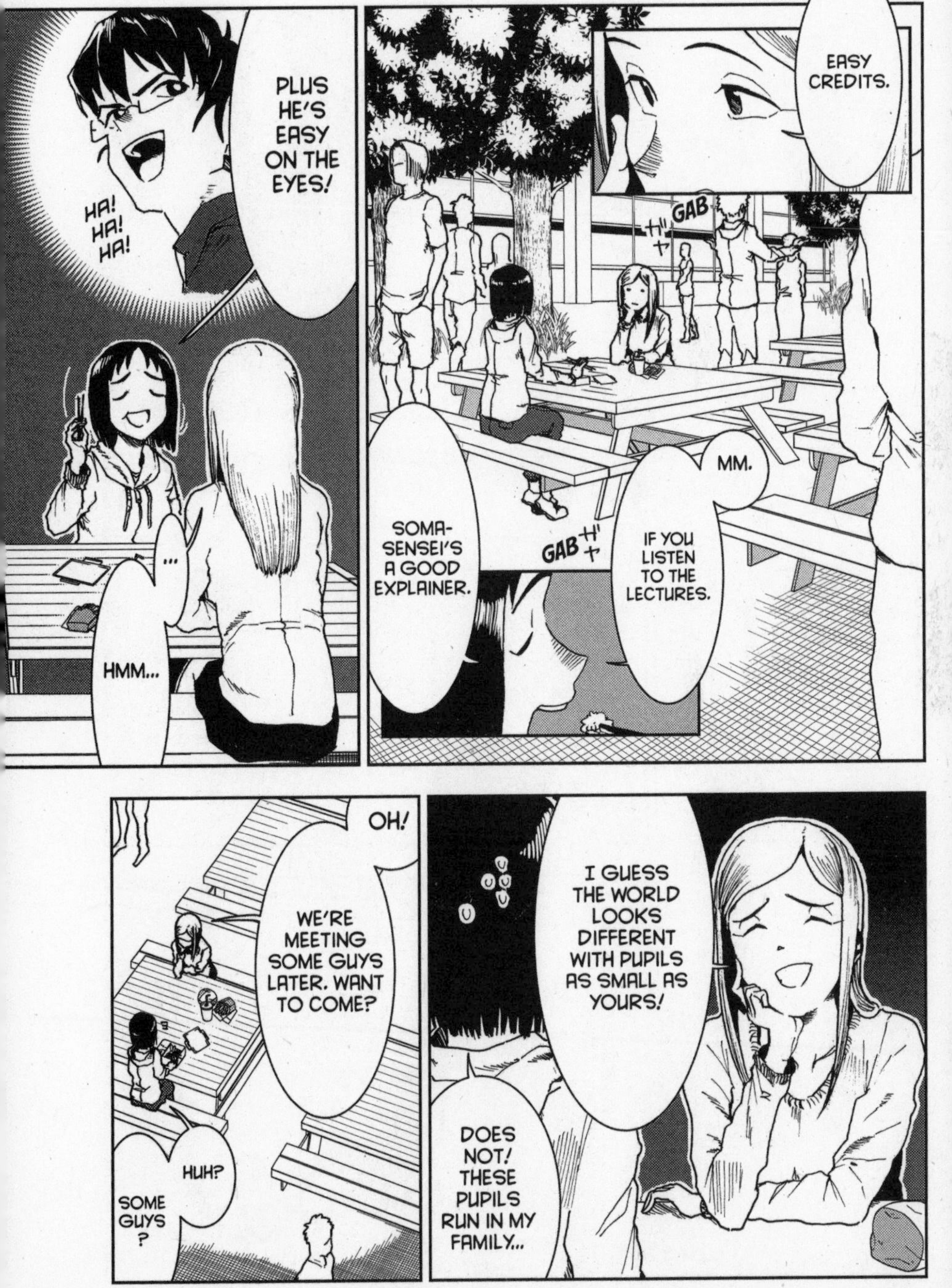
EASY CREDITS.
GAB ガヤ
MM.
IF YOU LISTEN TO THE LECTURES.
SOMA-SENSEI'S A GOOD EXPLAINER.
GAB ガヤ
PLUS HE'S EASY ON THE EYES!
HA! HA! HA!
...
HMM...
I GUESS THE WORLD LOOKS DIFFERENT WITH PUPILS AS SMALL AS YOURS!
DOES NOT! THESE PUPILS RUN IN MY FAMILY...
OH!
WE'RE MEETING SOME GUYS LATER. WANT TO COME?
HUH?
SOME GUYS?

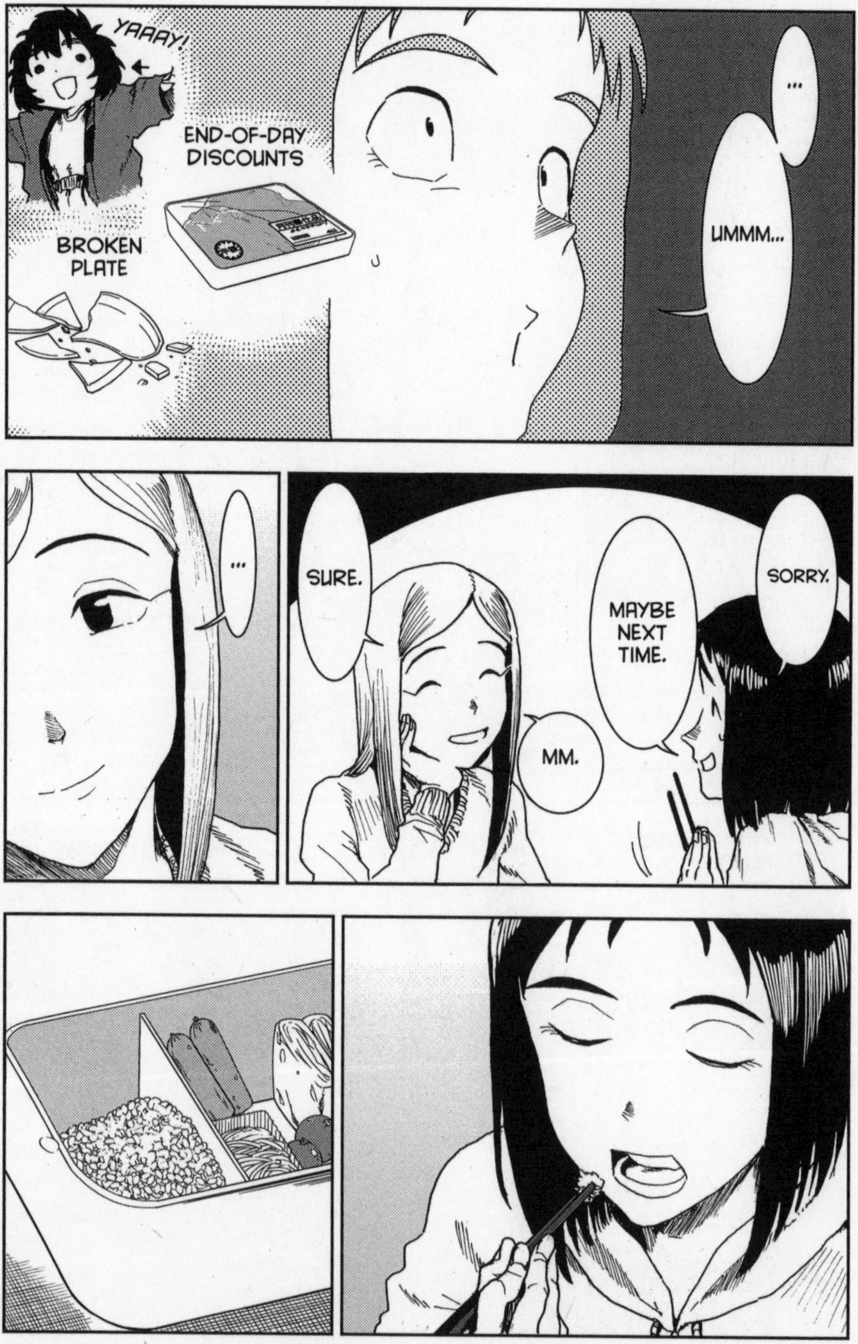
...
UMMM...
YAAAY!
END-OF-DAY DISCOUNTS
BROKEN PLATE
SORRY.
MAYBE NEXT TIME.
MM.
SURE.
...

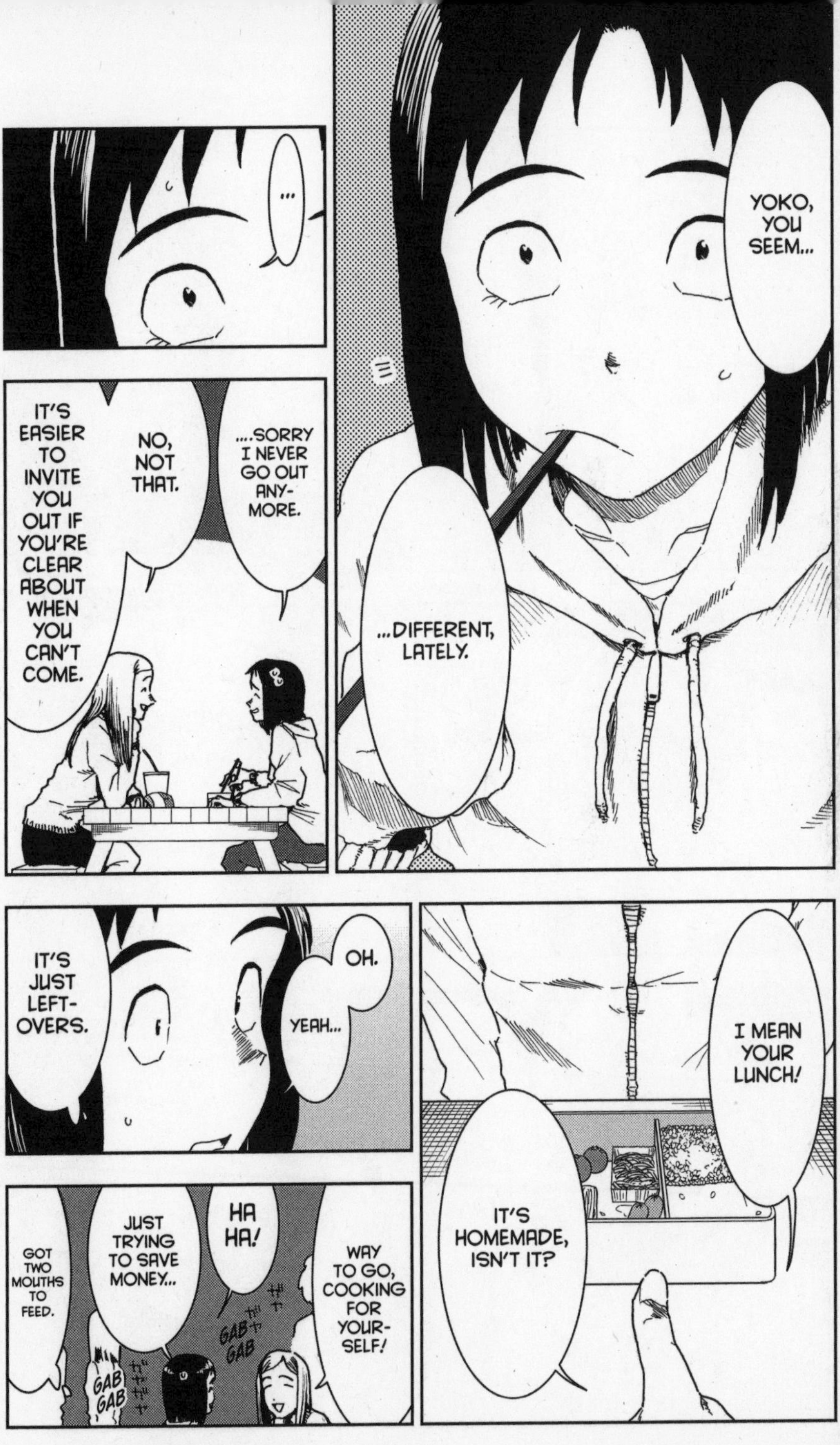
YOKO, YOU SEEM...
...DIFFERENT, LATELY.
...
....SORRY I NEVER GO OUT ANY-MORE.
NO, NOT THAT.
IT'S EASIER TO INVITE YOU OUT IF YOU'RE CLEAR ABOUT WHEN YOU CAN'T COME.
I MEAN YOUR LUNCH!
IT'S HOMEMADE, ISN'T IT?
OH.
YEAH...
IT'S JUST LEFT-OVERS.
WAY TO GO, COOKING FOR YOUR-SELF!
HA HA!
GAB GAB
JUST TRYING TO SAVE MONEY...
GAB GAB
GOT TWO MOUTHS TO FEED.

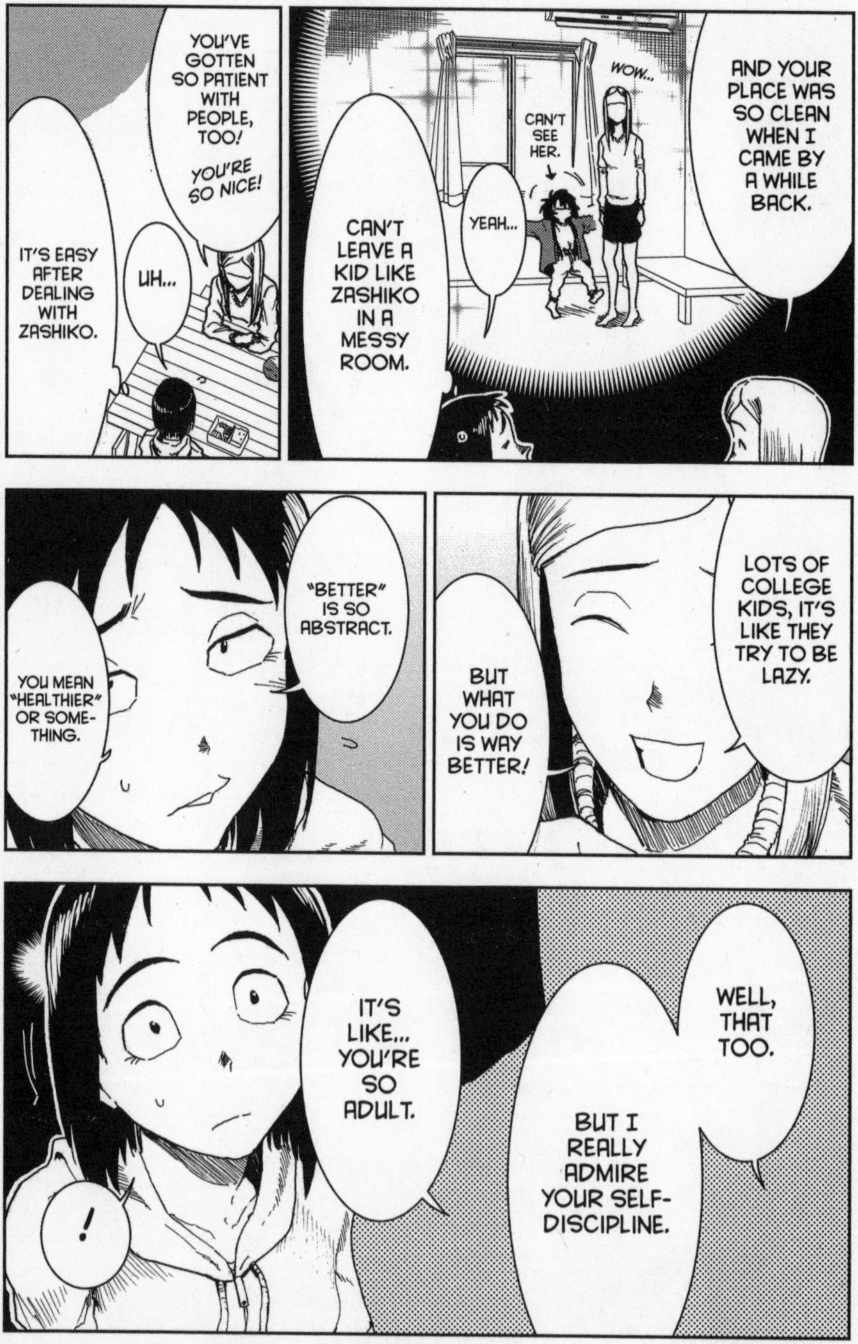
AND YOUR PLACE WAS SO CLEAN WHEN I CAME BY A WHILE BACK.
WOW...
CAN'T SEE HER.
YEAH...
CAN'T LEAVE A KID LIKE ZASHIKO IN A MESSY ROOM.
YOU'VE GOTTEN SO PATIENT WITH PEOPLE, TOO!
YOU'RE SO NICE!
UH...
IT'S EASY AFTER DEALING WITH ZASHIKO.
LOTS OF COLLEGE KIDS, IT'S LIKE THEY TRY TO BE LAZY.
BUT WHAT YOU DO IS WAY BETTER!
"BETTER" IS SO ABSTRACT.
YOU MEAN "HEALTHIER" OR SOME-THING.
WELL, THAT TOO.
BUT I REALLY ADMIRE YOUR SELF-DISCIPLINE.
IT'S LIKE... YOU'RE SO ADULT.
!

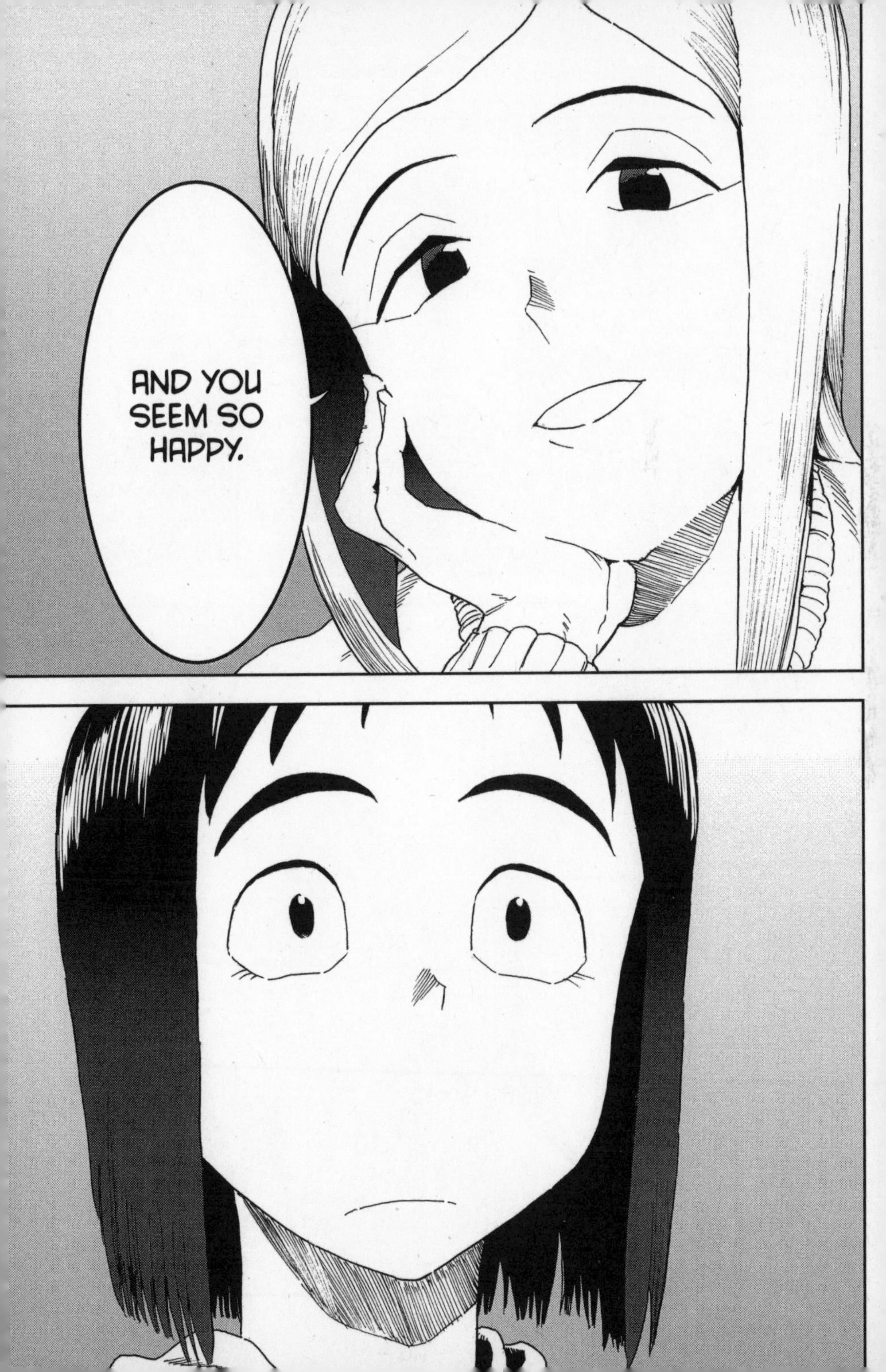
AND YOU SEEM SO HAPPY.

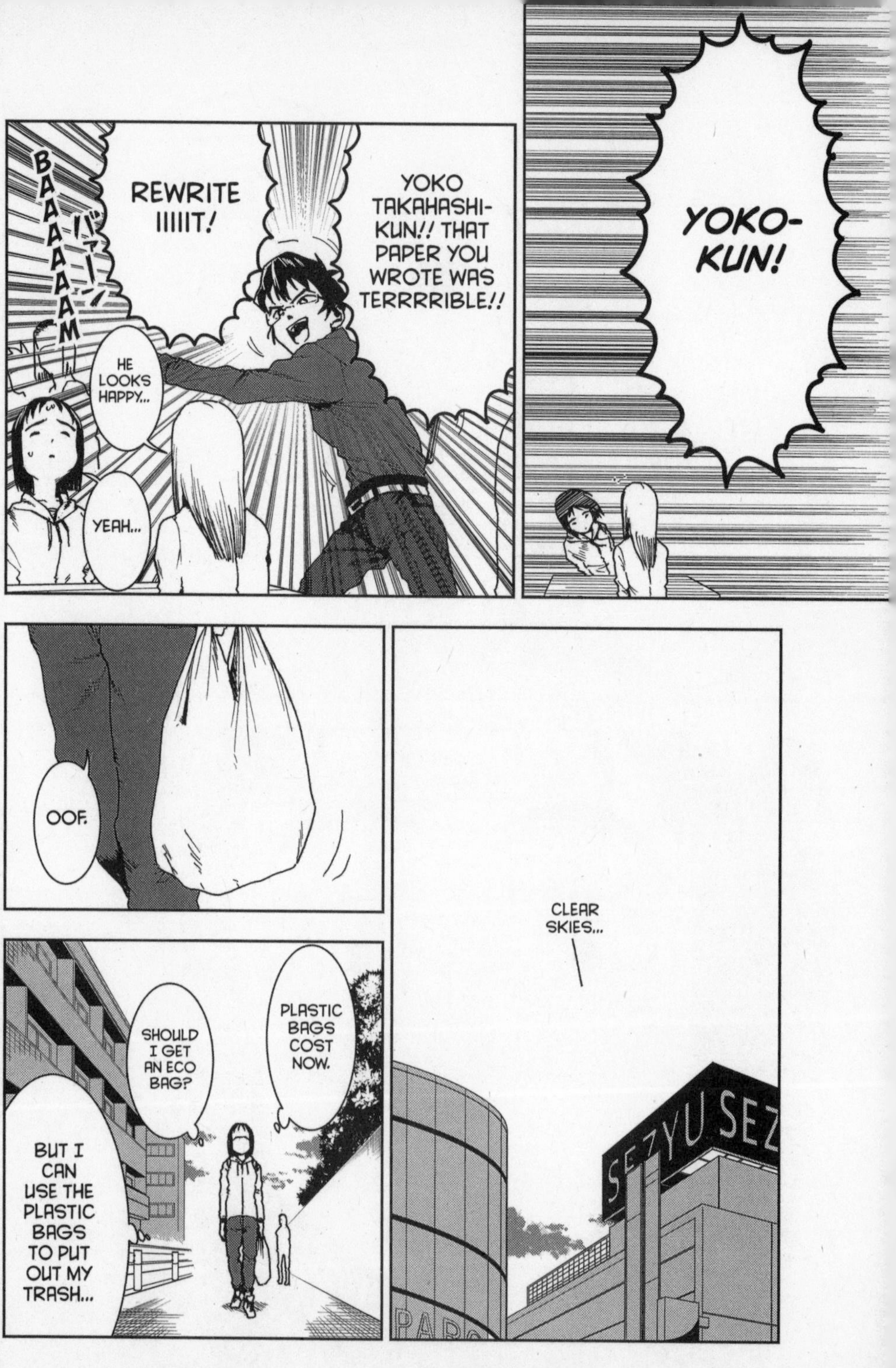
YOKO-KUN!
YOKO TAKAHASHI-KUN!! THAT PAPER YOU WROTE WAS TERRRRIBLE!!
REWRITE IIIIIT!
BAAAAAAAM
HE LOOKS HAPPY...
YEAH...
CLEAR SKIES...
OOF.
PLASTIC BAGS COST NOW.
SHOULD I GET AN ECO BAG?
BUT I CAN USE THE PLASTIC BAGS TO PUT OUT MY TRASH...

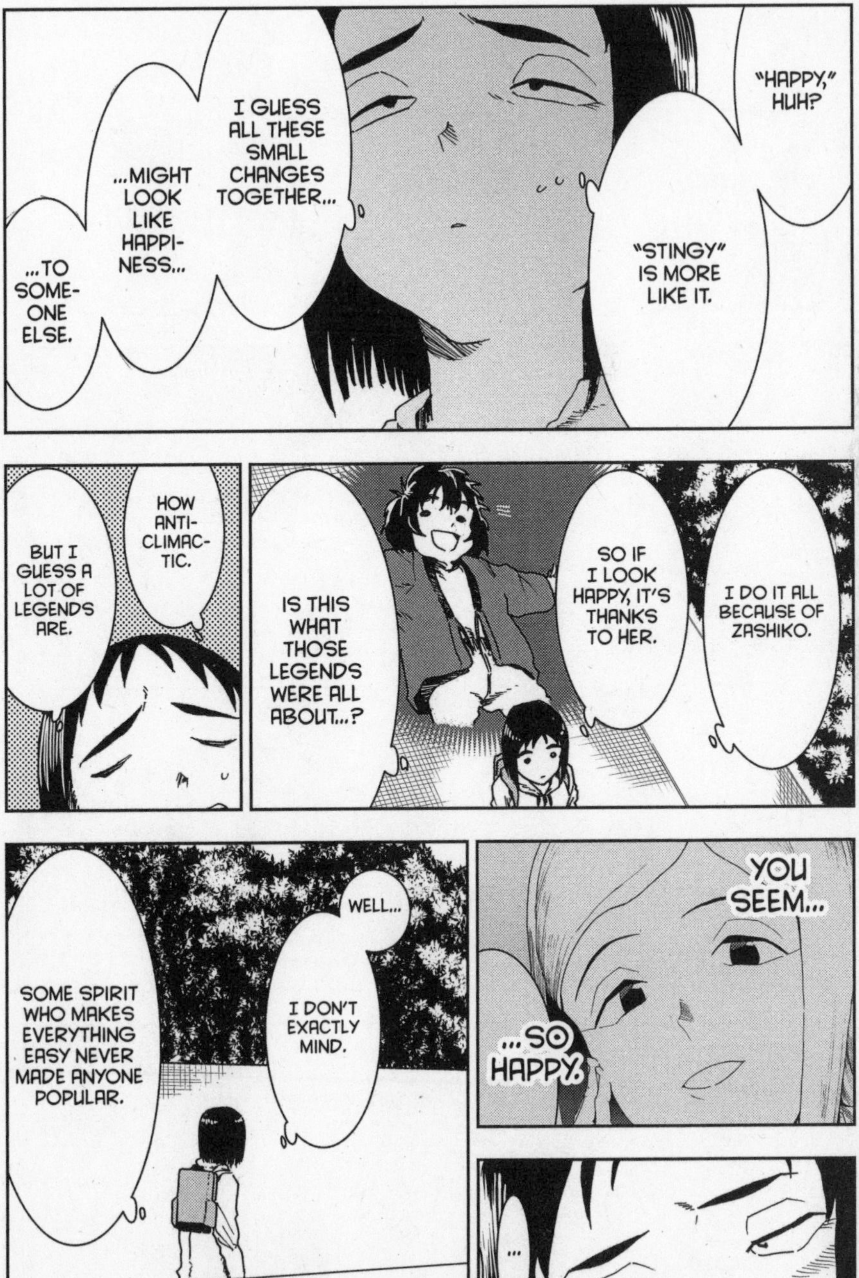
"HAPPY," HUH?
"STINGY" IS MORE LIKE IT.
I GUESS ALL THESE SMALL CHANGES TOGETHER...
...MIGHT LOOK LIKE HAPPINESS...
...TO SOMEONE ELSE.
I DO IT ALL BECAUSE OF ZASHIKO.
SO IF I LOOK HAPPY, IT'S THANKS TO HER.
IS THIS WHAT THOSE LEGENDS WERE ALL ABOUT...?
HOW ANTICLIMACTIC.
BUT I GUESS A LOT OF LEGENDS ARE.
YOU SEEM...
...SO HAPPY.
...
WELL...
I DON'T EXACTLY MIND.
SOME SPIRIT WHO MAKES EVERYTHING EASY NEVER MADE ANYONE POPULAR.

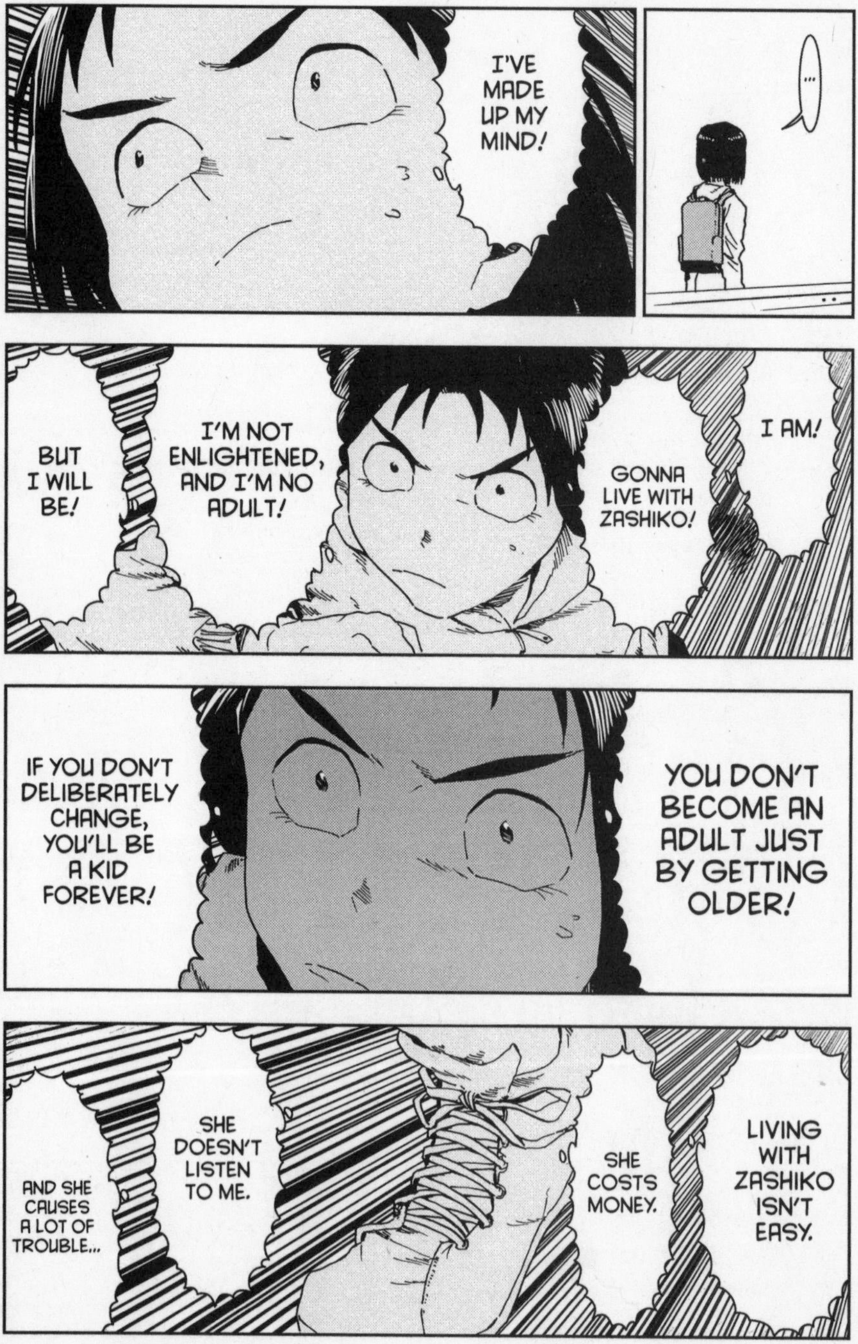
...
I'VE MADE UP MY MIND!
I AM!
GONNA LIVE WITH ZASHIKO!
I'M NOT ENLIGHTENED, AND I'M NO ADULT!
BUT I WILL BE!
YOU DON'T BECOME AN ADULT JUST BY GETTING OLDER!
IF YOU DON'T DELIBERATELY CHANGE, YOU'LL BE A KID FOREVER!
LIVING WITH ZASHIKO ISN'T EASY.
SHE COSTS MONEY.
SHE DOESN'T LISTEN TO ME.
AND SHE CAUSES A LOT OF TROUBLE...

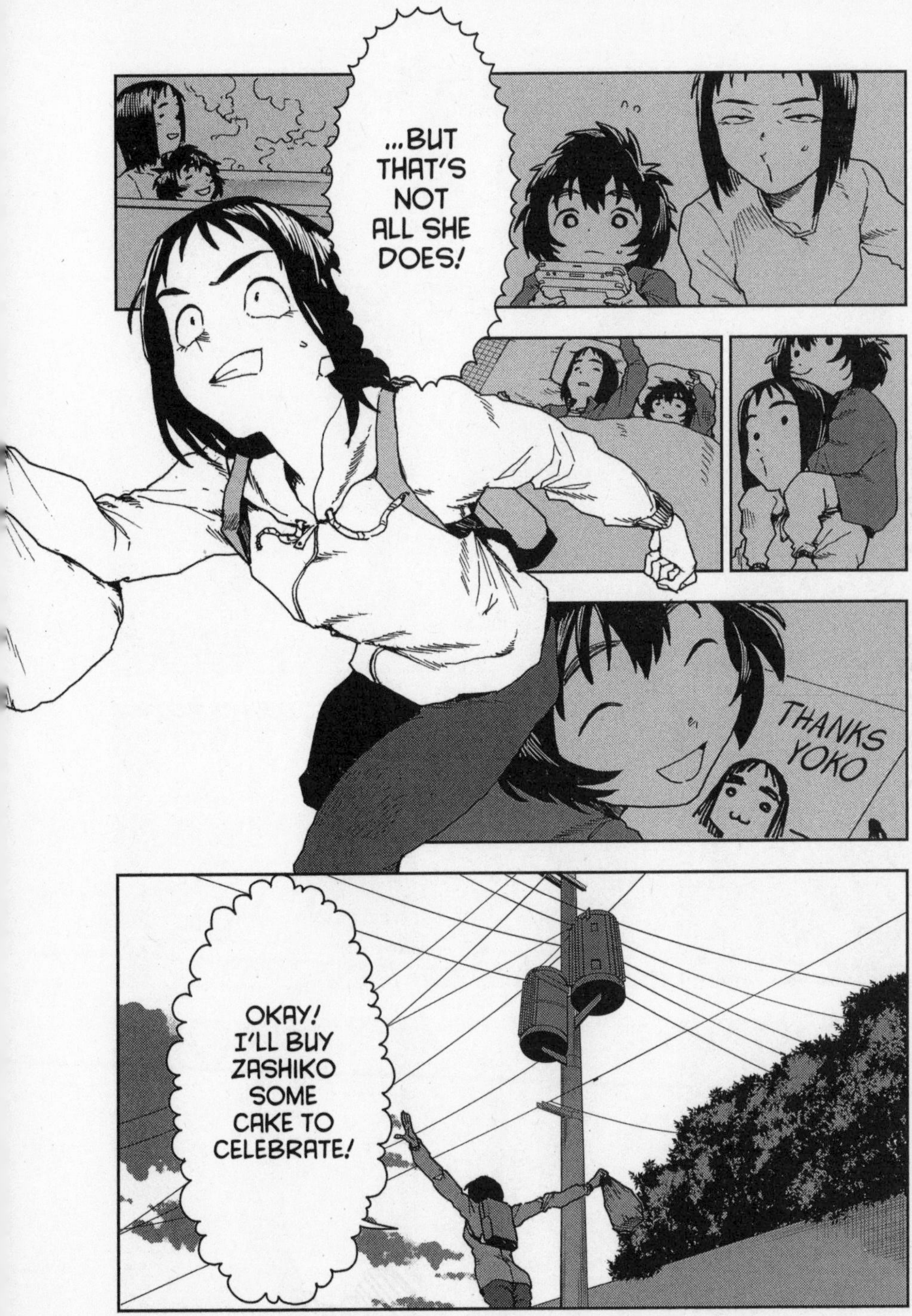
...BUT THAT'S NOT ALL SHE DOES!
THANKS YOKO
OKAY! I'LL BUY ZASHIKO SOME CAKE TO CELEBRATE!

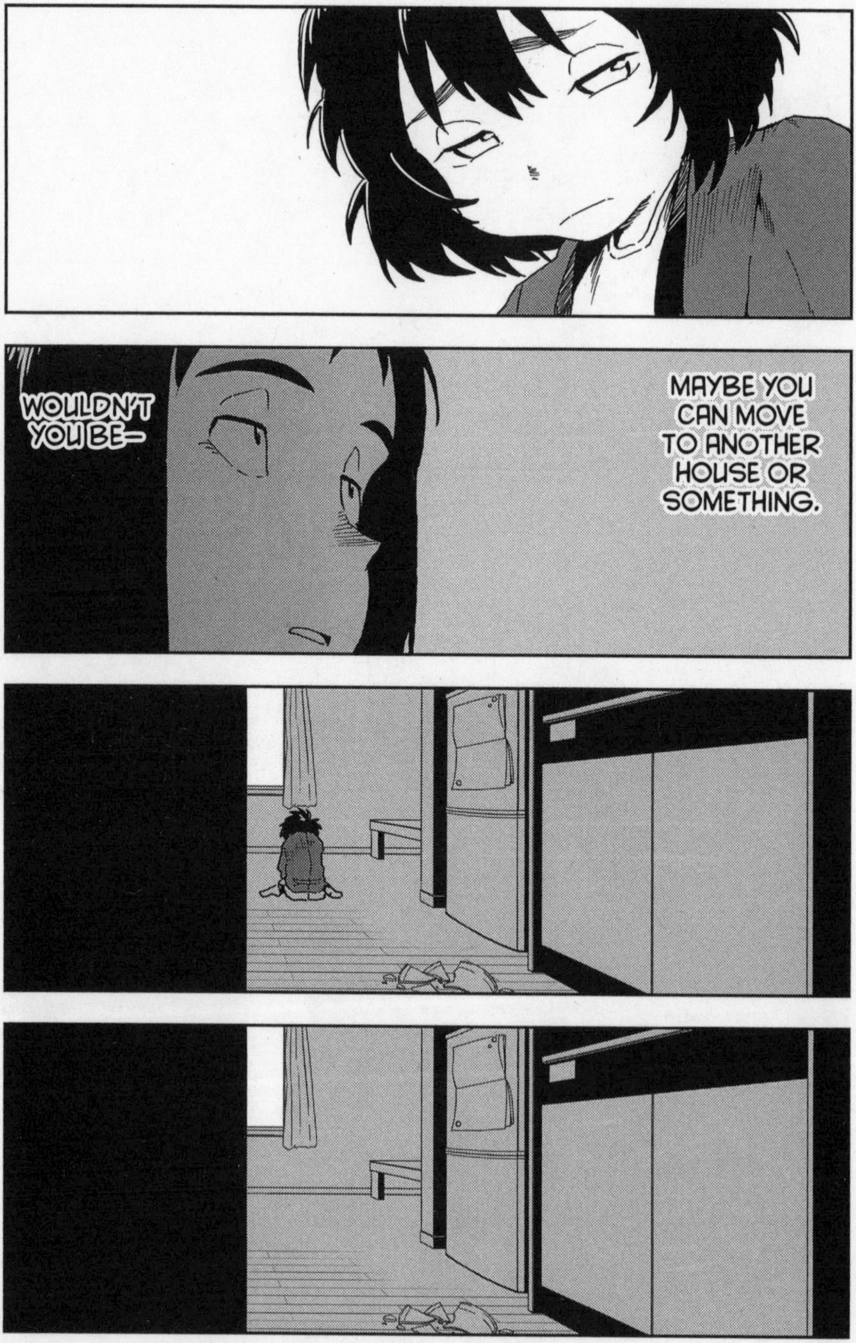
MAYBE YOU CAN MOVE TO ANOTHER HOUSE OR SOMETHING.
WOULDN'T YOU BE—

BY THE WAY, ZASHIKO'S JACKET IS PART OF HER BODY.
IT DOESN'T GET DIRTY OR NEED WASH-ING.
SPILLED MISO SOUP? GOES RIGHT THROUGH HER.
AND THROW IT OUT THE WINDOW, AND...
FLING
SHOOP

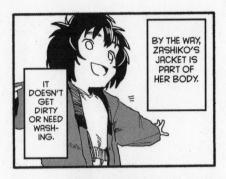

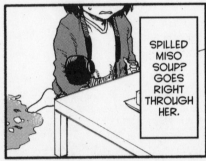

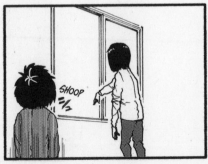

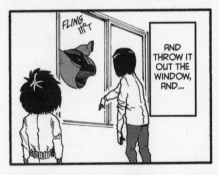

INTERVIEWS WITH
MONSTER GIRLS

Chapter 37: A Zashiki-warashi's Happiness (Part 2)

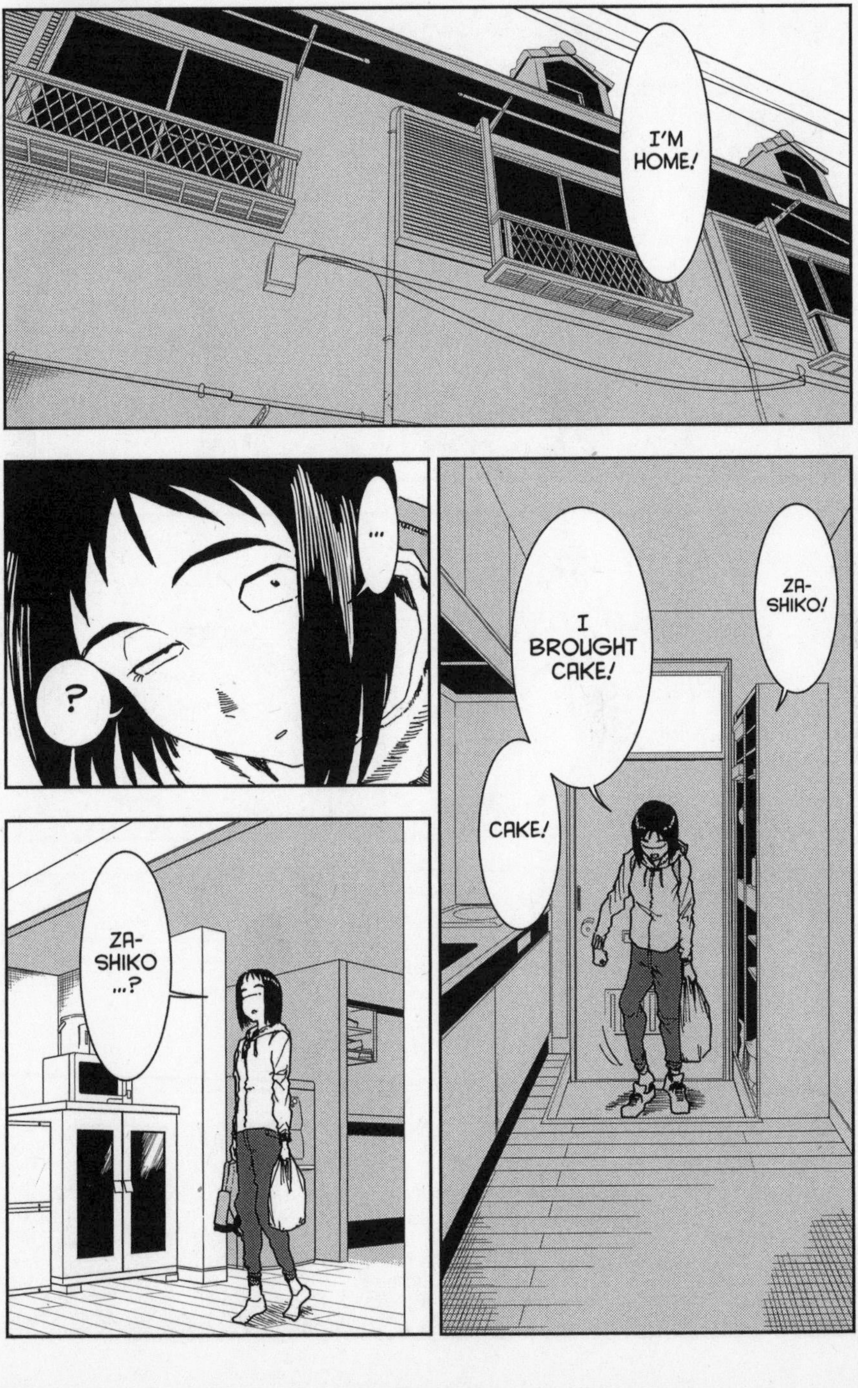
I'M HOME!
ZA-SHIKO!
I BROUGHT CAKE!
CAKE!
...
?
ZA-SHIKO ...?

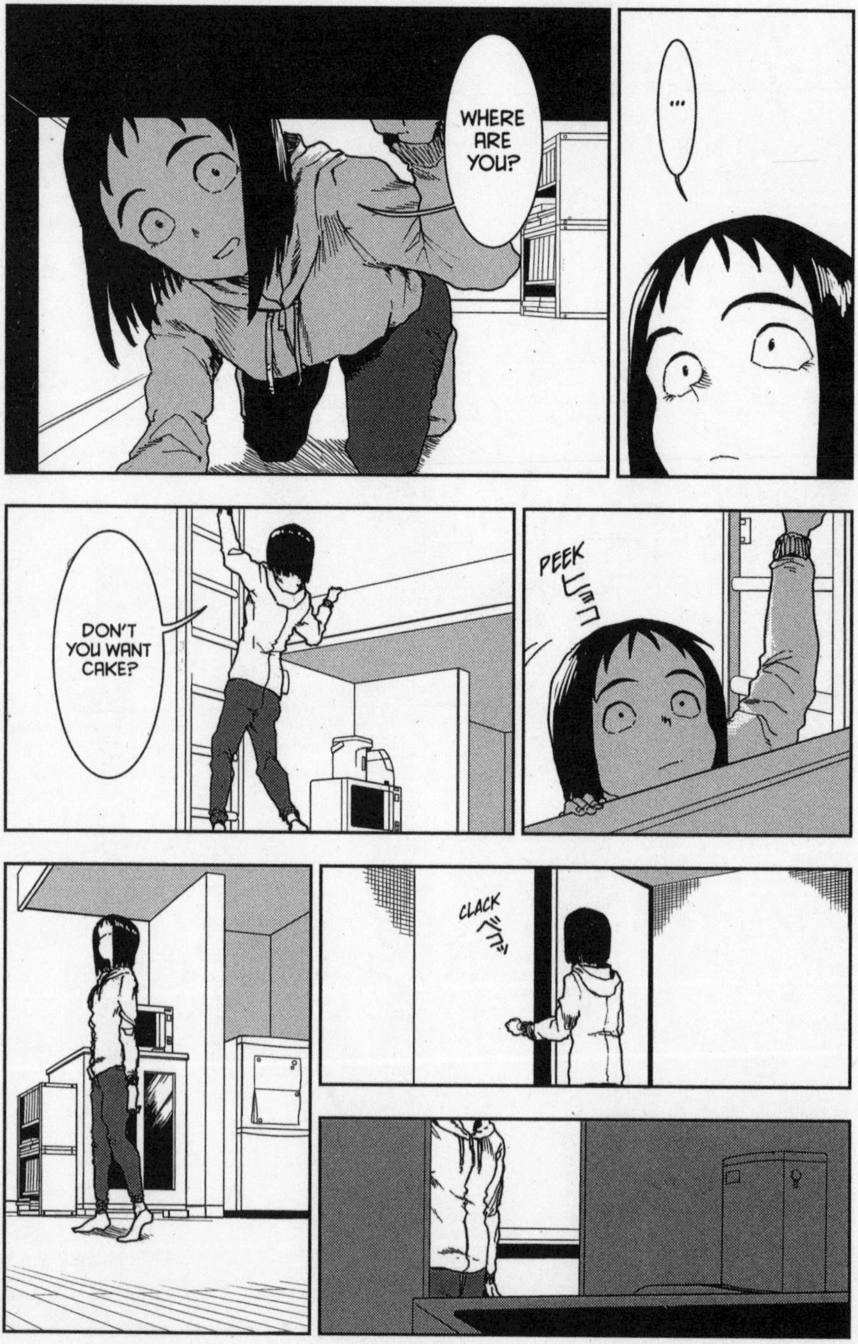
...
WHERE ARE YOU?
PEEK
ヒョコ
DON'T YOU WANT CAKE?
CLACK
ベタッ

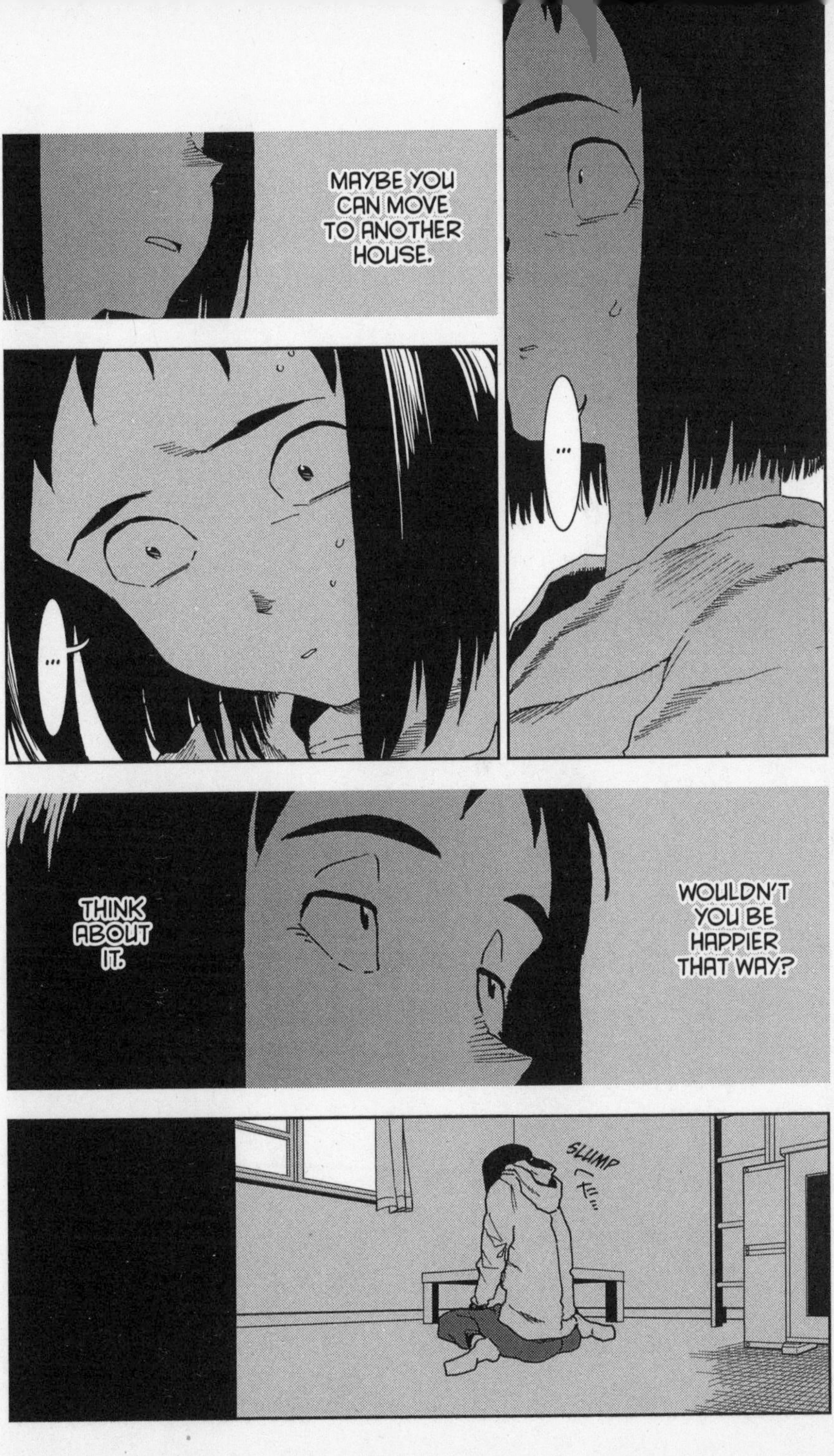
...
MAYBE YOU CAN MOVE TO ANOTHER HOUSE.
...
WOULDN'T YOU BE HAPPIER THAT WAY?
THINK ABOUT IT.
SLUMP

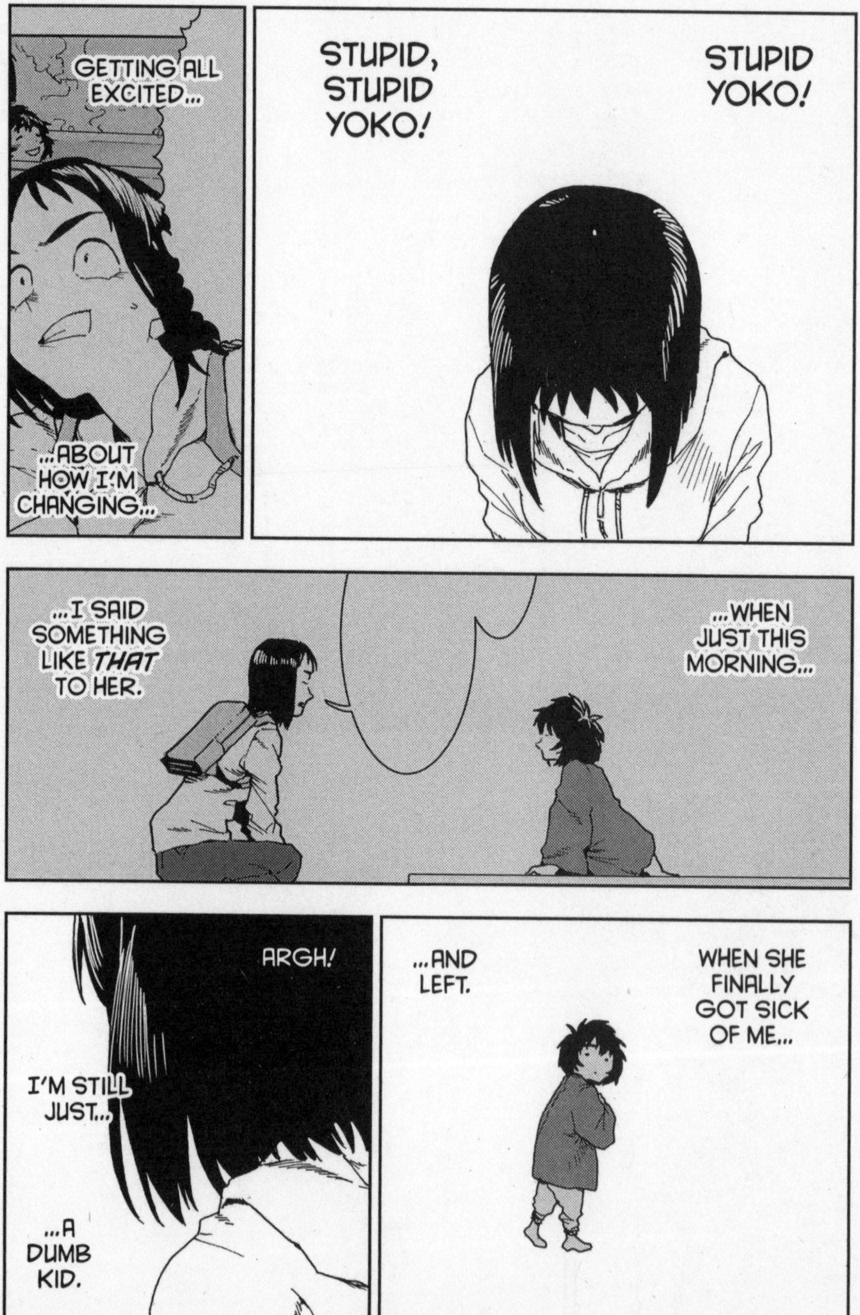
STUPID YOKO!
STUPID, STUPID YOKO!
GETTING ALL EXCITED...
...ABOUT HOW I'M CHANGING...
...WHEN JUST THIS MORNING...
...I SAID SOMETHING LIKE *THAT* TO HER.
WHEN SHE FINALLY GOT SICK OF ME...
...AND LEFT.
ARGH!
I'M STILL JUST...
...A DUMB KID.

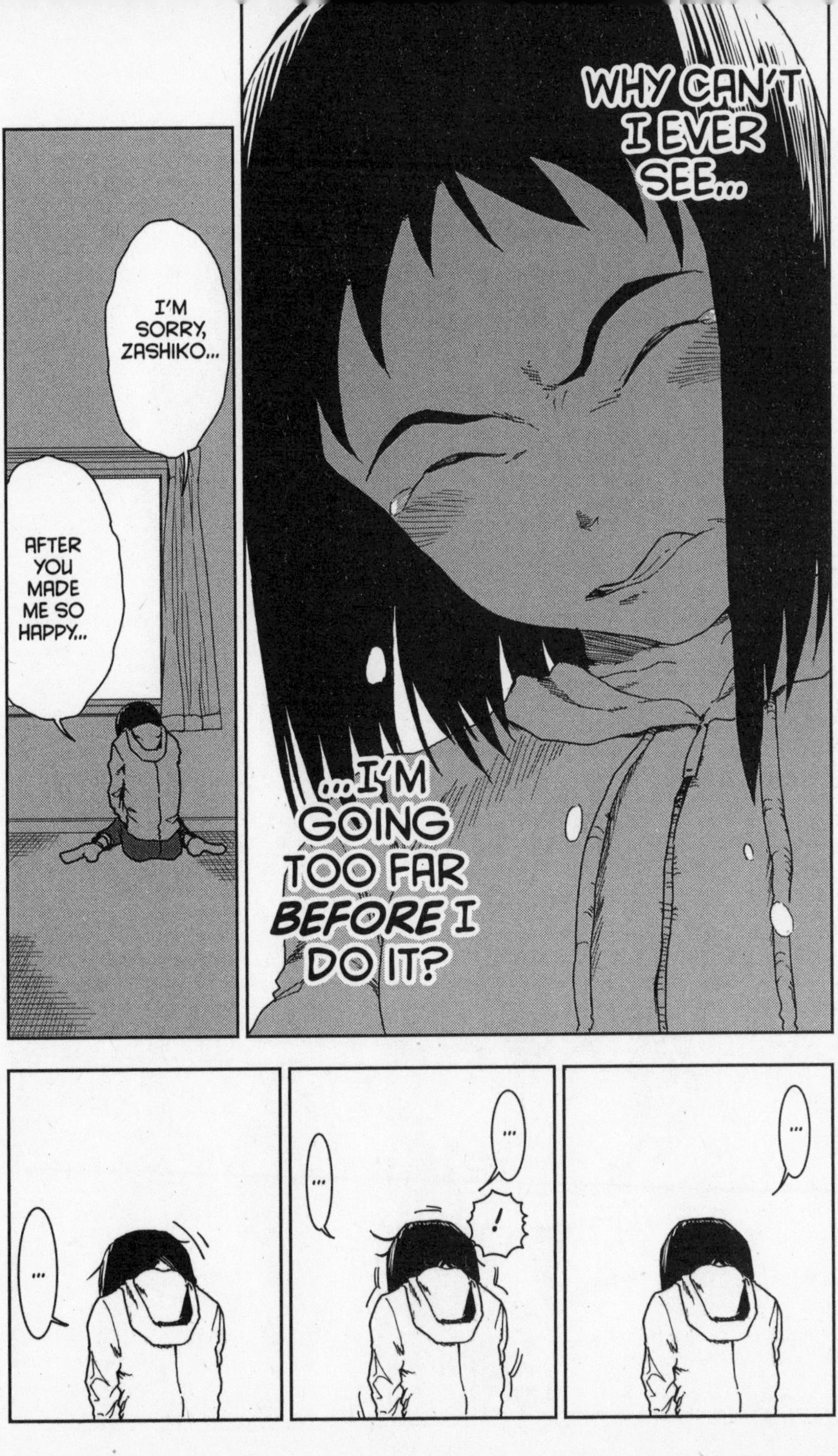
WHY CAN'T I EVER SEE...
...I'M GOING TOO FAR *BEFORE* I DO IT?
I'M SORRY, ZASHIKO...
AFTER YOU MADE ME SO HAPPY...
...
...
!
...
...

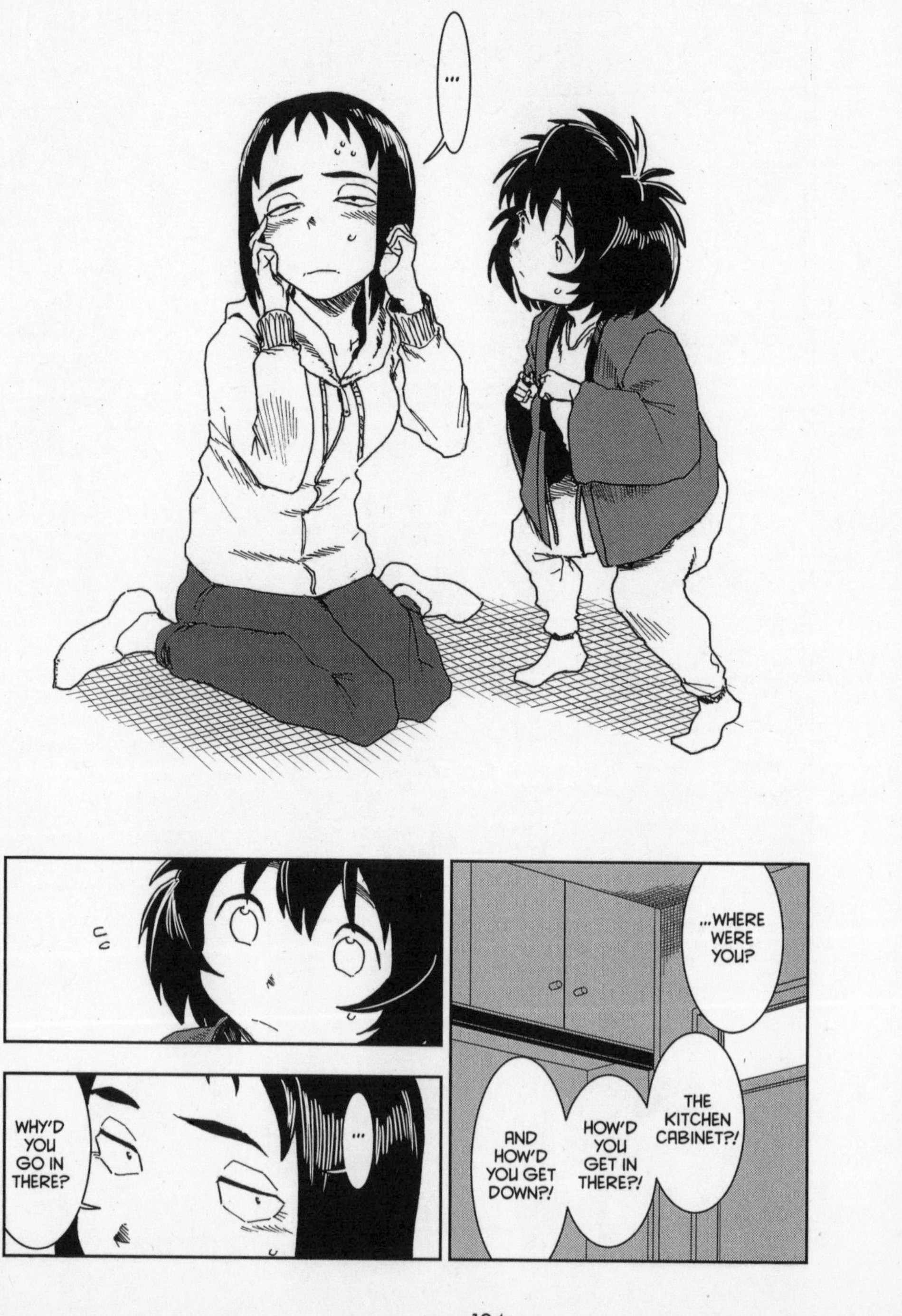
...
...WHERE WERE YOU?
THE KITCHEN CABINET?!
HOW'D YOU GET IN THERE?!
AND HOW'D YOU GET DOWN?!
...
WHY'D YOU GO IN THERE?

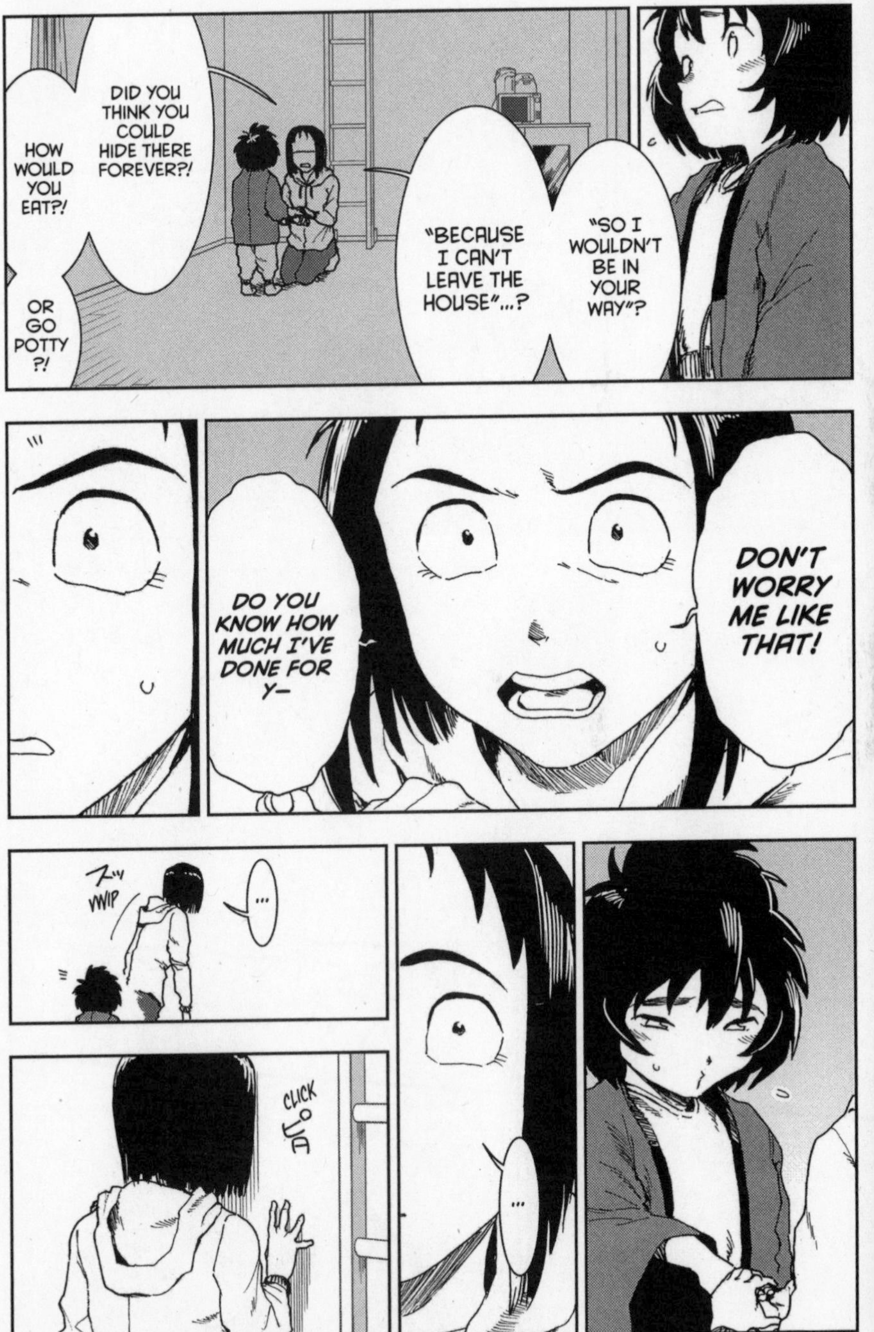
"SO I WOULDN'T BE IN YOUR WAY"?
"BECAUSE I CAN'T LEAVE THE HOUSE"...?
DID YOU THINK YOU COULD HIDE THERE FOREVER?!
HOW WOULD YOU EAT?!
OR GO POTTY ?!
DON'T WORRY ME LIKE THAT!
DO YOU KNOW HOW MUCH I'VE DONE FOR Y—
...
...
ズッ
VWIP
CLICK

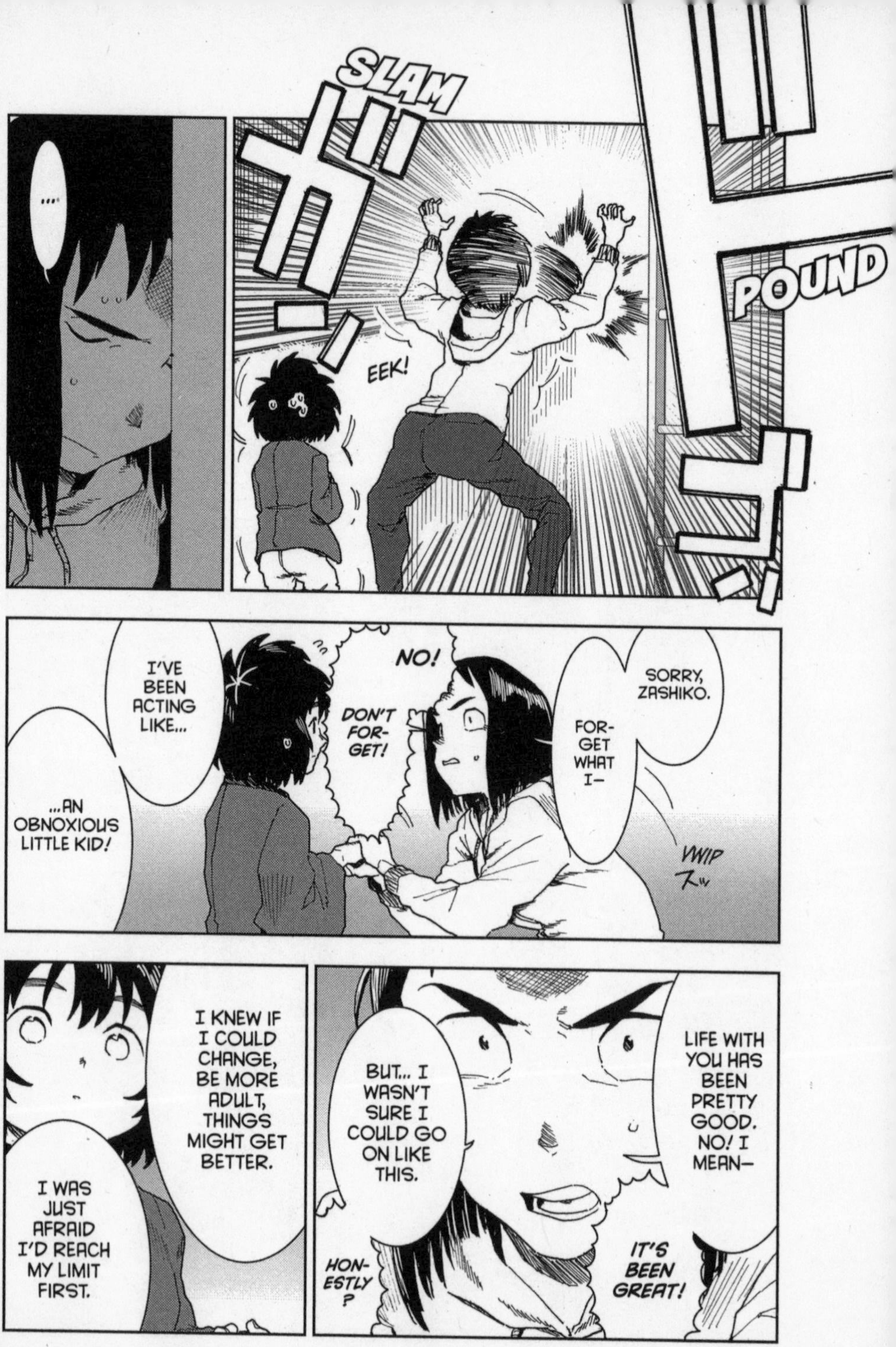
SLAM
POUND
EEK!
...
SORRY, ZASHIKO.
FOR-GET WHAT I—
VWIP
NO!
DON'T FOR-GET!
I'VE BEEN ACTING LIKE...
...AN OBNOXIOUS LITTLE KID!
LIFE WITH YOU HAS BEEN PRETTY GOOD. NO! I MEAN—
IT'S BEEN GREAT!
BUT... I WASN'T SURE I COULD GO ON LIKE THIS.
HONESTLY?
I KNEW IF I COULD CHANGE, BE MORE ADULT, THINGS MIGHT GET BETTER.
I WAS JUST AFRAID I'D REACH MY LIMIT FIRST.

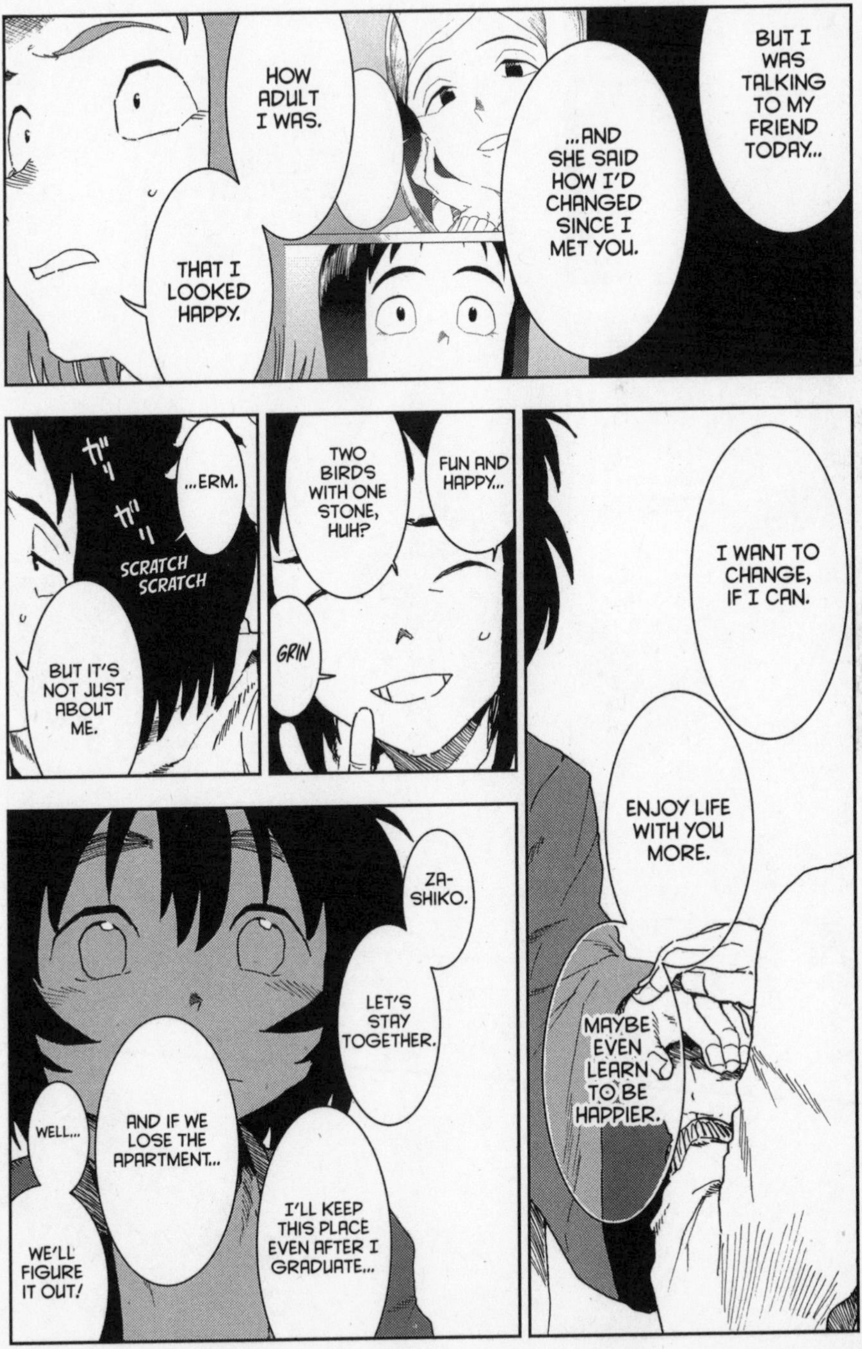
BUT I WAS TALKING TO MY FRIEND TODAY...
...AND SHE SAID HOW I'D CHANGED SINCE I MET YOU.
HOW ADULT I WAS.
THAT I LOOKED HAPPY.
I WANT TO CHANGE, IF I CAN.
ENJOY LIFE WITH YOU MORE.
MAYBE EVEN LEARN TO BE HAPPIER.
FUN AND HAPPY...
TWO BIRDS WITH ONE STONE, HUH?
GRIN
...ERM.
ガリ ガリ
SCRATCH SCRATCH
BUT IT'S NOT JUST ABOUT ME.
ZA-SHIKO.
LET'S STAY TOGETHER.
I'LL KEEP THIS PLACE EVEN AFTER I GRADUATE...
AND IF WE LOSE THE APARTMENT...
WELL...
WE'LL FIGURE IT OUT!

I'LL MAKE US BOTH HAPPY. I PROMISE.

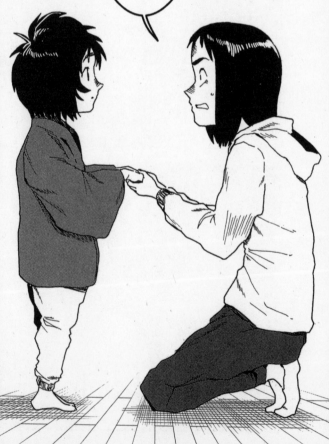

WHOOP!

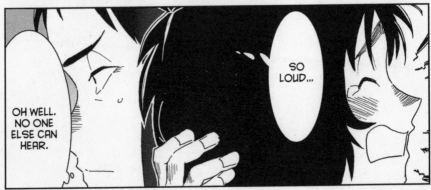

OH WELL. NO ONE ELSE CAN HEAR.

SO LOUD...

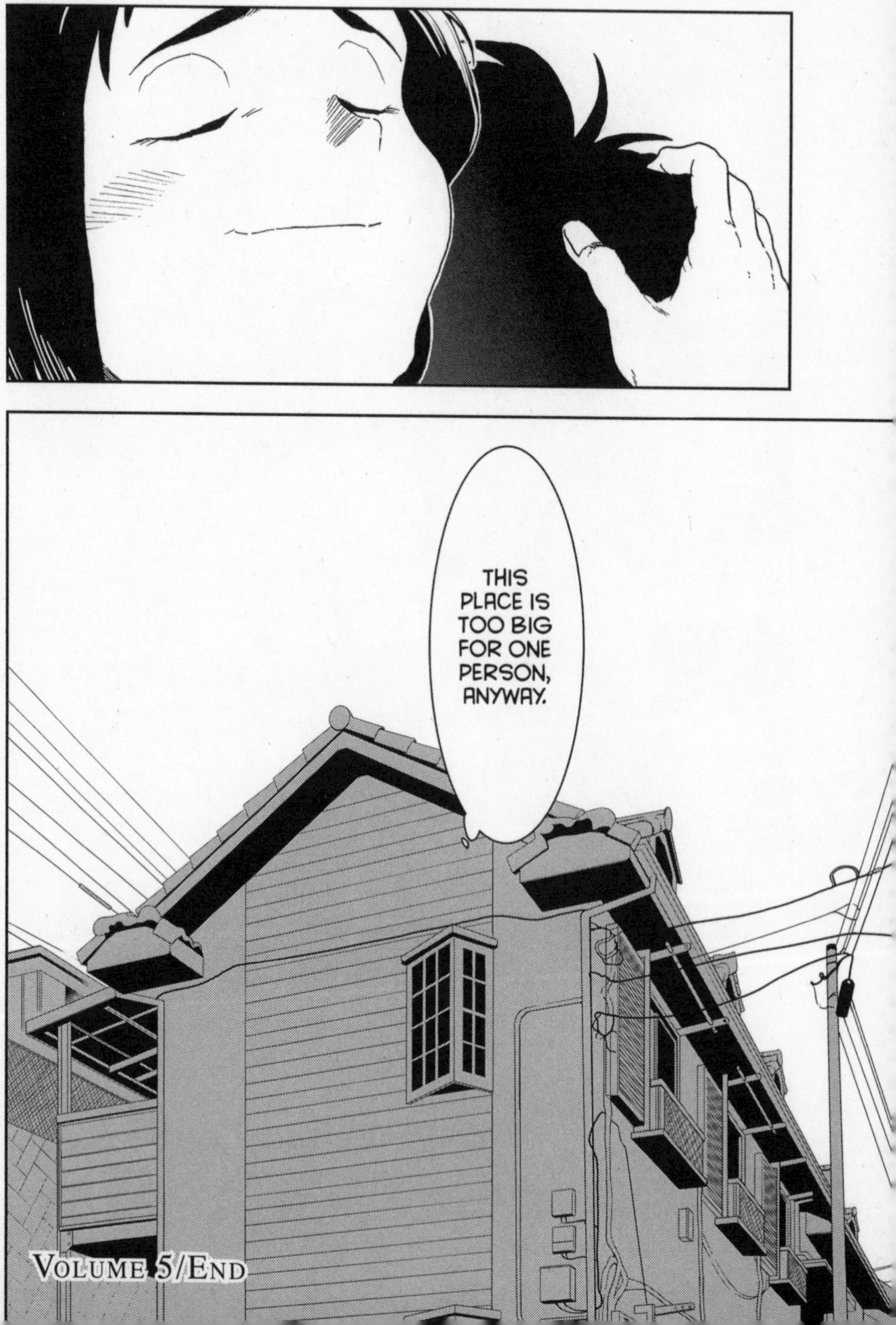
THIS PLACE IS TOO BIG FOR ONE PERSON, ANYWAY.
VOLUME 5/END

HM?
YOKO TAKA-HASHI...
AND THOSE DIS-TINCTIVE PUPILS...
...
SHEER COINCI-DENCE!

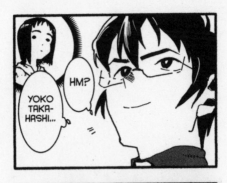

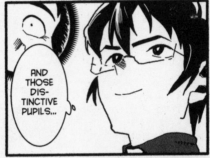

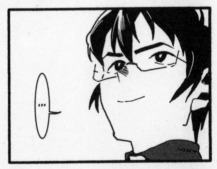

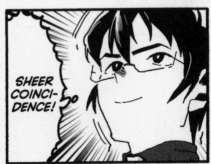

INTERVIEWS WITH MONSTER GIRLS

BONUS CHAPTER: UGAKI & KURTZ IN: THE FLUMMOXED FLATFOOT

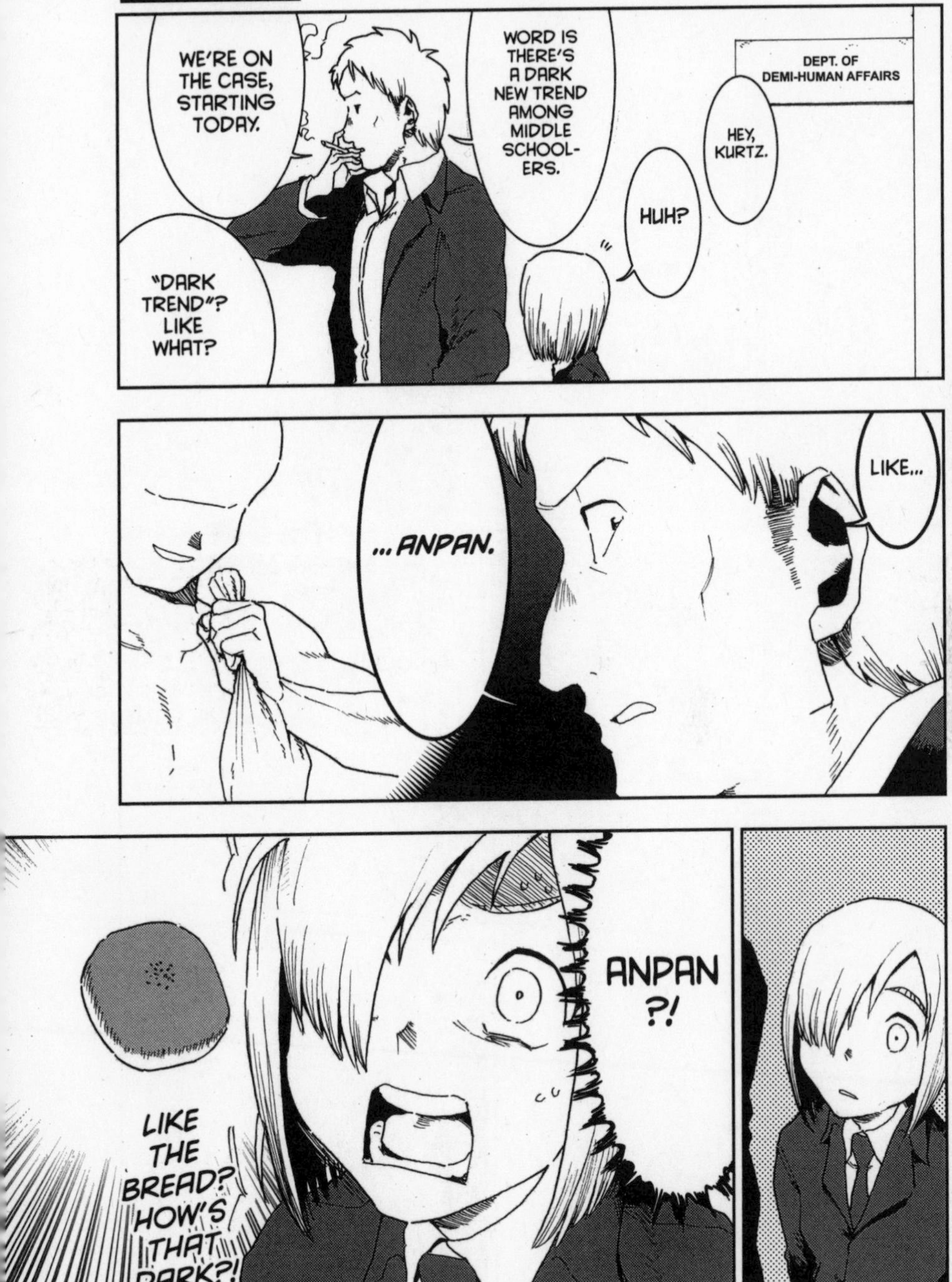
DEPT. OF DEMI-HUMAN AFFAIRS
HEY, KURTZ.
HUH?
WORD IS THERE'S A DARK NEW TREND AMONG MIDDLE SCHOOL-ERS.
WE'RE ON THE CASE, STARTING TODAY.
"DARK TREND"? LIKE WHAT?
LIKE...
...ANPAN.
ANPAN?!
LIKE THE BREAD? HOW'S THAT DARK?!

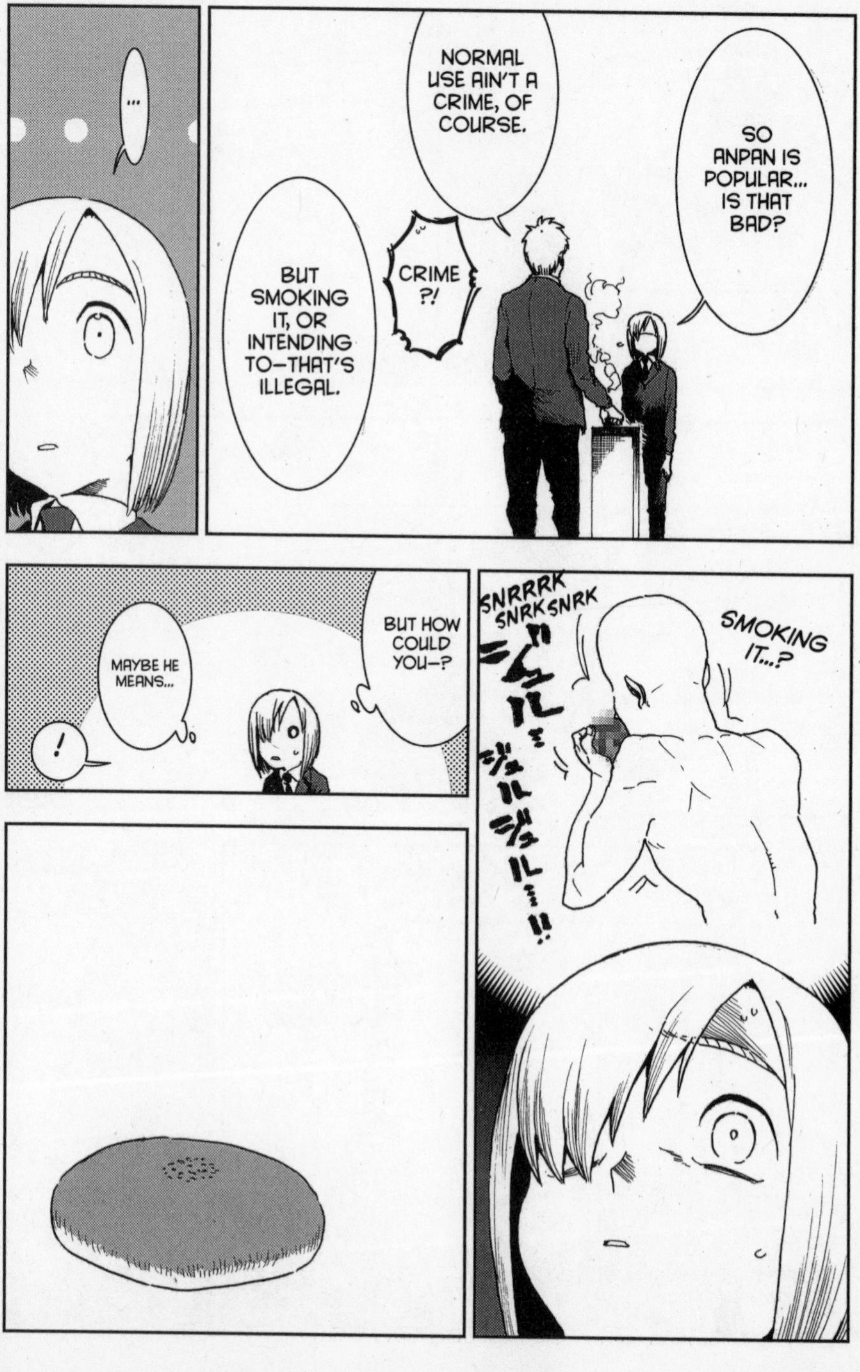
SO ANPAN IS POPULAR... IS THAT BAD?
NORMAL USE AIN'T A CRIME, OF COURSE.
CRIME?!
BUT SMOKING IT, OR INTENDING TO—THAT'S ILLEGAL.
...
SMOKING IT...?
SNRRRK SNRKSNRK
BUT HOW COULD YOU—?
MAYBE HE MEANS...
!

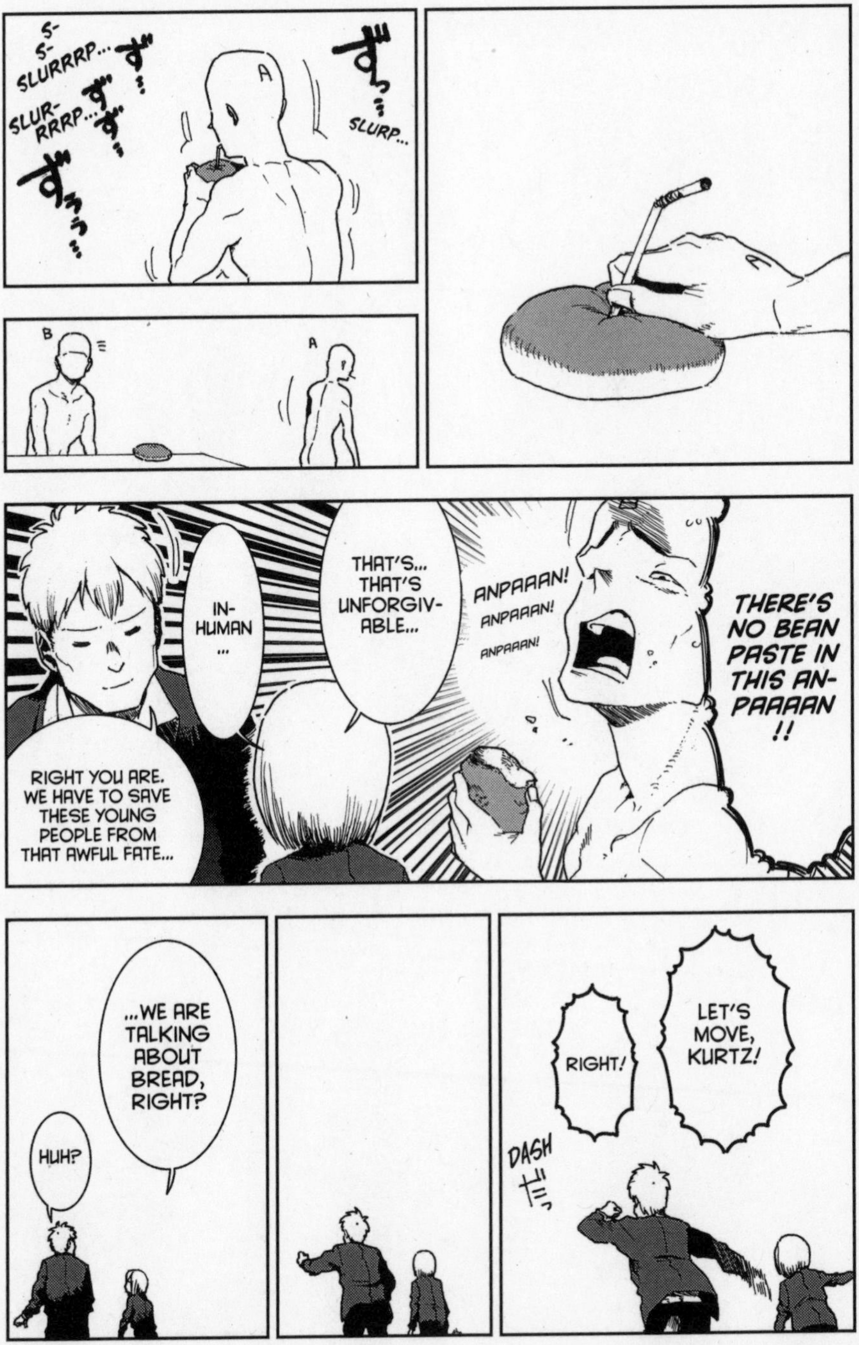
S-S-SLURRRP...
SLUR-RRRP...
SLURP...
THERE'S NO BEAN PASTE IN THIS AN-PAAAAN!!
ANPAAAN!
ANPAAAN!
ANPAAAN!
THAT'S... THAT'S UNFORGIV-ABLE...
IN-HUMAN...
RIGHT YOU ARE. WE HAVE TO SAVE THESE YOUNG PEOPLE FROM THAT AWFUL FATE...
LET'S MOVE, KURTZ!
RIGHT!
DASH
...WE ARE TALKING ABOUT BREAD, RIGHT?
HUH?

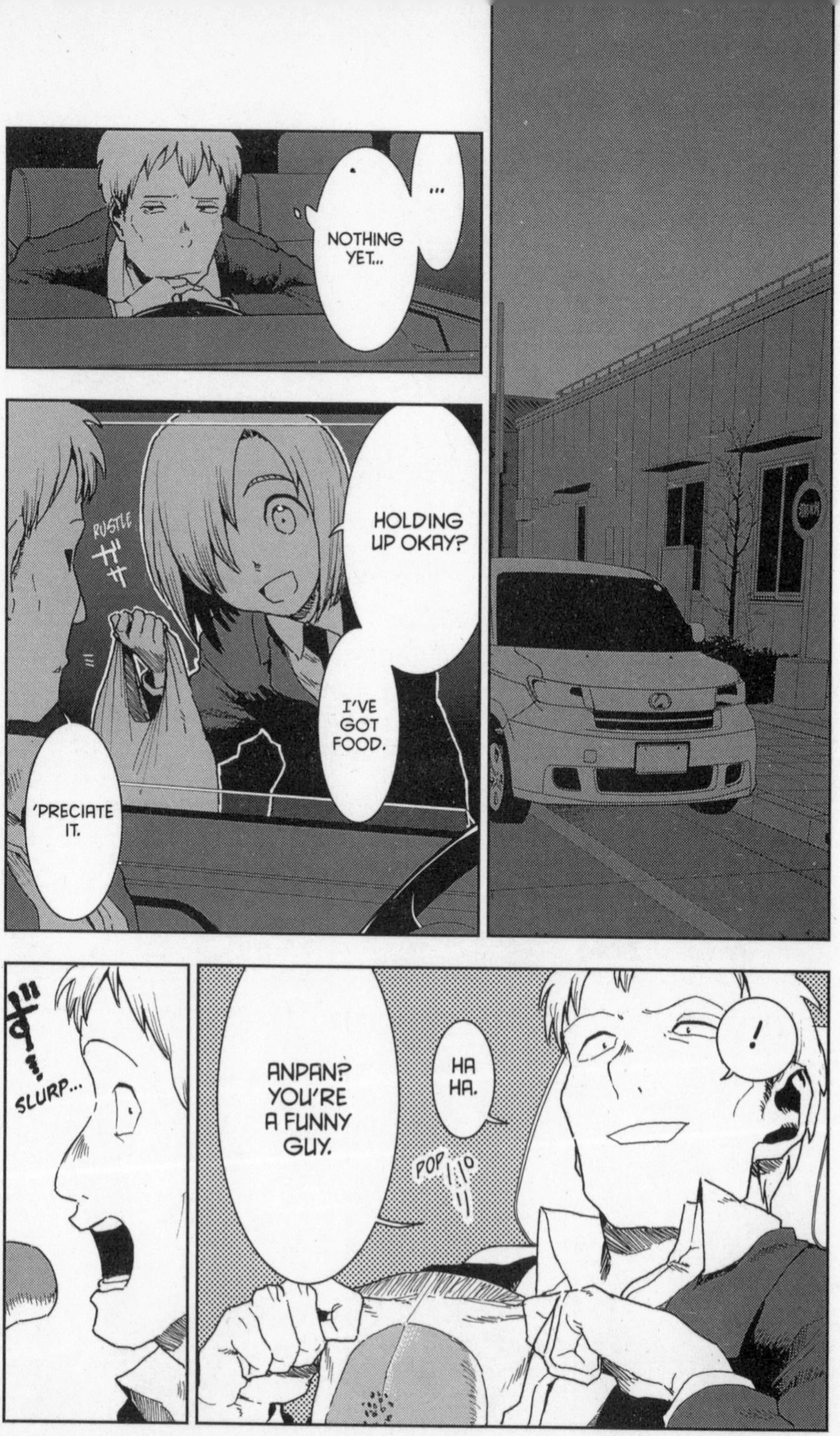
...
NOTHING YET...
HOLDING UP OKAY?
I'VE GOT FOOD.
RUSTLE
'PRECIATE IT.
!
HA HA.
ANPAN? YOU'RE A FUNNY GUY.
POP
SLURP...

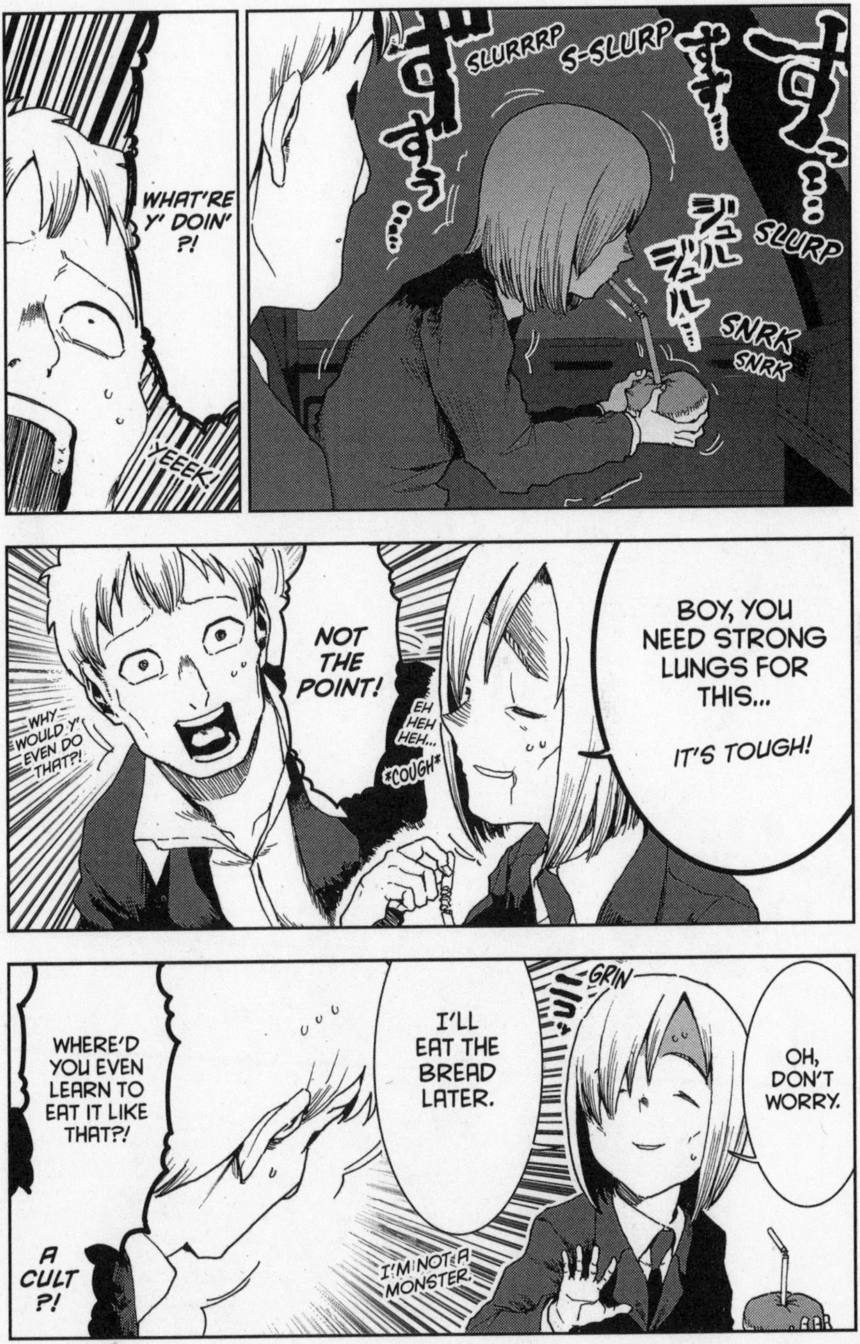
すっ…
すず…
S-SLURP
SLURRRP
ずずぅ…
ジュルジュル…
SLURP
SNRK SNRK
WHAT'RE Y' DOIN' ?!
YEEEK
BOY, YOU NEED STRONG LUNGS FOR THIS...
IT'S TOUGH!
EH HEH HEH...
COUGH
NOT THE POINT!
WHY WOULD Y' EVEN DO THAT?!
OH, DON'T WORRY.
ニヤッ
GRIN
I'LL EAT THE BREAD LATER.
I'M NOT A MONSTER.
WHERE'D YOU EVEN LEARN TO EAT IT LIKE THAT?!
A CULT ?!

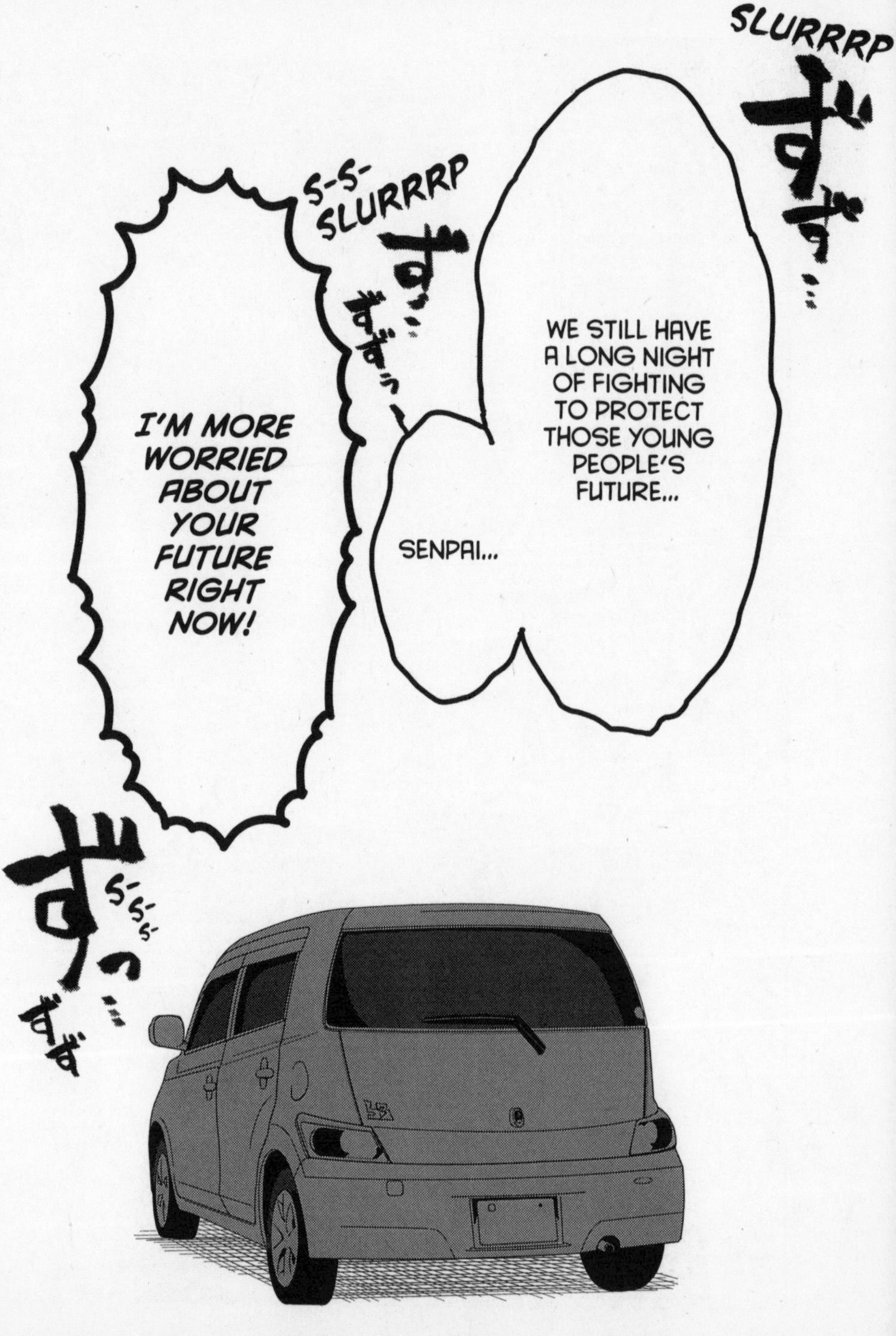
SLURRRP
ずず…
WE STILL HAVE A LONG NIGHT OF FIGHTING TO PROTECT THOSE YOUNG PEOPLE'S FUTURE...
SENPAI...
S-S-SLURRRP
I'M MORE WORRIED ABOUT YOUR FUTURE RIGHT NOW!

TRANSLATION NOTES

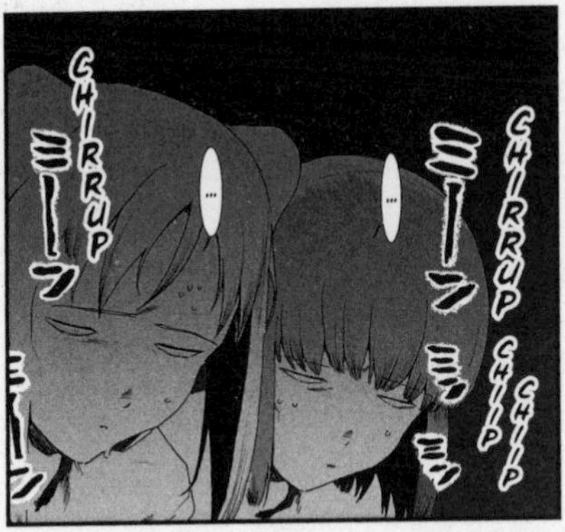
CHIRRUP
CHIRRUP CHIP CHIP
...
...

Cicadas, page 20
Cicadas and the shrill, scratchy sound they make (*min, min* is the onomatopoeia in Japanese) are endemic to Japanese summers. When you hear their distinctive stridulation in anime or manga, you can almost feel the heat on your skin!

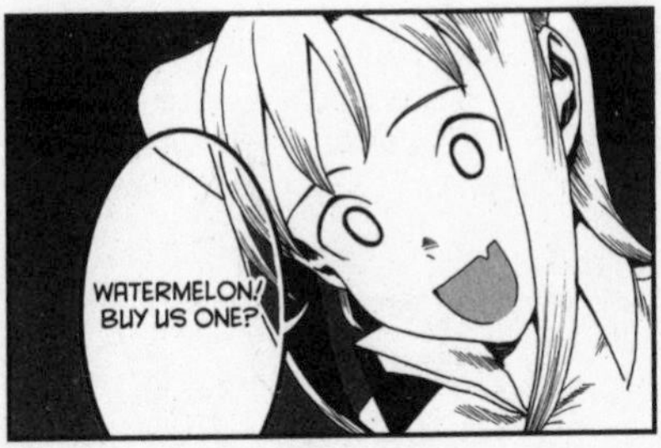
WATERMELON! BUY US ONE?

Watermelons, page 23
Eating watermelons is a popular way to beat the summer heat in Japan. However, fruit is often considerably more expensive in Japan than in the US.

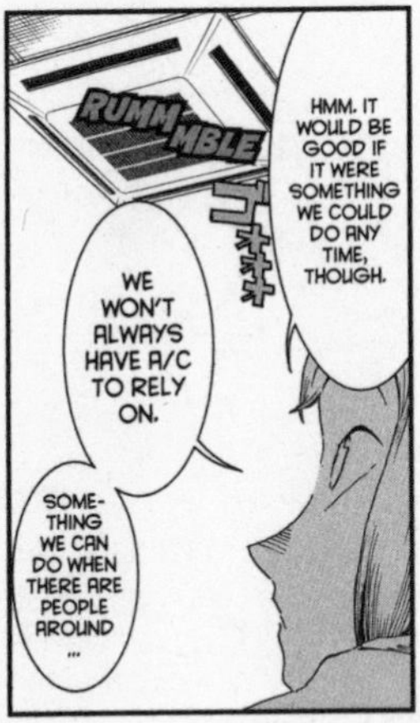
HMM. IT WOULD BE GOOD IF IT WERE SOMETHING WE COULD DO ANY TIME, THOUGH.
RUMMMBLE
WE WON'T ALWAYS HAVE A/C TO RELY ON.
SOMETHING WE CAN DO WHEN THERE ARE PEOPLE AROUND ...

We Won't Always Have A/C, page 25
Many Japanese classrooms have minimal climate control. A space heater in winter and an open window in summer are sometimes all that is available.

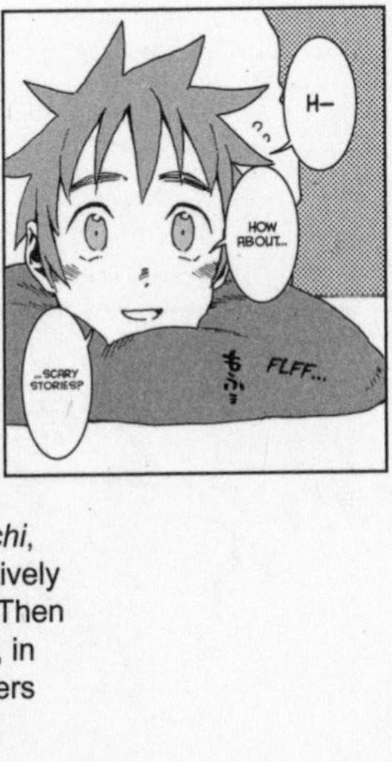
H—
HOW ABOUT...
...SCARY STORIES?
FLFF...

Scary Stories, page 25
In Japan, scary stories are a summertime, rather than fall, tradition.

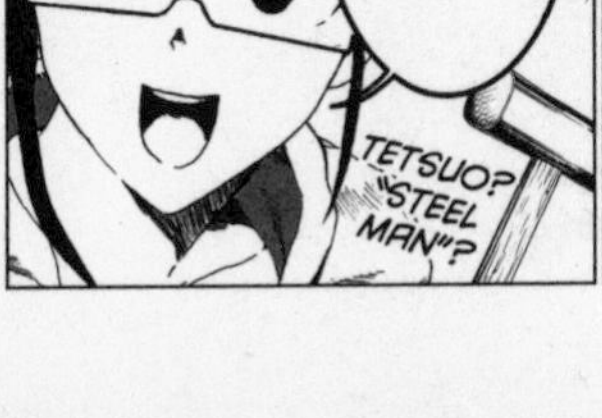
OR SHOULD I SAY...LIKE STEEL?
TETSUO? "STEEL MAN"?

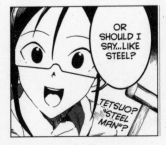

Like Steel, page 46
Sakie calls Tetsuo (panel 1) a *kanazuchi*, literally meaning a hammer, but figuratively referring to someone who can't swim. Then she puns on his name, "Tetsuo" which, in Japanese, is written using the characters for "steel" or "metal," and "man."

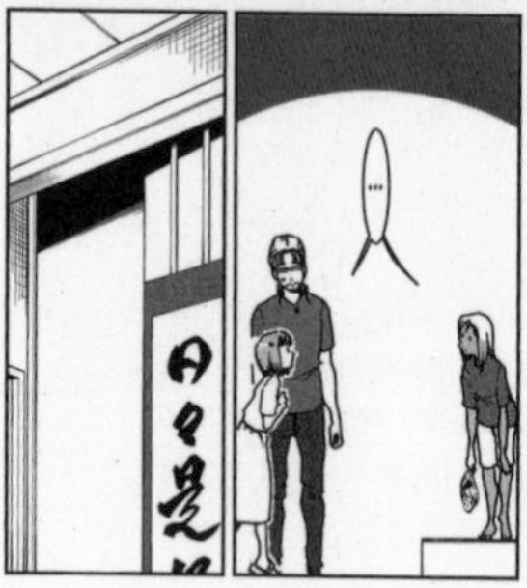
...
日々是

Calligraphy, page 75

A piece of calligraphy is partially visible in this panel (it can also be seen, again in part, on page 81). It is common for Japanese families to hang calligraphy somewhere in the house, often in the *tokonoma* (lit. "high place"), a raised area where items of special personal or spiritual importance are displayed. The visible part of the scroll in the Takanashi house reads "Every day is…" We can't say exactly what the rest of the phrase is, but it might conclude with something like "…new" or "…a good day."

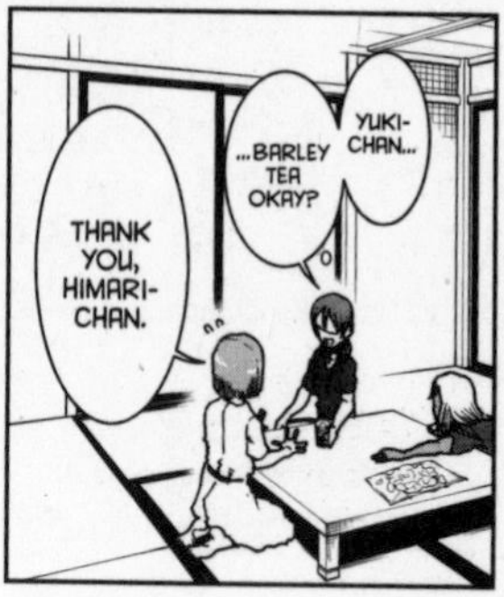
YUKI-CHAN...
...BARLEY TEA OKAY?
THANK YOU, HIMARI-CHAN.

Barley Tea, page 82

Barley tea (*mugi-cha*), typically served chilled rather than hot, is a common summer drink in Japan. Unlike green tea (*matcha* or *ryoku-cha*), it is brown and has an earthy flavor that's perfect for warm days.

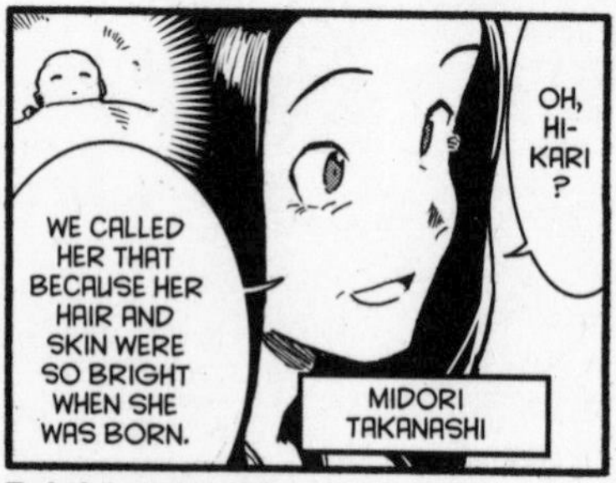
OH, HI-KARI?
WE CALLED HER THAT BECAUSE HER HAIR AND SKIN WERE SO BRIGHT WHEN SHE WAS BORN.
MIDORI TAKANASHI

Bright, page 89

Hikari's name in Japanese means "light." The name Midori means "green."

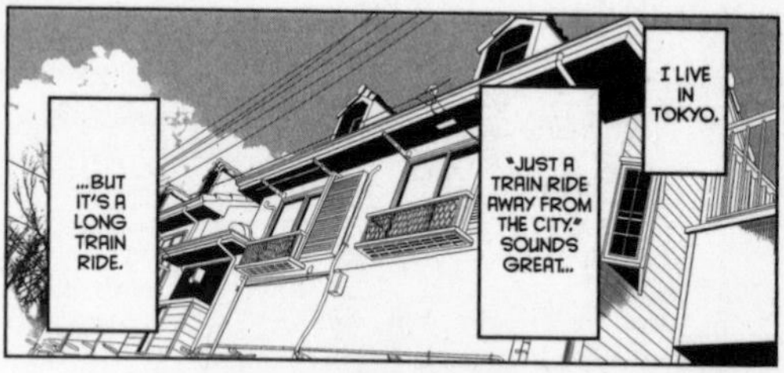
I LIVE IN TOKYO.
"JUST A TRAIN RIDE AWAY FROM THE CITY." SOUNDS GREAT...
...BUT IT'S A LONG TRAIN RIDE.

Just a Train Ride, page 91

The greater metropolitan area known as Tokyo covers a large swath of land, much of which is not the glittering city often associated with the name. Many residents of Tokyo live far away from downtown (often to avoid the astronomical housing prices) and make long commutes to work or school.

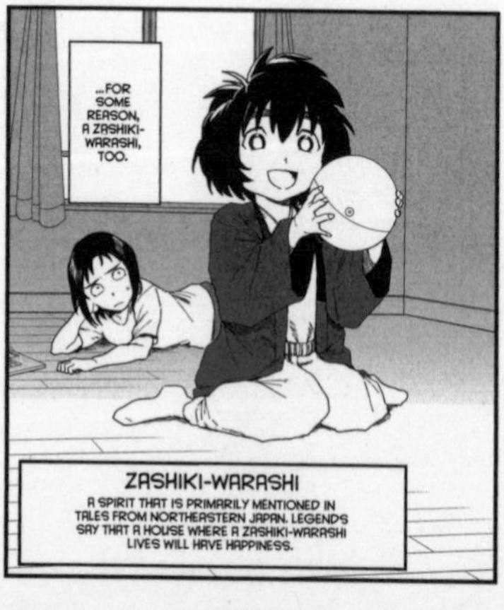
...FOR SOME REASON, A ZASHIKI-WARASHI, TOO.
ZASHIKI-WARASHI
A SPIRIT THAT IS PRIMARILY MENTIONED IN TALES FROM NORTHEASTERN JAPAN. LEGENDS SAY THAT A HOUSE WHERE A ZASHIKI-WARASHI LIVES WILL HAVE HAPPINESS.

Happiness, page 92

The word *shiawase* means a deep, abiding happiness, but it can also have nuances of good fortune or material abundance—making it harder for Yoko to know quite what to expect from her supernatural roommate.

Police Box, page 95

Police boxes, or *koban*, are small outposts staffed by one or two officers, often 24/7. They are found almost everywhere, so for many matters (including asking directions!), people can go to the police box instead of the police station.

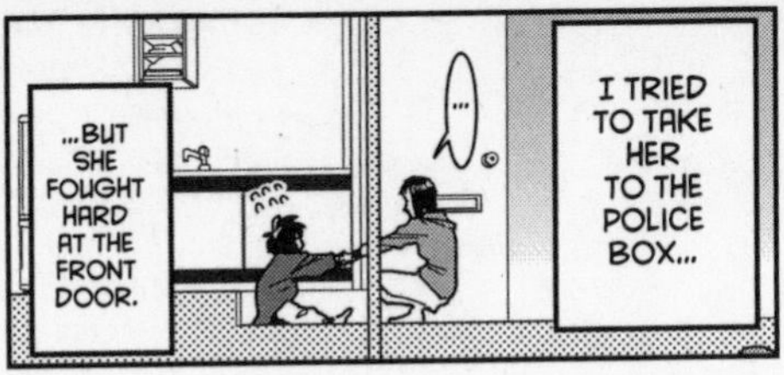
I TRIED TO TAKE HER TO THE POLICE BOX...
...
...BUT SHE FOUGHT HARD AT THE FRONT DOOR.

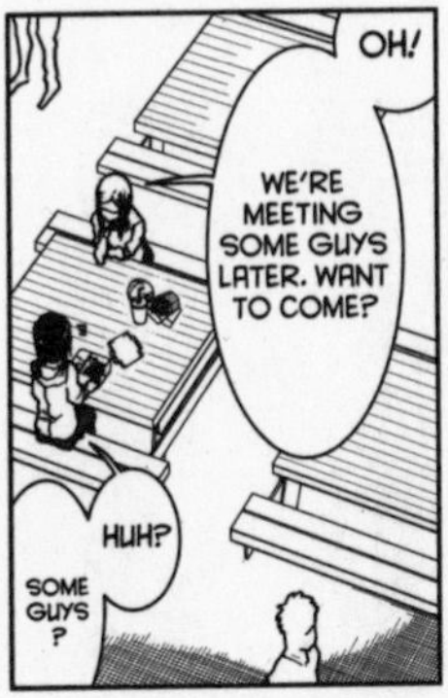
OH!
WE'RE MEETING SOME GUYS LATER. WANT TO COME?
HUH?
SOME GUYS ?

Meeting some guys, page 107

Yoko is actually being invited to a *go-kon*, or a group date, in which typically an equal amount of men and women go out to drinks, dinner, or other activities, and see who hits it off.

End-of-Day Discounts, page 108

Japanese supermarkets often discount fresh produce toward the end of the day in an attempt to move leftover stock. If she goes out with her friend, Yoko won't be able to snag the low-priced food.

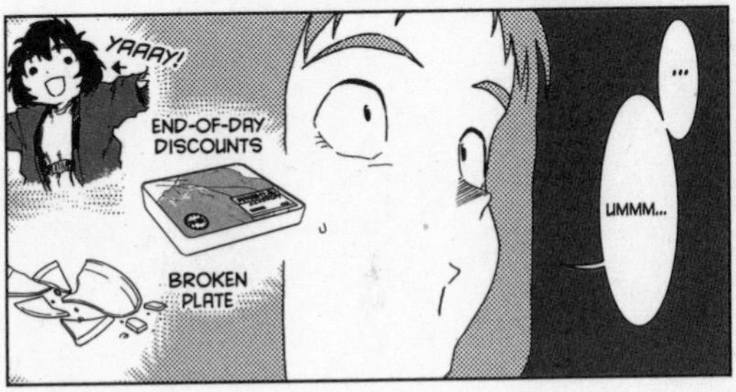
...
UMMM...
YAAAY!
END-OF-DAY DISCOUNTS
BROKEN PLATE

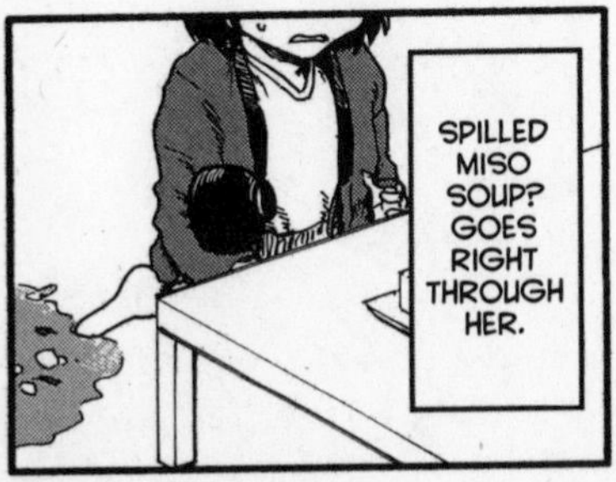
SPILLED MISO SOUP? GOES RIGHT THROUGH HER.

Miso soup, page 117

Perhaps the most famous Japanese soup, this is a soybean-based broth made with vegetables, tofu, and other ingredients.

Anpan, page 133

Anpan is a sweet bread filled with red bean paste (it's what Kurtz pictures on the first page of this story). An extremely widespread snack, one of Japan's most popular cartoon characters is Anpan Man, a superhero whose head is an anpan bun.

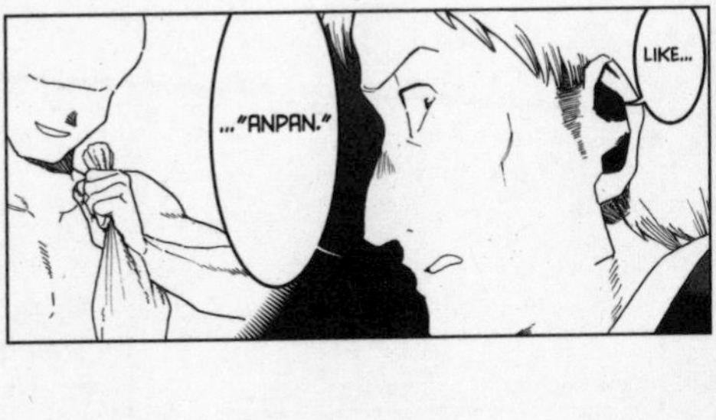
LIKE...
..."ANPAN."

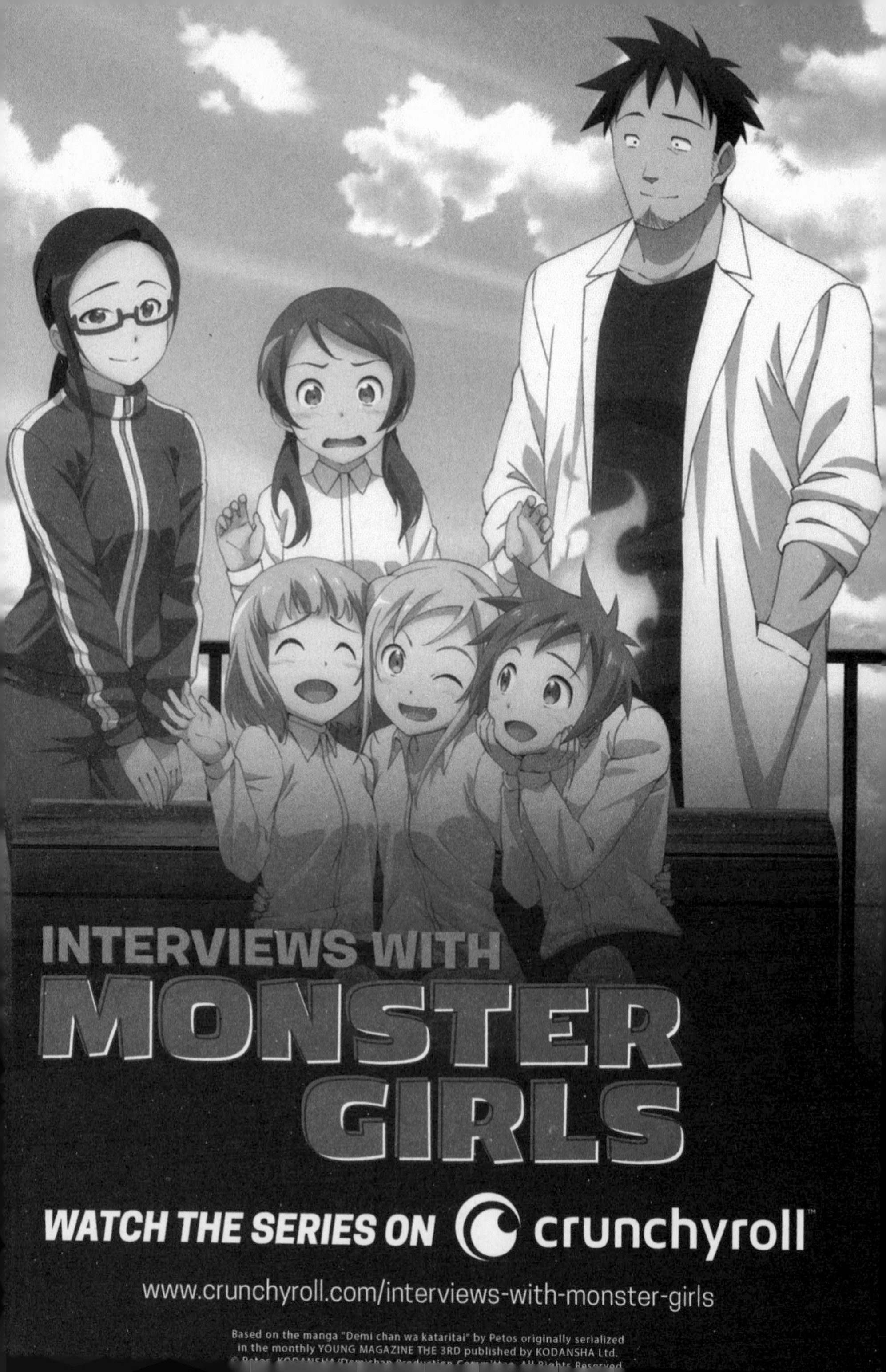

INTERVIEWS WITH
MONSTER
GIRLS
WATCH THE SERIES ON crunchyroll
www.crunchyroll.com/interviews-with-monster-girls
Based on the manga "Demi chan wa kataritai" by Petos originally serialized
in the monthly YOUNG MAGAZINE THE 3RD published by KODANSHA Ltd.

A Kodansha Comics Trade Paperback Original.

Published in the United States by Kodansha Comics, an imprint of Kodansha USA Publishing, LLC, New York.

Publication rights for this English edition arranged through Kodansha Ltd., Tokyo.

First published in Japan in 2017 by Kodansha Ltd., Tokyo, as *Demi-chan wa Kataritai*, volume 5.

ISBN 978-1-63236-435-7

Printed in the United States of America.

www.kodanshacomics.com

9 8 7 6 5 4 3 2 1

Translation: Kevin Steinbach
Lettering: Paige Pumphrey
Editing: Lauren Scanlan
Kodansha Comics edition cover design: Phil Balsman

STOP!

You are going the wrong way!

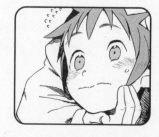

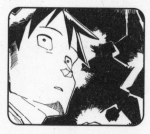

Manga is a completely different type of reading experience.

To start at the BEGINNING, go to the END!

That[redacted] Authentic manga is read the traditional Japanese
[redacted]
books a[redacted]'s easy to follow: just go to the other end of the
book[redacted] page and [redacted] from the right side to
th[redacted] you're experiencing
[redacted]

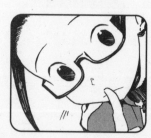

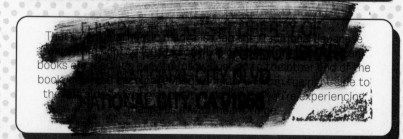